Profiles in Character

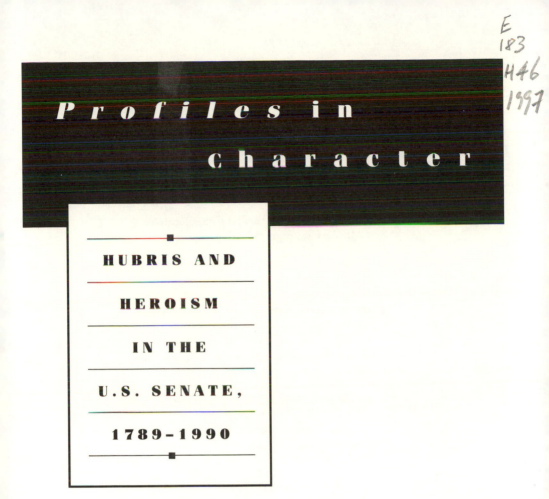

Profiles in Character

HUBRIS AND HEROISM IN THE U.S. SENATE, 1789–1990

Joseph Martin Hernon

M.E. Sharpe
Armonk, New York
London, England

Jacket photo credits: Kennedys: UPI/Bettmann.
All others: see pages following page 118.

Library of Congress Cataloging-in-Publication Data

Hernon, Joseph M.
Profiles in character : hubris and heroism in the U.S. Senate,
1789–1990 / Joseph Martin Hernon.
p.   cm.
Includes bibliographical references and index.
ISBN 1-56324-937-5
1. United States—Politics and government.
2. United States. Congress. Senate—History.
3. Legislators—United States—History.
I. Title.
E183.H46   1996
973—dc20   96-8940
CIP
Printed in the United States of America

To the memory of my father,
Joseph Martin Hernon (1901–1963),
a lawyer's lawyer;

my mother, Lucille Mearns (1902–1990),
a loving teacher of a sickly child;

Dr. Geoffrey Morrison (1948–1995), a historian's historian,
who challenged me to undertake the task;

and George Macaulay Trevelyan, O.M. (1876–1962),
whose inspiring artistry taught me the poetry
and irony of history.

Contents

Preface

Americans are not known for their sense of history or historical memory, though our national past spans little more than two centuries. So it should not be surprising to discover quite a few unsung political heroes, especially with our relatively recent obsession with the presidency to the neglect of Congress. But the end of the Cold War appears to mark the end of the imperial presidency and a greater balance of power between the executive and legislative branches.

My focus on character comes at the end of a national age of hubris as we are forced to downsize our patriotic ego. National demoralization has recently inspired a plethora of studies of the American character, but one must caution against easy, moralistic answers. It is hoped that this study demonstrates the way individual character can shape legislation and the course of historical events. Individual character does count for a lot.

Moving against the grain of conventional interpretations of American history, my study does not focus on a multiplicity of details but, rather, endeavors to paint in broad strokes a panorama of the great American political debate. Should not the study of history raise big moral questions with no facile answers?

Joseph M. Hernon
Amherst, Mass.
March 25, 1996

Profiles in character

Introduction

In 1956, Senator John F. Kennedy published a much-heralded book about "that most admirable of human virtues—courage," which he defined in a phrase of Ernest Hemingway's, "grace under pressure." The book's dust jacket headlined "Decisive Moments in the Lives of Celebrated Americans," who happened to be members of the United States Senate. Although I have also written about the lives of senators, I have done so in a considerably different way.

First of all, my heroes will be evaluated according to the Greco-Roman concept of "Virtue." It includes not only courage but also prudence, temperance, and justice, in our Founding Fathers' conception of their Greek and Roman heroes. This kind of courage is defined as the fortitude of a lifetime, which makes "grace under pressure" possible.

The young Thomas Jefferson wrote to a friend that "everything is useful which contributes to fix us in the principles and practice of virtue," and he recommended reading authors such as Jonathan Swift and Voltaire who would inspire an emotional, commonsense kind of virtue. In a letter to John Adams in old age, Jefferson wondered what a Julius Caesar, who "had been as virtuous as he was daring and sagacious," might "have done to lead his fellow citizens into good government." Very little, the Monticello sage concluded, because Rome's only concept of government was the "degenerate Senate" and the people were not "informed, by education" or encouraged "in habits of virtue."

Pierce Butler of South Carolina, a member of the Constitutional Convention and the first Senate, noted that the very concept of the office of president was shaped during the Philadelphia deliberations by a consensus about the "Virtue" of the expected first incumbent. George Washington's perceived virtue determined the powers given to the presidency itself.

Like the members of the first Senate, the young Washington was conscious of being taught "to put on the character and not just the clothes of a gentleman." Virtue and courage are part of character, but the historian must ascribe these characteristics with caution. Allan Nevins acknowledged in his "Foreword" to Kennedy's *Profiles* the need to look beyond moral courage to "that greater entity called character" because a person without character "may give fitful exhibitions of courage." Our "cynical society" of the 1990s has few criteria even to understand the concept, let alone live by it. And a study of a body intended as a forum for virtue must be an exploration into cultural as well as political history.[1]

Too much of our history centers on presidencies, and virtually every modern president has his own court historian with an extensive staff to exaggerate his importance and influence. Yet some senators who served unbroken terms for two to three decades were more politically significant than many of the presidents. And studying the contrasting careers of any two such senators provides a better understanding of the critical issues of their age.

Among the factors that determined my selections was length of tenure in the Senate. Thomas Hart Benton served from 1821 to 1851, John Sherman from 1861 to 1897, George Frisbie Hoar from 1877 to 1904, Henry Cabot Lodge Sr. from 1893 to 1924, William E. Borah from 1907 to 1940, George W. Norris from 1913 to 1943, and Strom Thurmond from 1954 to the present. Most of these men did not have presidential ambitions but through tenure and force of personality became historically significant. Sherman, on the other hand, illustrates a corollary to the theme: he was so busy running for president (three times) that he became a figurehead.

Significance is, of course, very much in the eye of the historical beholder. The collision course of the careers of Benton and John C. Calhoun within the Democratic Party led to their own, the party's, and the nation's crisis in the late 1840s. From the mid-1830s, they were at opposites on every issue that even indirectly involved slavery. Examining their conflicts provides a much clearer picture of the era, in my view, than a detailed assessment of the triumvirate of Webster, Clay, and Calhoun.

The two chapters on the Civil War and Reconstruction bear special notice. They contrast Charles Sumner, the famous antislavery leader, and William Pitt Fessenden, a truly unsung hero. Today's radical historians treat very favorably the bombastic Sumner but totally misunderstand the self-effacing Fessenden, especially his role in drafting the Fourteenth Amendment and in the impeachment trial of President Andrew Johnson. The temperamental differences between Sumner and Fessenden were as important as the political ones. Fessenden's heroism contrasts sharply with Sumner's demagoguery, or hubris, in 1866.

For the period from 1870 to 1900, I selected Hoar and Sherman. Hoar, though almost forgotten, was an obvious choice. He was one of a handful of

Lincolnian Republicans who had not abandoned their principles by 1890. George Edmunds of Vermont, serving from 1866 to 1891, and Justin Morrill, also of Vermont, whose tenure stretched from 1867 to 1898, were the other two. Edmunds retired in 1891, appalled at Senate ethics. Morrill, who had urged opportunism on Fessenden in the impeachment trial of 1868, became an outstanding legislator who lived just long enough to oppose the annexation of Hawaii. But, unlike ambitious cousin John Sherman, Hoar was more consistent over the years in supporting what the party of Lincoln had for a time advocated: civil rights. He became a champion of enforcing African American voting rights, woman suffrage, and rights for Chinese Americans, Irish Americans, and Filipinos.

Tom Walsh and Henry Cabot Lodge were of opposite parties and of almost opposite everything. Walsh demonstrated great cowardice as the author of the Sedition Act of 1918 but then stood up to Attorney General A. Mitchell Palmer and his assistant J. Edgar Hoover during the Red scare of 1919 and 1920 (something President-elect John F. Kennedy was afraid to do against FBI chief Hoover in 1960). Most significantly, Walsh, breaking with President Woodrow Wilson, almost achieved a compromise on the Treaty of Versailles. Perhaps the greatest parliamentarian in the history of the Senate, Lodge, out of crass personal and political motives, aided the "irreconcilables" and President Wilson in killing the treaty.

The 1920s in the Senate—and in many ways, in the country—were Borah's decade, and the 1930s were definitely Norris's. Both were progressive Republicans, though Norris supported Franklin Delano Roosevelt (FDR) in the 1932 presidential election and turned independent by 1936. Leader of the irreconcilables in defeating the Treaty of Versailles in 1920, successor to Lodge as chair of the Senate Foreign Relations Committee in 1924, and sponsor of efforts to "outlaw" war, Borah embodied the political issues of the twenties. His reputation would suffer as the result of his failure to understand the Nazi threat. The father of the Tennessee Valley Authority (TVA), Norris was a greater champion of the New Deal than most of the Democrats. He was the almost perfect progressive during his forty years in Congress, thirty of them in the Senate: as a final act in 1942, he fought for the elimination of the poll tax on southern African Americans.

Both Bob Taft and Arthur Vandenberg were Republicans, but their debates on foreign policy shaped national attitudes (including those of the Democrats) from 1950 to 1990. Vandenberg was a major architect of the bipartisan American foreign policy from 1945 to 1950, including the Truman Doctrine, the Marshall Plan, and the North Atlantic Treaty Organization (NATO). Skeptical of increasing American commitments to Europe and the Middle East, Taft became the chief opponent of NATO. The political jousts of the two ended with the triumph of the policy of collective security against international communism that Vandenberg had supported, though isolation would remain an enticing alternative down to the present.

Clearly, the Cold War and civil rights dominated the agenda of American politics from the Korean War to the present, and the careers of Hubert Humphrey and Strom Thurmond illustrate the theme. Though the ideological father of the New Frontier and Great Society programs, Humphrey found his career wrecked upon the shoals of presidential ambition and national security. Civil rights were subordinated to fighting communism in Southeast Asia. Thurmond modernized Calhoun's techniques, converting the white backlash of the 1960s into a political strategy. Thurmond's conversion from Democrat to Republican in 1964 was a prelude to a southern and Sunbelt strategy that elected Richard Nixon, Ronald Reagan, and George Bush. Knowing where power lies during an imperial presidency, Thurmond served in the Senate as a virtual one-man fifth column for the military-industrial complex.

The Cold War produced an arrogance of power in the nation and the executive branch, or what the ancient Greeks might call an age of hubris. But individual heroes emerged to check the abuse of power. Some acts of heroism flowed from the character of a lifetime, such as Sam Ervin's advocacy of constitutional rights during Watergate. On the other hand, three former professors, publicly perceived as virtuous—Wayne Morse, William Fulbright, and Mike Mansfield—differed from one another in word and action when heroism was desperately needed during the escalating Vietnam War. Gene McCarthy and Bobby Kennedy, motivated by both hubris and principle, acted out the political tragedy of 1968.

Although the dual portraits present a collage for each era of American history, I have placed them in a larger mosaic illustrating the roles of the executive and legislative branches. My book in this sense is a study of the Senate but not in a narrow institutional way.

Part I, "The Patrician Age," describes a period in which the Senate served as a kind of Privy Council to the president, with the vice president presiding. National reputations were to be made in the House, among them, those of James Madison and Henry Clay. The Senate was merely a springboard to the cabinet or preferably to the presidency, as it was for James Monroe and as Rufus King hoped it would be. But all that would change by 1820, when King led the opposition to the admission of Missouri as a slave state.

Part II, "The National Forum," portrays the Senate from 1820 to 1870 as the center stage in the national debate over slavery and emancipation. Here the South was able to maintain the balance between slave and free states, and the states' rights principles of Calhoun triumphed over Benton's opposition to the extension of slavery. For the sake of winning the presidency, the Democratic Party appeased the South in the 1850s, but to no avail. The Republicans gradually grew in strength from 1854 and controlled the Senate through the Civil War and Reconstruction. Two of their leaders, Fessenden and Sumner, not only shaped the Fourteenth Amendment and Reconstruction but also came close in 1862 and again from 1865 to 1868 to establishing something on the order of a parliamentary form of government.

Part III, "The Rise and Fall of the Senate Oligarchy," covers the broadest expanse of time, from 1870 to 1940. While the presidency was undoubtedly weak in the late nineteenth century, the House grew in political strength and the Senate played its traditional role in moderating legislation. But by 1900, a Senate oligarchy quietly wielded power sharing with an increasingly imperialistic presidency. Nelson Aldrich of Rhode Island was the chief oligarch, deeming it his role to serve the commercial and industrial interests. He was succeeded in 1911 by a loyal lieutenant, Henry Cabot Lodge of Massachusetts, who led the Senate Republicans until 1924. After six years of a Democratic-controlled Senate from 1913 to 1919, Lodge, the last of the old oligarchs, led the Republican Party of conservatives and progressives in defeating the Treaty of Versailles. Never had the Senate been so powerful, and it retained its power during the Jazz Age, when the country appeared to want a weak government. With a weak president, such as the inconsequential ex-Senator Warren G. Harding, Senator William Borah of Idaho became nationally and internationally powerful as chair of the Senate Foreign Relations Committee. Borah's power grew in direct proportion to the weakness of the president. The return to a strong presidency under FDR in 1933 marked the beginning of the decline of the power of the Senate. It was an era for strong independents, such as Senator George Norris of Nebraska, to star amid the turbulence of the depression and the divisive issues cutting across party lines. World War II and foreign threats to our national security strengthened the powers of the presidency, as the Senate slowly went into decline.

Part IV, "The Imperial Presidency and the Supine Senate," runs from 1940 to 1990. The power of the presidency was necessarily strengthened during wartime, especially during such a cataclysm as World War II, but the postwar effects were unforeseeable. The Cold War turned the Senate into little more than an appendage to the executive branch, but individual senators who realized this wielded much power. During the 1940s, the major contest was within the Republican Party. Senator Arthur Vandenberg of Michigan was a typical midwestern isolationist until his conversion to internationalism at the end of the war. Under President Harry S. Truman, he in effect was a second secretary of state, and the Vandenberg Resolution became the foundation for NATO and for the concept of collective security against the spread of communism. In opposition to NATO, Senator Robert Taft of Ohio worried about the weakening of the constitutional role of the Senate. And in the nuclear age, the power of the Senate was even further diminished in the name of national security and atomic secrecy: the careers of Senator Hubert Humphrey of Minnesota and Senator Strom Thurmond of South Carolina illustrate this. An imperial presidency that could break the logjam of civil rights bills during the 1960s could also lead the nation into foreign military ventures that would in the long run undermine our domestic economy.

Was the indirect election of senators by state legislators, as Alexis de Tocqueville put it in 1831, responsible for the Senate's enjoying "a monopoly of intelligence and talent" in contrast to the directly elected House, which was "remarkable for its vulgar elements"? Tocqueville argued that "this transmission of the popular authority through an assembly of chosen men operates an important change in it by refining its discretion and improving its choice." In his memoirs, Thomas Hart Benton disputed the value of indirect elections and Tocqueville's view that senators were chosen "by the wisdom of the State legislatures" and representatives "by the folly of the people." Senator Benton observed that the Senate was "in great part composed of the pick of the House." Did the Seventeenth Amendment, adopted in 1913, which called for the popular election of senators, drastically change the course of the Senate's history? This question is implicitly raised in assessing all of the senators before and after 1913.[2]

Henry Cabot Lodge, who was elected under both systems, thought that the passage of the Seventeenth Amendment would not change things. That remains a defensible claim. The old system elected Rufus King, "the last of the Romans," who could not win popular election to be governor of New York but could become senator. Six-year terms and indirect elections ought, in theory, to have given senators a certain freedom that the whims of popular opinion threaten. But was it easier to manipulate an Ohio legislature to elect a John Sherman or, in effect, bribe a Rhode Island legislature to reelect a Nelson Aldrich than it is to seduce a public? On the other hand, would that direct connection to the Founding Fathers, George Frisbie Hoar, have been easily reelected in a popular election? Were the popularly elected Keating Five less influenced by special interests than men of Aldrich's Senate?

Lodge was probably right. The progressive reform of the Seventeenth Amendment did not of itself improve the Senate. Some of the early progressives such as Walsh and Norris were remarkable senators, but often in spite of their populism. And plebiscitary elections can obviously undermine democracy; strongly contested primaries and general elections have increasingly become rarities. Ultimately, the virtue of the individual senator is crucial: any system can be corrupted.

On April 30, 1957, Senator John F. Kennedy, chair of the Special Committee on the Senate Reception Room, announced the selection of the five outstanding senators of the past whose portraits were to be hung there. The five selected were Henry Clay, Daniel Webster, John C. Calhoun, Robert M. La Follette Sr., and Robert A. Taft. It was a conveniently nonpartisan selection of two Whigs, one Democrat, one Progressive Republican, and one Republican. But the letters and comments of roughly 150 prominent historians and political scientists who were invited to nominate five senators is especially revealing. Out of 114 letters of recommendation, George Norris, though not selected, received the most votes, at 87; followed by Clay, 86; Webster, 83; Calhoun, 63; and La Follette Sr., 44. The remainder of the top ten were Stephen A. Douglas, 31; Benton, 26; Vandenberg, 25; Taft, 23; and Robert F. Wagner, 20. John Sherman was tied for eleventh place with 7 votes; Sumner received 6, and Borah, 4. Hoar and Walsh received 2 votes, and Fessenden, 1. These recommendations invite some revealing comparisons with my own selections, which I made about one year before seeing the 114 letters and total votes.[3]

Norris appears to have been an obvious choice for everyone but the senators on the committee, as were the triumvirate of Webster, Clay, and Calhoun for almost everyone but me. Their careers illustrate the proposition that those who were continually running for president weakened their position in the Senate. My choice Benton ranked seventh; his struggle with Calhoun over slavery, in my view, dominated their period both in and out of the Senate. The only other possible hero, besides Benton, to come out of the Compromise of 1850 was Senator Sam Houston of Texas, and certainly not Clay or Webster. It is worth noting that the Democratic majority today still has only one Democrat in that place of honor: John C. Calhoun, a choice of James M. Burns, Arthur M. Schlesinger Jr., and C. Vann Woodward, though Professor Wood Gray of George Washington University warned that it would be "unthinkable" to select Calhoun for "statesmanship transcending party and State lines."

For the 1850s and 1860s, I selected Fessenden, who had received one vote among the respondents to Senator Kennedy's committee, and Sumner, the recipient of seven votes. Fessenden is, perhaps, my chief unsung hero and should be a loudly sung hero to all members of Lincoln's party. Only

Professor John P. Holden, who was then chair of the Government Department of the University of New Hampshire, selected Fessenden as one of his
five: he "was without doubt the ablest debater the Senate has had" and
helped to "lead the country into a program to finance the Civil War and to
avoid the terror of runaway inflation" and was important in "the development of the phrasing of the 14th Amendment." Finally, Fessenden "upheld
the unquestioned power of the Senate in impeachment proceedings to be a
judicial duty and not a political opportunity" and "braved the wrath of his
party and State." Henry Steele Commager selected Lyman Trumbull of
Illinois, Fessenden's principal supporter, as one of his five outstanding
senators.

Seven historians, including Roy F. Nichols, dean of the University of
Pennsylvania Graduate School, selected John Sherman, and only two,
George Frisbie Hoar. But Sherman, with his longevity, was interchangeable
with any number of others of the era, whereas Hoar was unique for the
senate of the Gilded Age. Professor Thomas D. Clark of the University of
Kentucky selected Hoar: "In the Senate he brought dignity and professional
character to that body by his personal behavior and by his high standards of
decorum." Hoar knew "full well," according to Clark, that because of his
opposition to the salary grab and the American Protective Association, "his
position in the Senate would be injured." And I would include Hoar's
support for woman suffrage, Chinese immigration, and African American
voting rights and opposition to the annexation of the Philippines.

No historian or political scientist selected Henry Cabot Lodge, who obtained the first Ph.D. in history in the United States. The constitutional
scholar Edward S. Corwin of Princeton had considered him because of the
Lodge Reservations on the League of Nations but selected Norris instead.
Tom Walsh won two votes, including that of Professor Fred A. Shannon of
the University of Illinois, who wrote: "Walsh, a stalwart advocate of many
forward-looking policies, is best remembered as a conservationist and opponent of corrupt disposal of the public resources. He reached his climax in
the prosecution of the Teapot Dome miscreants." Quincy Wright of the
Carnegie Endowment for International Peace, who was the other admirer of
Walsh, called him "the ablest advocate of the League of Nations in the
Senate." Crucial in my selection of Walsh were his efforts to obtain a
compromise on the Treaty of Versailles and the League of Nations and his
growth during the Red scare. Lodge, though no hero of mine, is a central
figure in the history of the Senate and the country.

Norris and Borah were easy choices for the period 1920 to 1940, especially that "senator-at-large of the whole American people," Norris. Borah
won four votes of historians, among them Professor Dewey W. Grantham

Jr. of Vanderbilt: "Few Senators left a greater impression on their fellow Senators or upon the country as a whole than Borah."

The two senators dominating the first decade of the imperial presidency, from 1940 to 1950, by the sheer force of their personalities and intellects were Taft and Vandenberg. Taft was a hero to conservative Republicans and was chosen as one of the honored five, though he ranked ninth among the historians, just behind Vandenberg. Two well-known historians, Richard N. Current and Samuel F. Bemis, selected Vandenberg, Current pointing to Vandenberg's progress "from an intelligent isolationism to an understanding conception of the changing needs of American foreign policy."[4]

Future historians will assess the accuracy of my portraits of Humphrey and Thurmond. Could Humphrey, a one-man brain trust for the New Frontier and Great Society, have reached the level of a Norris had he not been selected vice president? Thurmond's significance and influence are obvious at a time when so many senators have been trying to use the Senate as a springboard to the White House.

This excursion through American history that focuses on virtuous senators is meant to counter an all too popular and cynical view that the study of history is irrelevant. Such a demoralizing philosophy is to be expected in an age of greed. W.E.H. Lecky wrote in *Democracy and Liberty* a century ago: "Where cynicism and scepticism have sapped the character, wealth comes too frequently to be looked on as the one reality of life, and atoning for every misdeed." It was a bad omen for the future of a nation, he thought, when men of "colossal fortunes" but questionable character became "the objects of admiration, adulation, and imitation." The words of Alexis de Tocqueville during the 1830s, fearing that democracy could turn to despotism, also carry much meaning today: "It really is difficult to imagine how people who have entirely given up managing their own affairs could make a wise choice of those who are to do that for them." In the principal address, "Historical Significance of the Occasion," at the unveiling of the portraits of the five "outstanding senators" on March 12, 1959, the words of Vice President Richard M. Nixon fell on many deaf ears, especially his own, with a delicious sense of irony: "We often hear that ours is a government of laws rather than of men. Certainly this is true. But, we also know that the most perfect law, the most perfect constitution, the most perfect rules of procedure may not be successful in operation unless there are men who are adequate to the tasks to which they are assigned."[5]

I

The Patrician Age (1789–1820)

Why did the U.S. Constitution provide for a two-house Congress? According to a popular story, Thomas Jefferson, upon returning from France, posed this question to George Washington over breakfast. "Why did you pour your tea into that saucer?" Washington replied. "To cool it," Jefferson answered. "Just so," Washington continued: "we pour House legislation into the senatorial saucer to cool it."

After the Philadelphia Constitutional Convention defeated the "Virginia Plan," in which members of a national Senate were to be elected by the House of Representatives in proportion either to the wealth or to the population of the states, the Federalists, or supporters of the Constitution, sought to disguise their aristocratic theory of mixed government in Roger Sherman's "Connecticut Compromise." Calling for the election of two senators from each state, it provided Federalists with the argument that "the people will be represented in one house, the state legislatures in the other." The Senate would thus restrain "the large states from having improper advantages over the small ones" and assuage the Anti-Federalist fear of the extreme consolidation of federal power. Even James Madison, who had fought the Connecticut Compromise the hardest in Philadelphia, defended it in the Virginia Ratifying Convention by arguing that the federal government would be "completely consolidated" if the Senate were to be "chosen by the people in their individual capacity, in the same manner as the members of the other house." Such an electoral process would destroy "the dissimilarity in the genius of the two bodies" that lay at the heart of the bicameral principle, Madison asserted in *The Federalist, Number 62.*

Alexander Hamilton, the leading Federalist, warned his fellow delegates in Philadelphia that "we need to be rescued from the democracy." "Nothing," he argued, "but a permanent body"—that is, a Senate for life—"can check the impudence of democracy." Because the Anti-Federalists, in his words, "so often" expressed their fear of "aristocracy," the Federalists felt compelled to deny any comparisons of the new Senate with the English House of Lords or the Roman Senate.[1]

Many of the Founding Fathers also made the mistake of equating oligarchy (rule of the few, actually the wealthy few, or plutocracy, in America) with aristocracy (rule of the elite best, usually an inherited nobility). Rufus King of New York, Hamilton's chief Federalist "gladiator" in the new Senate, frequently talked this way, which strengthened the coalition of urban workers and farmers, including new immigrants, beginning to support an opposition clique of Jeffersonian "Republicans." Jefferson called for a "party of virtue" to oppose "Rogues," and Madison saw two parties developing: a "republican party" founded on the belief that "mankind are capable of governing themselves" and an "antirepublican party," which had "debauched themselves into the persuasion that mankind are incapable of governing themselves."[2]

The Federalists slowly died out after 1800 because of their narrowing political base, and Rufus King was their last presidential candidate in 1816. But the last gasp of aristocratic Federalism, uttered by King in the Senate, was aimed at slavery, the great flaw in the democratic pretensions of the majority, Jeffersonian Republicans and their Democratic Party heirs. Wealthy northern aristocrats, whether Federalists like King, or their Republican heirs of Abraham Lincoln's day and later, such as William Pitt Fessenden and George Frisbie Hoar, would be free to oppose slavery and champion equal rights for African Americans and other ethnic minorities, as well as women. They were politically free to do so since they were not burdened by an alliance with southern white democracy, and their relative wealth and education gave them a psychological freedom to espouse large and just causes.

Like so many of the Founding Fathers, King sought to implement a Whig sense of history that he imbibed during the American Revolution. He emphasized experience and the pursuit of the practical in the life of the new nation. But like Edmund Burke, he became a conservative in opposition to the democratic extremes of the French Revolution. Its Democratic-Republican supporters, in the view of King's Federalists, sought to destroy history's "steadying" effect on the pursuit of liberty.[3]

Leading Anti-Federalists, such as Jefferson's alter ego, James Monroe, reacted to the oligarchic tendencies of the Federalists by forming a Republican alliance of workers in the North and West and plantation owners and supporters of slavery in the South. But this alliance would be increasingly threatened after 1820, as the Senate itself became the last bastion of an oligarchy, not of northern wealth but of southern land and slaves, which used fear of a consolidation of federal power to protect the tyranny of whites over blacks.

The Senate, that hoped-for forum for virtue, was largely an insignificant body with aristocratic pretensions until the Missouri Compromise of 1820 turned it into the chief political battleground between North and South. The "genius" of the Senate would not only protect smaller states against the larger ones but also defend tyrannical masters against their slaves.

Both King and Monroe are examples of politicians who used the Senate as a mere political stepping-stone. But King's return to the Senate, where he led the opposition to the Missouri Compromise, was, in perspective, the most significant achievement of either man, including anything Monroe accomplished in eight years as president. It remained, however, for Thomas Hart Benton to demonstrate the historical significance of a long, unbroken senatorial career.

1

"Last of the Romans"

Rufus King vs. James Monroe (1789–1820)

When the first U.S. Senate convened in December 1790 in its new quarters in Philadelphia, the two full-length portraits of Louis XVI and Marie Antoinette—1784 gifts of the French government to the Confederation Congress—were moved from the Senate's temporary chamber in New York. But because of divisive debates over the changing political conditions in revolutionary France, the portraits were hung with curtains that could be drawn for protection. Though symbols of *l'ancien régime* could be easily covered, the principles of the French Revolution began to permeate American politics and occasioned the rise of party politics in the United States. In the new Senate, two principal representatives of the emerging factions or parties, the pro–French revolutionary "Republicans" and the antirevolutionary "Federalists," were James Monroe of Virginia and Rufus King of New York.

Especially significant were their differences over slavery, as early as 1785, when they both served in the Confederation Congress. King led the fight to ban slavery after 1800 in the federal lands of the Northwest Territory. Though Thomas Jefferson supported the plan, Monroe dropped it in his Ordinance of 1787; but the Congress approved it, in exchange for concessions to southern planters prohibiting the growth of tobacco and indigo on the northwest side of the Ohio. On the extension of slavery question, Rufus King three decades later challenged the fragile "Era of Good Feelings" that enveloped the presidency of James Monroe.[1]

Born in 1758 into the tidewater aristocracy of Virginia that included George Washington, George Mason, "Light Horse Harry" Lee, and Richard Henry

Lee, James Monroe was three years younger than Rufus King. Their lives were closely intertwined, often in opposition, especially during the forty years from 1785 until 1825. Upon taking his seat as senator from New York in July 1789, Rufus King at thirty-four was the youngest senator, but that distinction would soon go to James Monroe at thirty-two, representing Virginia beginning in December 1790. But the Senate at that time, with its secret deliberations, was considered a graveyard for talented men, as James Madison enhanced his reputation in the more democratic House of Representatives, with its public debates. King had the longest career in the Senate in its first thirty years or so, serving from 1789 to 1796 and again from 1813 to 1825, and the two men confronted each other on the Senate floor only during Monroe's four years in the Senate from 1790 to 1794. But their differences during those years signaled the rise of party politics. Most significantly, both men were classic examples of politicians who used the Senate as a stepping-stone to higher office, particularly the presidency. In 1816, Monroe was the first former senator to be elected president, and his opponent was Senator King.

Rufus King was born in 1755 at Dunstan Landing, a part of the Maine frontier village of Scarborough, where his father, Richard, was a wealthy lumber merchant. King's boyhood memories were scarred when he was eleven, as a group of disgruntled debtors, disguised as drunken Indians and calling themselves Sons of Liberty, ransacked the family home and burned his father's papers, including deeds and securities. The family's attorney, John Adams, described the "Terror" and "Distress" of the scene as "enough to move a Statue, to melt an Heart of Stone." Such a scene might explain Rufus King's temperamental conservatism.

King's education strengthened his conservative Federalist views. First in his class at revolution-disrupted Harvard in 1777—with distinctions in math, language, and oratory—he then studied law under the conservative Theophilus Parsons at Newburyport. King developed into a Lockean empiricist, who believed that experience was the best teacher. He later commended the views of Edmund Burke and quoted that great opponent of the French Revolution: "We may not apply unqualified metaphysical principles to Affairs. Experience not abstraction ought to be our Guide in practice and in Conduct."

Interrupting his legal studies, King saw limited military service in Rhode Island as a major in General John Glover's brigade in 1778, but as the fighting shifted from New England to the South, King returned to his legal career. Monroe's military experience—better documented—was more formative for the teenager. He was certainly more interested in glory and advancement in the army than King, as Major Monroe became an aide to

Lord Stirling, one of Washington's brigade commanders. Monroe soon became acquainted with two other young aides, Lieutenant Colonel Alexander Hamilton and Colonel Aaron Burr. But his friendship with another eighteen-year-old, Pierre S. DuPonceau, secretary to Baron von Steuben, made a lasting impression.

DuPonceau introduced Monroe to the world of the *philosophes* and advanced the view that the American Revolution was acting out the theories of the Enlightenment. The young Frenchman encouraged the stoical streak in the naturally reserved young Virginian and also motivated Monroe's philosophical bent of mind, which would be greatly strengthened under the influence of Thomas Jefferson. Floundering in his legal studies at William and Mary after leaving the army, Monroe found a patron in the author of the Declaration of Independence and followed Governor Jefferson to his new capital at Richmond in 1780. Undoubtedly, Monroe's legal education under Jefferson was much broader than King's. The American *philosophe* advised his young protégé to read not only John Locke but Jean-Jacques Rousseau, and Cicero but also Plutarch. Monroe was a creature of Jefferson and worked for the rest of his life to turn the ideals of the American Revolution into a practical model for humanity.

The career of Monroe and that of King were remarkably parallel, each statesman becoming the other's principal political antagonist. Monroe was elected to the Virginia House of Delegates in 1782 and King to the House of Representatives of the Massachusetts General Court in 1783. Both married socially prominent New York women in 1786. Mary Alsop King was far wealthier, with her estimated 50,000 pounds dowry, than Elizabeth Kortright Monroe. At the beginning of his political career, King was handsome, with piercing eyes and haughty demeanor; and with his "high-toned" voice, he became a penetratingly eloquent debater. Monroe was physically impressive in a different way, broad-shouldered and of a massive over-six-foot frame. His plain face, wide-set eyes, and large Roman nose reflected his personality, which a younger contemporary described as "Plain, practical, didactic—a man of action, not words." In later life, he displayed a grave manner not unlike Washington's. King's connections with Adams and Hamilton shaped his career; Jefferson gave form to the career of Monroe.[2]

In 1786, Monroe doubted the political honesty of King as a member of the "most illiberal" delegation to the Confederation Congress, that of Massachusetts. But at the Philadelphia convention in 1787 drafting the Constitution, Monroe, who was not a delegate, would have to be content with reading about King's eloquence, if occasional rudeness, in presenting his views. King privately expressed the hope that the Massachusetts General

Court would "check the madness of Democracy" and send to Congress "men of Consequence, not Dunces." But King's "conservatism" and the Virginia delegation's "liberalism" were both bundles of contradictions. King, opposing the "rule of numbers," argued that property as well as population should determine the apportionment of representation in the new national legislature. Counting African American slaves as three-fifths of a person added to his hostility to representation by numbers. Both King and Madison, a Virginia delegate, opposed the "Great Compromise," proposed by Roger Sherman of Connecticut, which gave the states equal representation in the Senate and called for representation in the House according to population. But King and Madison agreed to the compromise since the only alternative was a breakup of the convention.

The outbreak of an antitax rebellion of western Massachusetts farmers under Captain Daniel Shays in 1786 strengthened King's skepticism about popular self-government and his support for a strong national government. He argued at the convention for the nationalist, or Federalist, view, including the need for a strong president and central government with separation of powers and checks and balances. King signed the Constitution in Philadelphia, having served as a member of the Committee of Style. As a delegate to the Massachusetts convention, he forcefully argued for its ratification.

Monroe, however, as a delegate to the Virginia Ratifying Convention, was a leading Anti-Federalist. Not an extreme opponent of ratification, Monroe focused on the controversial Jay–Gardoqui negotiations in 1786 regarding free navigation of the Mississippi. He maintained that under the Constitution, in the absence of a fixed quorum, seven states in the Senate could use their votes to close the Mississippi, in contrast to the nine states required to ratify a treaty under the Articles of Confederation. Madison, one of the principal authors of the Constitution and of twenty-nine of the *Federalist* papers, countered by arguing that western rights were better protected by the Constitution since treaties would be negotiated by the president and approved by a two-thirds vote of the Senate. Monroe's concern about manipulation of a Senate quorum Madison found to be absurd.

James Monroe perhaps convinced twelve of the fourteen delegates from the then Kentucky section of Virginia to vote with the Anti-Federalists. But the pressure increased when word arrived that eight states had already ratified the Constitution. Though not the decisive ninth, Virginia was a very important tenth, but its Anti-Federalists did win approval of a Bill of Rights to be submitted to the new Congress.

Monroe was pressured into running for the House of Representatives against Madison, but the soon-to-be author of the Bill of Rights outmaneuvered Monroe in proposing amendments to the Constitution as additional guarantees of individual liberties. With the support of the Baptists because of his advocacy of religious liberty, Madison easily won the House seat where he was to play a major role for the next eight years. But Monroe, at Jefferson's insistence, agreed to represent Virginia in the U.S. Senate, taking his seat in Philadelphia principally to enable his wife to be close to her family in New York. Monroe and Madison would soon become leaders of the "Republican" supporters of Jefferson in Congress.[3]

Largely because of his wife's family connections in New York and the birth of his children there, Rufus King moved to the city. After one month's official residence, he was elected to the New York Assembly; and after serving there for only ten days, backed by the Federalists as a compromise candidate, he was elected by the state legislature as junior U.S. senator. Taking his seat in the "upper chamber" at Federal Hall in New York City, King drew lots with the senior senator, General Philip Schuyler, Alexander Hamilton's father-in-law, and won the six-year term, the general drawing one for two years. King quickly became one of the leading Hamiltonian "Federalists" in the Senate.

The first Senate mustered a quorum on April 6, 1789, and immediately began debating rules and matters of protocol. It was soon to be vigorously, if not ludicrously, presided over by John Adams, inaugurated as vice president on April 21. Arguing that there were "no people in the world so much in favor of titles as the people of America," Adams from April 23 to May 14 led the Senate in a debate over titles for the president and other top officials of the government. He thought the word *president* was so commonly used that it was undignified by itself, but after several weeks of debate, the only title that stuck, temporarily, was the one bestowed by Senator Ralph Izard of South Carolina upon the stout vice president: "His Rotundity."

The austere propriety of General Washington added dignity no title could bestow to the office of president as he was sworn into office on April 30, 1789, on the balcony outside the Senate chamber in New York. Similarly, the demeanor of the first senators shaped customs and manners in the Senate. Selected by a process of filtration through the state legislatures, the Senate, conscious of its important name derived from Roman history, searched for an identity in those early years. Was it to be aristocratic by nature as many of the Federalists believed? Or was it to have the somewhat more modest but nonetheless weighty presence that Madison at the convention projected for it, a body proceeding "with more coolness, with more system, and with more wisdom than the popular branch" and therefore requiring "greater extent of information and stability of character"?[4]

As a leading Federalist, Rufus King quickly became a target for that acerbic critic of the First Congress and spiritual founding father of the Democratic Party, William Maclay, senator from Pennsylvania from 1789 to 1791. He described King's character as "detestable—a perfect canvas for the devil to paint on; a groundwork void of every virtue." Maclay called King one of the Hamiltonian "gladiators" adept at "smuggling" bills through the Senate at the behest of Secretary of the Treasury Hamilton. It was King's Hamiltonian defense of the business community that especially rankled Democratic-Republicans like Maclay and Monroe.

Shortly after entering the Senate, Monroe espoused Jefferson's opposition to the Bank of the United States, which Hamilton proposed, as based upon "implied powers" in the Constitution, and King strongly supported. The bank was a stabilizing force for the new government, attracting capital from merchants and winning their much-needed confidence. But it also benefited speculators and thereby attracted the opposition of agrarian interests. The bank further delineated differences between King's Federalists and Monroe's Republicans and would reemerge as an issue in the 1830s.[5]

Monroe sharpened the party profiles in 1791 when he introduced a bill to open the Senate debates to the public. In his only Senate speech to be preserved, he called for exposing "the trustees of the publick . . . confidence to the publick view" to prevent enacting legislation "dangerous to the publick liberty." "Let the jealous, the prying eye of their constituents uphold their proceedings, mark their conduct, and the tone of the body will be changed," he asserted. With considerable naïveté, he argued that under the scrutiny of public debates, a senator "whose heart was devoted and whose mind pursued with unceasing ardor the establishment of arbitrary power" would "change his style and from motives of private interest become the fervent patron of the publick liberty." Though he initially lost the battle, the controversy raged on until 1794, when he succeeded in winning public admission to the debate over the seating of Albert Gallatin as senator from Pennsylvania. The Federalists, led by Rufus King, sought to deny Gallatin his seat on the grounds that he had not been a citizen for the requisite nine years when elected, as required by the Constitution.

A "sparrowlike" man, the French-speaking Swiss aristocrat Gallatin was opposed by some of the Federalists on bigoted, nativist grounds that would lead to their triumph and downfall over the Alien and Sedition Acts of 1798. The real motive, however, was the Federalist desire to strengthen a precarious one-vote control of the Senate. Gallatin, who had arrived in America in 1780 and taught French at Harvard, did not take an oath of allegiance until 1785 to the state of Virginia, which then owned the part of western Pennsylvania where he owned land. More important to the Federalists, however, was Gallatin's leadership of the farmers of western Pennsylvania in opposing Hamilton's excise tax on whiskey. And while serving unofficially in the Senate until the vote, Gallatin, who had a keen understanding of finances, launched an attack on Hamilton's fiscal policies in a sharp French accent. A future secretary of the treasury under President Jefferson, Gallatin was a symbol of the French Revolution the Federalists so despised; and by a strict party vote of 14 to 12, the "Democratic" Republican from Pennsylvania was unseated.[6]

Another major controversy that shaped the two-party system and highlighted the differences between King and Monroe was the "Citizen Genet" affair. Edmond Genet, as the French Republic's new minister to the United States, landed at Charleston, South Carolina, in April 1793, shortly after the execution of Louis XVI and Marie Antoinette and the French declaration of war against Great Britain, Spain, and Holland. President Washington had already issued a neutrality proclamation, though the word *neutrality* was not used. As the French minister journeyed toward Philadelphia, he was warmly greeted by Democratic societies and Anti-Federalist newspapers. When Genet arrived in Philadelphia, he received an icy reception from the president. Despite his promise to Secretary of State Jefferson, Genet ordered a captured English ship refitted as a French privateer, to sail in violation of American neutrality. The cabinet then decided to order Genet's official recall but to grant him asylum to escape the guillotine that awaited him in France.

Rufus King and Chief Justice John Jay published a letter in the New York newspaper *The Diary,* accusing Genet of planning to "Appeal to the People" over the head of the president. The Federalists had personalized the issue as a conflict of Genet against Washington, and Jefferson privately worried that the controversy might "sink the republican interest" and advised Madison and Monroe to abandon the Genet cause. According to Madison, Monroe could "hardly bring himself absolutely and openly" to condemn Genet; but along with other Republicans, the Virginians dissociated themselves from the Frenchman's conduct. Monroe still believed the philosophy he had espoused enthusiastically in essays under the pen name "Aratus" in 1791, linking the American and French revolutions: "Whoever owns the principles of one revolution must cherish those of the other. . . . As a friend of humanity, I rejoice in the French Revolution, but as a citizen of America, the gratification is greatly increased." Monroe warned that the failure of the Revolution in France would endanger liberty in America—a cardinal principle of Jeffersonian republicanism.[7]

The question of the French Revolution continued to shape the policies and attitudes of both King and Monroe through 1815, until the overthrow of

Napoleon and the end of potential and actual war with the United Kingdom. Monroe appropriately left the Senate in 1794 to become minister to France, and King in 1796 to serve as minister to the Court of St. James. Each man also found his life entangled at times in a conspiratorial web woven by the chief plotter within his party, the Federalist Secretary of State Timothy Pickering and Republican Senator Aaron Burr.

Burr connived to become minister to France in 1794 to succeed Gouverneur Morris, recalled at the request of the French government. But Washington, at that precarious moment in Franco-American relations, after the Genet affair and the Reign of Terror, was not about to appoint Burr; and Monroe served for the next two years. He was most successful in rescuing Tom Paine and Madame Lafayette from prison and the guillotine but alienated Secretary Pickering and even President Washington for excessive admiration of the French government. Yet he was unable to calm French anger over the treaty with Great Britain negotiated by Chief Justice John Jay in November 1794. His Republican friends at home were equally angry at granting Britain most-favored-nation status, with no provision for settling the question of the impressment of American sailors, among other issues. When Timothy Pickering replaced the pro-French Edmund Randolph as secretary of state because Washington believed Randolph had intrigued to block ratification of Jay's Treaty, Monroe's ministerial days were numbered. The president recalled him in 1796 during the growing controversy over Jay's Treaty.

While stationed in Thermidorian France, Monroe's chief flaw was his eagerness to see broad principles, rather than private ambitions, shaping political motives. He shared this trait with many other Jeffersonians and their heirs. He even sympathized with the negative French reaction to Washington's "Farewell Address" against "entangling alliances," including the long-standing one with France. Upon leaving his post, Monroe in a formal address praised the principles common to the American and French revolutions. Pickering found his comments "unpardonable."

King had an easier time as minister in England. More tactful but less witty than Monroe, King served ably and cultivated many friendships, including that of the abolitionist William Wilberforce. But the Federalist minister was also more strongly supported at home by the ruling Federalists in John Adams's administration. He was even kept on by Jefferson, until, on the advice of Hamilton, King resigned in 1802 to return home to aid the dwindling fortunes of the Federalists.

King's years in London coincided with the temporary triumph of the Federalists from 1796 through 1798. The Alien and Sedition Acts of 1798 spelled the beginning of their downfall and extinction. Silly ideology proved even more harmful to King and the Federalists than to Monroe and the Republicans. In 1790, the virtuous King was among those who defeated in the Senate a motion to wear mourning upon the death of that, in his words, "Old Rogue" Benjamin Franklin. But it was less for being a libertine that the homespun philosopher had lost the favor of Federalist senators, than for being a Francophile.

So extreme in his opposition to the French Revolution was King that he personally prevented many of the Irish revolutionaries of 1798, sentenced to be exiled, from seeking asylum in the United States. Back home, his Federalist allies, during the threat of war with France, were pushing through Congress the Alien and Sedition Acts, which raised the period of residency for full citizenship from five to fourteen years and led to the arrest of twenty-five people for sedition, most of them editors or printers. Former Senator George Cabot of Massachusetts praised King for "the great service you have rendered the Country in shutting its doors against Irish Desperadoes." King boasted that his intervention had won him the "honor" of the "cordial and distinguished Hatred" of Irish leaders.

That "hatred" would be repaid a hundredfold as the new immigrants flocked to the Democratic-Republican Party and helped to elect Jefferson president in 1800. From there, it was a slow death for the Federalists over the next twenty years, while Rufus King, their last leader, was bitterly opposed by Irish immigrants, who aligned themselves with the slaveholding Democrats.[8]

Monroe was like King in one respect: whether from virtue or shrewdness, he kept at arm's length the principal conspirator of his party. Aaron Burr—the charismatic, womanizing grandson of New England's fiery evangelist Jonathan Edwards—served as senator from New York from 1791 to 1797 and eventually was elected vice president in 1801. But he had his eye on the highest office as early as his contest for vice president in 1792. A leading Democratic-Republican, Burr had prevented a duel between Alexander Hamilton and James Monroe in 1791, only to become notorious by killing Hamilton himself in a duel in 1804.

King, meanwhile, was keeping his independence from Timothy Pickering, who served as secretary of state under Washington and for more than three years under Adams, until that president fired him for extreme hostility to France. Pickering was elected by the decrepit Federalists as senator from Massachusetts and served from 1803 to 1811. With scarcely a good word in later life for any of the Founding Fathers, except Hamilton, Pickering was especially critical of Washington's incompetence. While in the Senate, he fanned secessionist flames in New England in 1804 and, as part of the secession plot, even urged Federalists to back Republican Vice President Burr for governor of New York.

Pickering continued to plot the secession of the northeastern states up to the Hartford Convention of 1814, pitifully maintaining a rather pro-British attitude even after the burning of Washington. Burr—rumored to be involved in various conspiracies, including one that would make him king of Mexico—was hounded by President Jefferson and his allies. The president had only to remember the way his running mate of 1800 had tried to "steal" the election, replace Jefferson as president, and frustrate the intentions of the electors—all of which necessitated the passage of the Twelfth Amendment, providing for separate balloting for president and vice president. In 1807, Jefferson succeeded in getting Burr indicted for treason. At his trial in Richmond, Virginia, with Chief Justice John Marshall presiding, Burr was found not guilty; but he went into exile in Europe.

Burr became a legendary rogue in American history. A popular toast of 1807 runs, "Aaron Burr—may his treachery to his country exalt him to the scaffold, and hemp be his escort to the republic of Dust and ashes." But Burr also leaves the legacy of delivering one of the most memorable speeches in Senate history. He had stoically presided over the Senate during the counting of electoral votes from the 1804 election in which George Clinton replaced him as Jefferson's vice president. And in leaving his office of presiding officer, the diminutive Burr moved many senators to tears in his tribute to their chamber as a forum for good or evil. The Senate, he declared, was "a sanctuary; a citadel of law, of order, of liberty: and it is here—it is here, in this exalted refuge; here, if anywhere, will resistance be made to the storms of political phrensy and the silent arts of corruption; and if the constitution be destined to perish by the sacrilegious hands of the demagogue or the usurper, which God avert, its expiring agonies will be witnessed on this floor."[9]

Also using the Senate as a stepping-stone while representing Massachusetts from 1803 to 1808 was John Quincy Adams, the first "profile in courage" in John F. Kennedy's study. Portrayed as a hero by Kennedy, Adams voted for Jefferson's embargo, despite the opposition of home-state Federalists, and resigned his Senate seat afterward. But J.Q. Adams's heroism had the reinforcement of his father's approval: the ex-president distrusted extreme Federalists like Pickering. Quincy Adams also attended the Republican caucus that nominated Madison for president and soon was appointed minister to Russia by Jefferson. A political realist and careerist, Adams abandoned the moribund Federalists and eventually became President Monroe's secretary of state and presidential successor—the third secretary in a row to step into the presidency.[10]

While Adams was in the Senate, Monroe replaced King at the Court of

St. James. The Virginian enhanced his public reputation by his role in negotiating the purchase of the full Louisiana Territory. But as minister to the United Kingdom, he suffered the humiliation of having the Monroe–Pinckney Treaty of 1806 not even submitted for ratification by Jefferson. In the view of the president and Secretary of State Madison, Monroe had ignored his instructions in negotiating a treaty with Britain that did not deal with impressment and indemnity payments for the British seizure of American ships. When Monroe resigned and returned to America in December 1807, he received a rather chilly reception from Jefferson and Madison and no promise of political preferment. In 1808, Jefferson witnessed the calamity of having the "two principal pillars of my happiness," Madison and Monroe, compete for the presidency. Madison easily defeated Monroe among Virginia electors and then won nationally, heading the Republican ticket with George Clinton against the Federalist ticket of Charles Cotesworth Pinckney and Rufus King. Monroe declined an informal offer of the governorship of Louisiana as beneath his status or, in Jefferson's words, paying "close attention to his honor and grade," and had to wait until 1811, when conditions were right, for Madison to appoint him secretary of state, whereupon he resigned as Virginia governor.

Rufus King twice served as Federalist vice presidential nominee, in 1804 and 1808. After an antiwar coalition of Federalists and northern Republicans carried most of New England and the Middle Atlantic States, King was returned to the Senate from New York, where he served from 1813 to 1825. President Madison even considered appointing King secretary of state during the desperate days of 1814, when the invading British burned the nation's capital. Such an appointment of a moderate Federalist would, it was argued, deflate support for the Hartford Convention and unite the country behind Madison's administration. But Monroe opposed the appointment of his lifelong antagonist, who as secretary of state would be in a stronger position to succeed Madison as president. Instead, Monroe, while serving as secretary of war in 1814, remained as acting secretary of state.

Monroe returned to his position at the State Department in 1815, now clearly heir apparent to Madison. In the presidential election of 1816, Monroe easily defeated King, the Federalist standard-bearer: the Federalists entered electors in only three states, and Monroe drubbed King by an electoral vote of 183 to 34. With anti-British feeling sweeping New York after the War of 1812, King, though still in the Senate, was defeated in the 1816 gubernatorial race as a symbol of "British thralldom," amid a rumored assassination plot involving Irish immigrants.[11]

The last of the Federalists, King was elected to the Senate in 1820 with the support of "Bucktail" Republicans led by Senator-elect Martin Van

Buren. A Federalist newspaper, the Boston *Columbian Centinel,* on July 12, 1817, had coined the phrase "Era of Good Feelings" to describe the presidency of James Monroe. He modified his republicanism into support for a national consensus, after the sectional divisiveness of the War of 1812. But the superficial unity only lasted his first term. After his unopposed reelection in 1820, when he won all but one electoral vote, including that of the father of his secretary of state, the last Federalist president, John Adams, factions were forming around three cabinet members and others. It was, however, Monroe's old antagonist, Rufus King, who exposed the president's Achilles' heel: the extension of slavery to states carved from the Louisiana Purchase.

Monroe was a good symbol of the national dilemma over slavery. Staunch advocate of the democratic principles of the French Revolution, he nevertheless permitted the execution of "about thirty-five" slaves as governor of Virginia after the Gabriel Uprising of 1800. The planned rebellion centered on a plantation about six miles from Richmond owned by Thomas Prosser, who was known for treating his slaves with "barbarity." The reputed leader of the insurrection was one of his slaves named Gabriel, described by another prisoner as "a fellow of courage and intellect above his rank in life." Having a divided council and being unable to cast a tie-breaking vote, Monroe was boxed in politically. Though he favored pardons, Monroe was not about to sacrifice his political career by resigning in protest, though there were mitigating circumstances calling for leniency. He wrote to his friend Jefferson: "When to avert the hand of the Executioner, is a question of great importance. It is hardly to be presumed, [that] a rebel who avows it was his intention to assassinate his master, etc., if pardoned will ever become a useful servant. And we have no power to transport them abroad, nor is it less difficult to say whether mercy or severity is the better policy in this case, tho' when there is cause for doubt it is best to incline to the former policy." Jefferson pathetically commented: "We are truly to be pitied."

Like many southerners who hated slavery, Monroe eventually became an advocate of relocating freed slaves in Africa. He supported the aims of the American Colonization Society, whose directors named the first settlement in their newly acquired territory of Liberia, Monrovia. But two decades after, in Governor Monroe's words, the "unpleasant incident" of the Gabriel Uprising, at the end of Monroe's first presidential term, the slavery question assumed new political importance in the debates over the admission of Missouri as a slave state.[12]

In 1819, twenty-two states were represented in the Senate, eleven slave and eleven free. Northerners were politically anxious as territories being carved from the Louisiana Purchase threatened to open themselves to slavery, later becoming states that would tip the Senate in favor of slavery. As antislavery ranks increased in the House from the more populous northern states, southerners looked upon the Senate as their last bastion against abolitionism.

At that time, Secretary of State John Quincy Adams noted in his diary that "at our evening parties we hear nothing but the Missouri question and Mr. King's speeches." Adams, the staunch antislavery advocate of the 1830s and 1840s in the House, in 1820 believed that although the Missouri Compromise was "all that could be effected under the present Constitution," "perhaps it would have been a wiser and bolder course to have persisted in the restriction on Missouri until it should have been terminated in a convention of the states to revise and amend the Constitution." Jefferson worried about a new "schism" based on "the coincidence of a marked principle, moral or political, *with a geographical line.*" He described the Missouri agitation as "a fire bell in the night."

Ringing that bell was Rufus King. President Monroe was concerned about the old Federalist King's forming a new party with dissident antislavery Republicans and thought that King's antislavery ardor reduced his reputation not only "for talents and patriotism" but "indeed for morality." The fiscally conservative King, however, was merely renewing the commitment he had made as early as 1787 in the Confederation Congress. At the Constitutional Convention, he also disliked the "three-fifths compromise" on the representation of slave states in Congress, although he defended it in urging ratification at the Massachusetts convention. But by 1819, he realized that opposition to the extension of slavery in newly admitted states was becoming increasingly popular in New York. In the end, it was the support of his new fellow senator Martin Van Buren that ensured his return to the Senate. King's views were an early version of those of the Free-Soil Party, whose candidate ex-President Van Buren would become in 1848.

King was not a strict abolitionist but opposed the continued expansion of slavery, mainly because of the resulting shift it might make in the political balance of power in the Senate, away from the North to the South. Nevertheless, King realized the national psychosis that slavery encouraged: "Freedom and slavery are the parties which stand this day before the Senate, and upon its decision the empire of the one or the other. . . . If, instead of freedom, slavery is to prevail and spread, as we extend our dominion, can any reflecting man fail to see the necessity of giving to the general government, greater powers to enable it to afford the protection that will be demanded of it; powers that will be difficult to control, and which may prove fatal to the public liberties?"

But President Monroe disputed King's "morality" in opposing the admission of Missouri as a slave state. Like Jefferson, he thought King was using the slavery question to divide the nation along geographical lines and to resurrect the Federalist Party. Certain of his own moral correctness, King argued before the Senate its moral obligation to ban slavery in the new territories: "Mr. President, I have yet to learn that one man can make a slave of another. If one man cannot do so, no number of individuals can have any better right to do it. And I hold that all laws or compacts imposing any such condition upon any human being are absolutely void, because contrary to the law of nature, which is the law of God, by which he makes his ways known to man, and is paramount to all human control."[13]

President Monroe, anxious for reelection in 1820, had become a nationalist and abandoned many of his early Republican principles. He even consorted with Nicholas Biddle, a director of that hated institution the Bank of the United States, to change the votes of three Pennsylvania members of the House to ensure the admission of Missouri. The balance of power was maintained in the Senate with Maine admitted as a free state. Slavery was to be prohibited north of the 36°30′ parallel in the territory of the Louisiana Purchase.

Though unanimously reelected in 1820, save one New Hampshire elector, Monroe was largely a figurehead in his second presidential term, which ushered in an era of bad feelings. Senator Samuel L. Southard of New Jersey, who became secretary of the navy, told John Quincy Adams that "the President was so harassed that he scarcely knew where to set his foot." Three members of his cabinet hoped to succeed him as president: Secretary of State John Quincy Adams, Secretary of the Treasury William Crawford, and Secretary of War John C. Calhoun. The election campaign of 1824 began almost immediately after Monroe's reelection and was joined by Henry Clay and Senator Andrew Jackson. Rufus King noted that Monroe in his second term had no friends in Congress to "support" his "recommendations," and Clay candidly remarked to Quincy Adams: "Mr. Monroe has just been reelected with apparent unanimity, but he has not the slightest influence in Congress. His career was considered as closed. There was nothing further to be expected by him or from him."[14]

As his valedictory in the Senate in 1825, King proposed a plan to encourage the emancipation and emigration of slaves through payments from the federal government. A fund would be established from the sale of public lands to aid in manumission. On a motion of Senator Thomas Hart Benton of Missouri, the resolution was printed. But it never reached the floor for discussion.

If Monroe was the "last of the cocked hats"—the Revolutionary War heroes who served as president—in Senator Harrison G. Otis's words, King was the "last of the Romans," or those patrician Federalists who hoped to model the American Senate upon the aristocratic body of the Roman Republic and to keep the plebeian House in check. Senator William Pinkney of Maryland described King, with his courtly manner and pompous airs, as "an old woman out of fashion." King appeared in the Senate dressed in knee breeches, silk stockings, and buckled shoes at the dawn of a new democratic era of trousers. But this symbol of the old manners and ways even made an impression on that rude but sophisticated frontiersman Benton, upon whom King urged "moderation and forbearance" in Senate debates.[15]

Both Monroe and King acted upon their own conceptions of virtue. Monroe, in his Era of Good Feelings, presented himself as a second Washington who governed above party politics. But his nonpartisan virtue turned to vice, as his cabinet disintegrated to infighting. During his second term, Monroe reigned but did not rule. In contrast, the Burkean conservative King, who had become a man without a party in the Senate, found an issue that gave his life new meaning toward its end. An elitist and an opponent of universal male suffrage as "in the highest degree dangerous," he nevertheless called slavery "contrary to the law of nature, which is the law of God." The last of the Federalists, King saw a need to limit suffrage according to property and education but found slavery abhorrent. Virtue demanded both for him at the dawn of a new democratic age with a racist hue.[16]

II

The National Forum (1820–1870)

The Senate came of age between 1819 and 1821 in the debates over the admission of the territory of Missouri to statehood. In 1819, there were twenty-two states in the Union, eleven slave and eleven free. Even with the three-fifths ratio for counting slaves boosting the representation of the slave states, they held only eighty-one votes in the House of Representatives, against its 105 seats from free states. Also worrisome to southern slaveowners was the more rapidly growing northern population: about 5.2 million people in free, to 4.5 million in slave, states.

The South looked to its equal vote in the Senate to preserve the sectional balance, and a compromise was concluded only with the support of the "doughfaces"—free-state representatives who defected from earlier support for the abolition of slavery in the state of Missouri. The mutual agreement provided for the admission of Maine, separated from Massachusetts, as a free state, and Missouri, as a slave state, which maintained the free/slave balance in the Senate. The Missouri Compromise also called for the exclusion of slavery from all territories carved from the Louisiana Purchase north of the parallel line 36°30′.

Slavery, often disguised in the form of sectional power struggles, shaped American politics from 1820 to 1850. And the political journey of one of the first two senators from Missouri, Thomas Hart Benton, clearly illumines the history of the United States over the thirty years he spent in the Senate until his defeat in 1851.

Benton's nemesis, as he rose to national prominence during the 1830s and 1840s, was John C. Calhoun of South Carolina. With their contrasting positions on slavery, they were fighting for the future of the Democratic Party, the only national party by the 1850s. Benton, a slaveowner, gradually opposed an extension of slavery westward that might threaten the Missouri Compromise. By 1850, he had inched toward denouncing slavery as an evil that should not be permitted to spread. Calhoun even defended slavery as a positive good; and the Democratic Party, to survive nationally, appeased the South. Benton warned the nation upon Calhoun's death in 1850 of the vitality of his principles and their threat to the Union. The Calhoun factor still shapes American history.

From the beginning of Andrew Jackson's second term as president, Benton and Calhoun took opposite positions on almost every issue. And most questions at least indirectly involved slavery: whether the postmaster general could seize "inflammatory" abolitionist literature sent into the South, whether slaveowners could bring their slaves into the free territory of Oregon, and how many slave states would be carved from the Republic of Texas. Even the personal lives of the two men exacerbated the sectional tensions.

Many surveys of American history feature the three decades from the Missouri Compromise to the Compromise of 1850 as the era of the triumvirate of Daniel Webster, Henry Clay, and Calhoun, the perennial presidential candidates who were using their Senate careers to pursue the higher office. But Benton, forsaking presidential ambitions, became the first senator to achieve greater historical significance than most of the presidents of his time. In fact, once Calhoun abandoned his pursuit for the presidency in 1844, he became more powerful and consequential in his final years in the Senate. At a time when the Senate dominated the national stage, Benton and Calhoun shared the spotlight.

The intertwined lives of two Republican senators from New England present a uniquely revealing portrait of the period 1850 to 1870. Both William Pitt Fessenden of Maine and Charles Sumner of Massachusetts opposed the scrapping of the Missouri Compromise in the passage of the Kansas–Nebraska Act of 1854. Both as chair of the Senate Finance Committee and then secretary of the treasury, Fessenden became, in effect, Lincoln's prime minister; and Sumner, the country's leading opponent of slavery, thought *he* was. From 1865, when Fessenden was elected chair of the Joint Committee on Reconstruction, to 1868, the personal antipathy of the two men shaped national politics: the drafting and passage of the Fourteenth Amendment, attitudes toward Reconstruction of the South, and the Senate trial of President Andrew Johnson on impeachment charges.

Fessenden's vote prevented President Johnson's conviction, though his motives for casting it and events leading up to it have been widely misunderstood by historians. Fessenden's "conservatism" and Sumner's "radicalism" from 1865 to 1868 have been overstated, and the picture is more complex. Fessenden saw no inconsistency in advocating honesty and hard work and in championing racial equality. Sumner's radicalism was occasionally self-serving. Fessenden's acerbic wit and personal integrity had no time for "humbug," such as the long-winded speeches, sometimes *ad hominem,* of Sumner.

The godson of Daniel Webster, Fessenden was a Whig convert to Republicanism and shared some of the aristocratic values of the old Federalists, such as Rufus King. Sumner, elected as a Free-Soiler and an opponent of the Webster Whigs, was more politically independent from the Republican Party but more dependent on his constituency, the abolitionists. Fessenden possessed an especially sovereign sense of integrity. He was definitely "his own man," devoid of ambition except to keep his home in the Senate, where he became a major power and influence. Sumner represented a special-interest group and, after his brutal beating in 1856, became the personification of the abolitionist movement. During the Civil War and Reconstruction, "Bleeding Sumner" was the prisoner as well as the champion of the Garrisonian abolitionists. Though considerably more radical than President Abraham Lincoln on slavery and emancipation, with one son killed and two others fighting in the war, Fessenden possessed a strong pragmatic streak, like the president. In pursuing "the practical" during Reconstruction, Fessenden, as conciliator, took a path similar to what Lincoln's might have been and suffered for it. In many ways, Fessenden's career was more virtuous and heroic than Lincoln's.

Both Fessenden and Sumner were victims of the Civil War and Reconstruction. Understanding their relationship presents a new perspective to a turbulent period; each to his admirers exhibited a special heroism. But the ideals of both men were quickly abandoned, following the Reconstruction, in the new industrial America, which had a Senate oligarchy to do its bidding.

2

"Samson and the Temple of Slavery"

Thomas Hart Benton vs. John C. Calhoun
(1820–1850)

Perhaps no one epitomized an age the way Thomas Hart Benton captured the prevailing spirit and contradictions of the period 1820 to 1850. He became the first senator to serve for thirty consecutive years, representing the border state of Missouri, whose controversial admission to the Union in 1821 triggered the first debate over slavery. Theodore Roosevelt, in his biography of Benton, remarked: "No other American Statesman, except John Quincy Adams—certainly neither of his great contemporaries, Webster and Clay—kept doing continually better work throughout his term of public service, or showed himself able to rise to a higher level at the very end than at the beginning."

But another imposing figure stalked Benton in counterpoint to the Missourian's growing concern about slavery, Senator John Caldwell Calhoun of South Carolina, the philosopher of states' rights and champion of slaveowners. During the 1840s, the two men contested for the future of the Democratic Party, and Calhoun won. But in the words of the abolitionist Horace Greeley, Benton, through losing his Senate seat in 1851 over opposition to the extension of slavery, became "a Samson falling and carrying down the pillars of the [slavery] temple with him."[1]

More than anyone except Andrew Jackson, Benton was an advocate and a representative of the democratic movement of his age. Clay served the narrow interests of midwestern and eastern commerce, Webster the interests of manufacturing and capital, Calhoun the concerns of southern plantation slaveowners. Benton championed the values of small, freeholding farmers, urban workers, and small trades- and businessmen. He was an early champion of free homesteads for free men and won the nickname "Old Bullion" for his advocacy of gold and silver currency in the interests of western farmers against eastern land speculators backed by paper money. But he was not an unblemished populist. He speculated in real estate and had acquired a "small fortune" before he was twenty-one. And he came to the Senate in 1821 almost as much a representative of John Jacob Astor's American Fur Company, which secured his one-vote margin of victory in the Missouri legislature. Though more historically significant than most of the presidents of his time, he was hardly the "greatest man in the world," as young Tom Sawyer supposed one "Glorious Fourth" in Hannibal, Missouri. In fact, errors in Benton's youth haunted him through adulthood.[2]

Benton was born on March 14, 1782, in the piedmont area of North Carolina, just four days before the birth of his great nemesis, Calhoun, in the uplands of South Carolina. The Benton family was descended from English, Episcopalian stock, whereas the Calhouns were Calvinist Presbyterians from County Donegal, Ireland. Though neither man was particularly religious, Benton was temperamentally Episcopalian, whereas Calhoun bore the very demeanor of a Presbyterian minister. Both at an early age voraciously read the classics. Benton's mother, Jessie, had him read widely in British history, especially about the tyranny of King Charles I and the English Civil War, and the young boy developed a passion for progress and liberty in the English Whig sense. Plutarch's *Lives* were also read to inspire a sense of history. And in later life, Benton would frequently demonstrate he was a one-man library, as in 1812, when he pompously wrote Andrew Jackson, major general of the Tennessee Militia, to volunteer: "I think with Tacitus, that every man should aim at doing something worthy of being written, or at writing something worthy of being done."

While Calhoun methodically studied in South Carolina and Georgia schools and then decided on the very best education at Yale and reading law in Connecticut, Benton set out for the University of North Carolina. Calhoun never deviated from the personally righteous path he maintained through life, but Benton exhibited a youthful delinquency that tormented his adult life.

At the age of sixteen, young Benton—head of his household of mother and seven brothers and sisters since his father's death when Tom was eight—entered the University of North Carolina at Chapel Hill. But a few months later, he was expelled for petty thievery from his roommates and sent home to widow Benton's in humiliation. Legend has it that the young miscreant turned on the jeering crowd as he was departing Chapel Hill, shouting: "I'm leaving here now, but damn you, you will hear from me again!"

Two years later, the widow and her children sought a new life trekking to Tennessee. They settled on a 2,500-acre homestead about twenty-five miles south of Nashville and next to the great trail known as the Natchez Trace. After six years of reading and occasionally teaching, Benton at twenty-four was sworn in as a lawyer in Tennessee.

In January 1812, attorney Benton—about to turn thirty—wrote to his friend Andrew Jackson, commander of the Tennessee Militia, and volunteered to recruit troops for the war against the British. Benton quickly worked his way up to the position of colonel in the militia and aide to General Jackson. After the militia was disbanded in 1813, Benton won a commission in Washington as lieutenant colonel in the regular army and was authorized to recruit a regiment in Tennessee.

But in the summer of 1813, Benton felt forced to defend his family's honor. His brother Jesse had been wounded in a duel with a friend of Andrew Jackson's while the general was a second. In an angry exchange of letters, Jackson advised Thomas Benton that men of honor do not "quarrel and brawl like the fish woman." But Jackson still instigated a melee with the brothers at Talbot's Hotel in Nashville. Thomas Benton shot Jackson in the arm, as Jackson's bullet left a hole in the colonel's sleeve. While the general recovered, Thomas and Jesse strutted in front of Talbot's; and Thomas, before a crowd, broke Jackson's sword in two.[3]

Though Lieutenant Colonel Benton saw some action during the War of 1812 in skirmishes around Mobile Bay and Pensacola, just when Jackson was preparing for the battle of New Orleans, he ordered Benton back to a recruiting mission in Tennessee. Benton then angrily proceeded to Washington to seek permission to lead an invasion of Canada. But his efforts to be free from Jackson's control proved futile when news reached the capital of the Peace of Ghent and Jackson's glorious victory at New Orleans.

Benton obviously could not return to Nashville to practice law as the man who had wounded the local, now national, hero Andrew Jackson. So the thirty-three-year-old Benton decided to move west in the fall of 1815. He crossed the Mississippi to settle in the budding new town of 2,000 people, St. Louis. Society in the Missouri Territory was fluid like that of most of the new West and ideal for the advancement of the still-young lawyer, who desired to escape his past in North Carolina and Tennessee.

In the meantime, John C. Calhoun had taken a more respectable and conventional course and had already achieved national prominence. After graduating in 1804 from Yale, where he was elected to Phi Beta Kappa, and then spending a year at Judge Tapping Reeve's law school in Connecticut, he returned to practice law in Charleston, South Carolina. But for all of his intellectual rejection of his Presbyterian heritage, it was an important psychological part of him. He frowned upon the "intemperance and debaucheries" of the people of Charleston: "It was Cavalier from the start; we were Puritan." And in 1807, Calhoun returned to the uplands of South Carolina to practice law and farm at Abbeville, just a few miles from where he was born. Unlike Benton, Calhoun was not on the move, except in politics.[4]

In 1808, Calhoun was elected to the South Carolina legislature, and in 1810, he won election to the national House of Representatives. He solidified his political support among plantation owners and wealthy Charleston merchants by marrying his cousin, a Huguenot descendant and wealthy Charleston belle, Floride Bonneau Colhoun.

Calhoun quickly became known in the Twelfth Congress as one of the "War Hawks," along with Henry Clay, in supporting the Madison administration. Soon he was celebrated as "the young Hercules who carried the war on his shoulders." While Benton failed to win glory on the battlefield and alienated a great war hero, Calhoun was covering himself with glory in Congress and appointed to James Monroe's cabinet in 1817 as secretary of war. At thirty-five, he was the youngest cabinet member, and he soon earned the title "father of the War Department" with his great efficiency and organizational skills. He ordered military posts to keep detailed records of diseases treated and to compile statistics on weather, population, and trade. By 1821, when Benton was entering the Senate, Calhoun had become, in John Randolph's sarcastic words, "the army candidate for the Presidency."[5]

Meanwhile, in St. Louis, Thomas Hart Benton had quickly developed a reputation as an aggressive and successful lawyer. But in 1817, in a duel, he shot and killed a young attorney, Charles Lucas, son of the powerful Judge Jean Baptiste Charles Lucas, in a dispute over rumors about Benton's past in Tennessee and North Carolina. The duel dogged Benton for the rest of his life and provided more ammunition for his political opponents. Nevertheless, he was elected one of the first two senators from Missouri; David Barton was the other. And while Benton was waiting to take his seat as senator-elect, on March 20, 1821, he married Elizabeth McDowell, the daughter of a prominent Virginia family. He always treated "our dear Betsy" with tenderness, especially after she suffered from what was diagnosed as epilepsy in 1842 and spent the next twelve years, until her death in 1854, in a sort of "twilight of both mind and body."

In the Senate, Benton made a reputation on frontier issues. He pointed out to his colleagues that the Anglo-American agreement for joint occupation of the huge Pacific northwest would expire in 1828. Benton urged the United States to encourage de facto American "occupation" of the Oregon country. He also championed frontier interests with a plan to reform national land policy. His "graduation–donation" bill provided that any lands offered for public sale that remained unsold for five years would be offered again at a reduced, or "graduated," price. Furthermore, any settler of such unsold land who had occupied and cultivated it for three years would be entitled to receive the plot as a "donation." Although such a proposal won considerable support in the West, many eastern politicians saw it as a threat to their region's supremacy in population and political power.

Fortuitously, in early 1824, Benton also proposed electoral reform on the principle *"demos krateo."* "Democracy," he argued, meant literally governed by "the people" or majority rule; consequently, "the people can vote for a President as easily as they can for an elector." Yet his compromise proposed that the popular vote in each congressional district be used to cast one electoral vote. But the presidential election of 1824 flew in the face of the democracy principle.

Andrew Jackson was elected senator from Tennessee in 1823 over one of Benton's friends, and the presence of the two enemies in the Senate forced upon them a gradual reconciliation. Benton was appointed to the Military Affairs Committee, whose chairman was Andrew Jackson, and the two men were seated next to each other on the Senate floor. Before long, Benton had introduced his wife to the man he had tried to kill a few years earlier.

When the deadlocked presidential election of 1824 was thrown into the House of Representatives, Benton was forced to choose between Jackson and John Quincy Adams. In supporting Jackson, Benton broke with his in-law Henry Clay and also his Missouri colleague David Barton. Barton commented: "Of all the unnatural coalitions (not to say the most insincere) is that of our Senator Pomposo, of imperial port and mien, with the General!"[6]

Though Benton lost influence with the executive branch for four years, his backing Jackson—with 152,901 popular votes to 114,023 for Adams—proved popular in Missouri. In Benton's view, Adams's election by the House was "a violation of the *demos krateo* principle." A new political party sprang up. Benton's and Jackson's new Democratic Party would make political democracy the key issue—except for slaves, of course.

Curiously, in 1826, after Henry Clay's appointment as secretary of state was viewed by Jackson's supporters as part of the "corrupt bargain" of 1825 in the House of Representatives that elected John Quincy Adams president, Thomas Hart Benton still attempted to head off a duel between Clay and John Randolph of Virginia. Benton was, perhaps, doing penance for his much-regretted killing of Charles Lucas and also striving for respectability.

John Randolph, in a speech to the Senate, had ridiculed the House's election of Adams: "Let Judas have his thirty pieces of silver!" And he suggested that they might "go to buy a Potter's field, in which to inter this miserable Constitution of ours, crucified between two gentlemen, suffering for 'conscience sake,' under the burthen of the two first offices of this Government." He then referred to "young Kentucky—not so young, however, as not to make a prudent match, and sell her charms for their full value" to "Old Massachusetts."[7]

The cousin of Clay's wife, Lucretia, daughter of his uncle Thomas Hart, Benton ended his political estrangement from the Clays by attempting to prevent the "affair of honor." But the duel took place, despite Benton's efforts, fifty yards from the Old Chain Bridge over the Potomac on the Virginia side across from Georgetown. Both men missed twice, with Randolph firing in the air the second time. But the incident further fueled the campaign for "democracy": Andrew Jackson, victim of the "corrupt bargain," was the standard-bearer, and Thomas Hart Benton his new champion.

In the 1828 presidential race, Andrew Jackson easily defeated John Quincy Adams, as a coalition of interest groups with a popular-democratic base in the western states organized around the slogans of Jacksonian Democrats against the alleged moneyed oligarchy supporting the Adams–Clay alliance. Benton's land-reform proposals, in the view of Adams, contributed to Jackson's success in the West against Clay.

The hoi polloi Democrats quickly changed the national mood as the famous "military chieftain," in the view of the quasi-aristocratic National Republicans, ushered in the reign of "King Mob." And to strengthen his hold on government, Andrew Jackson was the first president to employ a patronage system on a large scale, with between 10 and 20 percent of government officials replaced by Jackson supporters. The Democratic Party became the first modern political party, and Thomas Hart Benton became, in effect, "majority leader" in the Senate.

The career of John C. Calhoun paralleled the rising sectionalism growing out of the so-called Tariff of Abominations of 1828. He had served as vice president for one term under John Quincy Adams but then switched allegiance to the sixty-two-year-old Andrew Jackson, who had pledged to serve only one term as president. But South Carolina's nullification of the tariff drove Calhoun away from his "nationalism" of the early 1820s toward support for states' rights. He was on a collision course with Jackson, as his heir apparent.

Much to the surprise of Jacksonian Democrats, who aimed the tariff of 1828 at raw materials imported by New England manufacturers, New England supported the tariff because it embodied protectionism. It was the cotton-growing southern states that were especially opposed, particularly South Carolina, whose legislature adopted a set of eight resolutions calling the tariff unconstitutional and unjust. The resolutions were accompanied by an essay, "The South Carolina Exposition and Protest," written but not signed by Jackson's newly elected vice president, Calhoun. His "Exposition" discussed the theory of state sovereignty and expounded the doctrine of nullification by a single state. Vice President Calhoun had identified himself with the "particularist" views of his state and section.

Amid the famous debate on the tariff and nullification between Senators Daniel Webster of Massachusetts and Robert Hayne of South Carolina, Benton in early 1830 at first took the position of states' rights, as an advocate of a southern-western alliance. The "colonel," as he was popularly known, denounced New Englanders for their dis-Unionist attitudes during the War of 1812 and the Hartford Convention. The northeastern "*quondam* friends of the Negro*" had kept Missouri out of the Union for "one whole year," he said, and now falsely claimed to be a friend of the West on tariffs and internal improvements.[8]

But by April, at a banquet to celebrate Thomas Jefferson's birthday, organized by Benton and Hayne, the nature of the federal Union became an issue dividing the president and vice president. In the 104 toasts made, various southerners denounced the tariff as "unequal taxation," with one observing "there is no treason in resisting oppression." Finally, toward the end of the evening, President Jackson, distressed at the nullification sentiments expressed, proposed a dramatic toast: "Our Federal Union: It must be preserved." Vice President Calhoun then volunteered a toast: "The Union: Next to our liberty most dear; may we all remember that it can only be preserved by respecting the rights of the states and distributing equally the benefit and burden of the union." A deep fissure was opening in the Jackson administration and cabinet. Benton, in his memoirs, overlooked his role in organizing the dinner and described it as a sounding board for nullification. And Secretary of State Martin Van Buren even asserted that Jackson had used the words "Our Union" and that Senator Hayne had inserted the word "Federal" for the record.[9]

By 1831, the ideological rift widened on an issue of personal morality. Floride Calhoun and several cabinet wives snubbed the new wife of Secretary of War John Eaton, Peggy O'Neale, a barmaid whose premarital chastity had been questioned. President Jackson gallantly defended Mrs. Eaton. But the rift grew even wider with the publication of the 1818 correspondence of then Secretary of War Calhoun, which showed that he was highly critical of Jackson's military campaigns in Florida.

Secretary of State Martin Van Buren and Jackson then hatched a plan whereby the whole cabinet resigned to give the president a free hand and to show Calhoun in his true colors. The Senate then rejected Van Buren's nomination as minister to the Court of St. James, Clay and Webster voting against Van Buren, and Calhoun twice casting a tie-breaking vote as vice president in opposition. But the defeat of Van Buren did not kill him politically as Calhoun predicted. The Democratic National Convention in Baltimore renominated Jackson for president, with Van Buren replacing Calhoun as the vice presidential nominee. And the Democratic ticket easily defeated Henry Clay and John Sergeant, the National Republican nominees, in the presidential election of 1832.

Virtue and morality were debated along class lines during the 1830s. The principal issue of the 1832 election was Andrew Jackson's veto of a new charter for the Second Bank of the United States. Thomas Benton had earlier led the attack on the "Monster": the Bank of the United States, headed by Nicholas Biddle in Philadelphia, was "too great and too powerful to be tolerated in a Government of free and equal laws." It would "make the rich richer, and the poor poorer." The bank was also "injurious to the laboring classes" because, through speculation on banknote credit, the price of land or property was "raised to the paper maximum" while "wages remain at the silver minimum." "Old Hickory," in his veto, echoed Benton's sentiments. The bank was unconstitutional, said Jackson, and he would not sign legislation making the wealthy "richer by act of Congress."

During Jackson's second term, Benton was clearly the administration leader in the Senate, and he took great delight in ridiculing Clay and Webster as "the duplicate Senators." By 1834, the "Whig Party"—a coalition of banking, commercial, and slaveholding interests—had formed in opposition to "King Andrew." Webster and Clay joined Calhoun in opposition to Jackson's "executive despotism." And Clay succeeded in pushing through the Senate a resolution of censure against President Jackson for removing government deposits from the Bank of the United States. Benton denounced the Clay–Calhoun effort to restore the bank as a threat to the "property and liberty of the American people."[10]

Benton also launched a hard-money campaign and called for suppressing all banknotes under twenty dollars. His hard-money position was to become a rallying point for radical Democrats through the 1830s. Surprisingly, Benton's bill that established a new bimetallic standard was even supported by Webster and Calhoun. "Dr. Benton's yellow lozenges" soon appeared as five-dollar gold pieces, and Andrew Jackson declared that the "gold bill" had done more for the nation's economy than all other legislation since 1789. Benton would soon proudly accept the nickname "Old Bullion."

In 1836, the Democrats of Mississippi nominated Martin Van Buren for president and Thomas H. Benton for vice president. Benton declined the honor, however, the same way he had quashed Whig rumors that Andrew Jackson would appoint him chief justice to succeed John Marshall. Benton successfully backed his friend Secretary of the Treasury Roger B. Taney for the Court. "Old Bullion" was content to be the second most powerful man in the Democratic Party, as Martin Van Buren was elected president against three Whig candidates.

The Whigs, running against the despotism of "King Andrew," united Webster–Clay National Republicans in the North, some dissident Democrats, and Calhoun nullifiers in the South. But Jackson, having abolished the national debt and the Bank of the United States, found his ultimate triumph in the election of Van Buren.

Benton also won his almost three-year effort to expunge from the Senate record Henry Clay's resolution of censure against President Jackson. Along strict party lines, the Senate voted 24–19 to "expunge" the censure from the record, despite Calhoun's reference to the "times of Caligula and Nero" and Clay's description of the expunging as "a foul deed which, like the blood-stained hands of the guilty Macbeth, all ocean's waters will never wash out."[11]

"Old Bullion" witnessed the inauguration of Van Buren in 1837, as Andrew Jackson left office to a great ovation on the Capitol steps. Benton called the moment the grandest scene of his life: "a man and the people—he, laying down power and withdrawing through the portals of ever-lasting fame;—they, sounding in his ears the everlasting plaudits of unborn generations." The men were much alike, alternately harsh and kind, vindictive and forgiving, personifying some of the best and worst of their America.

President Van Buren begged Benton to join his cabinet, but the senator declined. The debate over the "expunging" resolution revealed Benton's vulnerability in any confirmation process or contest for higher office. His Achilles' heel—expulsion from the University of North Carolina—was revealed by Senator Benjamin Leigh of Virginia when he shouted that "in that catechism which I learned at my mother's knee, I was taught 'to keep-to keep-to keep' my hands from picking and stealing, and my tongue from evil speaking!"[12]

Though Benton was psychologically, and perhaps politically, prevented from running for higher office, he was the first to appreciate the power of longevity in the Senate. Unlike Clay, Calhoun, and Webster, Benton had policies and principles that did not need to be trimmed to suit presidential ambitions. And as the two major parties, Whigs and Democrats, by the 1840s became fragmented alliances of contradictory interests, increasingly threatened by third parties, Benton became the symbol of unity among the Democrats against the divisive, proslavery views of John C. Calhoun.

The great moral question of slavery could no longer be avoided, however much Benton tried. In his "State of the Union" message to Congress in

1836, Andrew Jackson warned of incendiary abolitionist publications, such as William Lloyd Garrison's *Liberator,* circulating by mail throughout the South. Since they might incite slave revolts, a law suppressing them might be in order. When Calhoun presented a bill authorizing postmasters to seize the publications, Benton objected. Although he condemned the abolitionists, he warned that investing 10,000 postmasters with censorship powers might lead to regrettable events. The bill was defeated.

The Senate also debated, for two months, the right of abolitionists to petition the Congress to abolish slavery in the District of Columbia. Calhoun denounced the right to petition, saying that it would admit that Congress had a right to grant the petition. Benton denounced Calhoun for giving the abolitionists publicity and notoriety. And the Senate overwhelmingly accepted the petitions but rejected their "prayer."

Also in 1836, after the Republic of Texas had won its independence, Calhoun called for its immediate annexation to extend slavery and restore the balance within the Union. Benton supported the recognition of the Texas Republic but opposed immediate annexation and denied that the Texas revolt against Mexico had anything to do with slavery.

Benton had many ties to Texas. Two of his brothers lived there, and General Sam Houston, the republic's first president, had served as an ensign under Colonel Benton's command in 1814. But Benton argued that discussion of annexation in 1836 would bring the nation into conflict with Mexico, whose gold and silver filled U.S. demand for a viable hard currency. Furthermore, in his view, advocates of annexation, like Calhoun, were inflaming the slavery controversy and weakening the Union. Though the Senate supported Benton's position in 1836, Calhoun had only fired his opening shots on Texas and the slavery question.

Both men supported Van Buren as president between 1837 and 1840, especially on the establishment of an Independent Treasury to replace the Bank of the United States. But the Whig opposition was united in the presidential election of 1840 under General William Henry Harrison, who ran a "log cabin and hard cider" campaign against the frontier perception of an "effete, effeminate, cologne-scented, Eastern aristocrat" Van Buren. Harrison, however, stood for northeastern industrial interests, and the New Yorker Van Buren, for western policies; but most of the West voted for Harrison, one of their own, against "little Van, the used-up man."[13]

One month after his inauguration, Harrison died, and the almost four-year ordeal of the Whigs under President John Tyler began. A Virginia nullifier who had resigned from the Senate rather than support Benton's "expunging resolution," Tyler left the Democrats because of enmity for Jackson, not support for Whig principles. But the expansion of slavery into the newly admitted states of the West would be the dominant issue in the 1840s. The two principal antagonists in the Senate debate were Benton and Calhoun, fighting to control the future of the Democratic Party.

Each member of the triumvirate of Webster, Clay, and Calhoun in the early 1840s, however, had higher ambitions. Webster became Harrison's and then Tyler's secretary of state until 1843, and Clay resigned from the Senate in 1842 to run for president as the Whig nominee in 1844, since Tyler was a president without a party. Calhoun since 1840 was planning to seek the Democratic nomination in 1844 and was even courting northeastern protectionists, by supporting a moderate tariff, and westerners, by advocating federal support for internal improvements.

But events quickly bypassed the triumvirate. All three were out of office in 1843, as the controversy over the annexation of Texas and the creation of new "slave states" heated up. In 1842, President Tyler had rejected two annexation offers from President Sam Houston of Texas because of the opposition of Congress and Secretary of State Webster. But by 1843, Webster had resigned and was replaced by Calhoun's friend Abel Upshur, who offered Texas a treaty of annexation. And then Providence intervened on February 28, 1844.

A Sunday outing down the Potomac on the USS *Princeton* turned to disaster when a new gun was exhibited and, on its final testing, exploded into the audience, killing Upshur and Secretary of the Navy Thomas Gilmer. Benton barely escaped death, suffering shock and a burst eardrum.

President Tyler, in the midst of the Texas negotiations, found no prominent Whig or Democrat to replace Upshur, other than Calhoun. Aware by then that his presidential drive had failed, Calhoun "reluctantly" accepted the appointment and moved quickly to secure the annexation of Texas after stepping into Upshur's shoes on April 1. The South Carolinian saw an opportunity, in James G. Blaine's words, to attain "an historic revenge which the noblest minds might indulge" on Martin Van Buren. On April 12, a secret treaty was signed, annexing the Republic of Texas without reference to boundaries. Calhoun informed Mexico that the United States was ready "for all possible consequences," giving the Mexican government the choice of war or humiliating surrender.[14]

After the treaty was signed, but before it was submitted to the Senate for ratification, Calhoun made a bold move. Citing an old dispatch of the British foreign minister, Lord Aberdeen, seeking "the general abolition of slavery throughout the world," Calhoun in a letter to the British minister in Washington, Lord Pakenham, called Britain's policy on Texas a direct threat to the United States.

Calhoun's letter to Pakenham was extremely racist in tone, maintaining that the ratio of deaf, dumb, blind, and insane among African Americans of the free states was 1 : 96, compared to 1 : 172 in the slave states. In fact, in the South, Calhoun argued, blacks, under slavery, had attained their highest levels of morals, intelligence, and civilization.[15]

The "Pakenham letter" flushed out Clay and Van Buren, who had secretly agreed to neutralize the Texas issue in the presidential campaign of 1844. They both opposed the immediate annexation of Texas, but Calhoun's policy succeeded in dividing both the Whigs and the Democrats along the Mason–Dixon line. Van Buren's candidacy faded in the South as the result of Calhoun's tactics, and he was unable to win the two-thirds needed for the nomination at the Democratic National Convention in Baltimore. Instead, on the ninth ballot, the Democrats nominated a "dark horse," the Speaker of the House, Congressman James K. Polk of Tennessee. Calhoun was delighted. Polk was an annexationist, and his nomination would unite the South. Clay would be eliminated as a factor in the South and would have great difficulty in arguing against annexation in the West.

Benton at first fought immediate annexation and strongly denied that slavery was an issue for anyone but abolitionists and Calhoun supporters. He argued that the treaty clearly annexed Mexican territory without consulting its government. Impressed with Benton's attack, the Senate defeated the treaty by a 35–16 vote. He then proposed his own plan for annexing Texas. It called for a well-defined boundary, leaving the Rio Grande Valley in Mexico. The "State of Texas" would be no larger than the largest existing state, with equal division of the remaining area into slave and free territories. Mexican consent would be negotiated by treaty, unless Congress, not the president, should decide that Mexican approval was unnecessary. Benton's bill, however, was tabled by a vote of 25 to 20, along party lines, with opposition coming from those opposed to any form of annexation. These opponents, including the abolitionists, however, won a Pyrrhic victory, which ensured the passage of a measure even more opposed to their interests.

After Senator George McDuffie of South Carolina compared Secretary Calhoun's dead treaty to the ghost of Caesar that haunted Brutus, "Sir Oracle" Benton, as McDuffie tagged him, condemned the Calhoun treaty for dividing all of Texas into potential slave states (as many as four, besides Texas, were proposed). It was "an open preparation for a Missouri question, and a dissolution of the Union." Claiming to be the oldest champion of Texas, Benton denounced "the criminal politicians who prostituted the question." He then pounded McDuffie's desk, defiantly shouting, "The senator . . . compares the rejected treaty to the slain Caesar, and gives it a ghost, which is to meet me . . . as the spectre met Brutus at Philippi . . . and the enemies of the American Union triumph over me. . . . I shall not fall upon my sword, as Brutus did . . . but I shall save it, and save myself for another day, and for another use—for the day when the disunion of these States is to be fought—not with words, but with iron—and for the hearts of the traitors who appear in arms against their country."

As the galleries applauded, an old enemy, ex-President and Congressman John Quincy Adams, walked up to Benton's desk and congratulated him, while Benton replied: "Mr. Adams, you are passing off the stage, and I am passing away also, but while we live, we will stand by *The Union*."[16]

Benton managed to get reelected to the Senate in 1844, though his standing in his home state as well as the country declined as he was overshadowed by Polk and the Texas annexation issue. Ironically, the abolitionists helped to elect Polk. The Liberty Party—opposed to slavery and annexation—gave more than 62,300 votes to James G. Birney, its presidential candidate, and Polk won by only 38,180 votes. If fewer than 6,000 votes for Birney in New York had shifted to Clay, he would have won the state and the election.

When the Senate convened in December 1844, debate raged between supporters of Benton's bill and those advocating Calhoun's treaty. But on February 5, 1845, Benton offered a substitute bill, omitting all references to Mexico and slavery, that called for admission of a state of Texas and cession of all excess territory to the United States. The new bill depended on Polk's ability and goodwill.

But the House passed a joint resolution calling for the annexation of Texas and separating from it not more than four additional states, with those north of the Missouri Compromise line "free." This would make almost all of Texas "slave," whereas Benton's substitute plan would leave the question undecided.

"Old Bullion" finally agreed to support a joint resolution annexing Texas, with the understanding that the newly elected President Polk would choose between the House plan and Benton's. But with only three days left in office, President Tyler, upon Calhoun's advice, implemented the House plan to annex Texas. As Polk was sworn in, the annexation was a *fait accompli*.

Benton later charged that he and four senatorial friends had been tricked into affirmative votes by assurances that Tyler would let Polk adopt Benton's plan. In any case, the Democratic Party had been divided and the ruling dynasty of Benton and Van Buren overthrown. War with Mexico was probable, and increased sectional conflict over the extension of slavery was inevitable.[17]

From 1845 to 1847, Benton played the role of a one-man "Kitchen

Cabinet" in the Polk administration. And the dispute between the United Kingdom and the United States over the Pacific northwest served as Benton's bridge back to power. Polk's campaign had promised "Fifty-four Forty or Fight," annexing present-day British Columbia, all the way to the Alaskan border. But Benton—Oregon's strongest advocate in Congress for twenty-five years—had always maintained that the 49° parallel should serve as the boundary.

During the first half of 1846, Benton met with the president and secretly with the British minister. By June, the Senate, under Benton's leadership, advised the president to accept the British offer of a 49° boundary, which Polk proceeded to do, especially since the United States was already at war against Mexico.

Benton at first opposed Polk's declaration of war, after Mexican soldiers attacked General Zachary Taylor's army on the Rio Grande. Benton insisted that Taylor had been encamped on Mexican soil, and the senator told Polk that he would vote to defend our own territory but not to make aggressive war on Mexico. Nevertheless, Benton voted for the declaration of war, while Calhoun—now back in the Senate after being rejected by Polk as his secretary of state—abstained. Calhoun feared the effect of a war in strengthening the powers of the federal government.

Polk soon asked Benton for a written summary of his views on conducting the Mexican war. His report urged General Taylor and his soldiers to behave honorably to convince Mexicans that Americans only wanted an honorable, negotiated peace. The senator argued that Americans should exploit the divisions among races, classes, and parties in Mexico: "the Spaniards, who monopolize the wealth and power . . . and the mixed Indian race who bear its burthens . . . the lower and the higher clergy, the latter of whom have the dignities and the revenues, while the former have poverty and labour . . . the political parties . . . some more liberal, and more friendly to us than others." The war should "leave no lasting animosities behind" nor permit "injurious reports to go forth to excite the ill will of the other Republics of Spanish origin, against us."[18]

Daniel Webster and Henry Clay lost sons in the war, and the Whigs won control of the House of Representatives in the 1846 election. But while Calhoun supported the policy of "masterly inactivity" of the Whig generals, Zachary Taylor and Winfield Scott, Benton was appalled at the lack of direction in the war, which was also weakening the Democratic Party. So he made a bold, perhaps foolhardy, proposal that Congress create a new rank of lieutenant general, whose incumbent would serve as chief of staff to coordinate military policy and negotiate for peace. Still longing for military glory, the "colonel" proposed himself for the job. But the opposition of the

Whigs and Calhoun's supporters killed the bill, and the senator finally turned down an appointment as a field commander with the rank of major general.

After Mexico City finally fell to Scott's troops, the Mexican government sued for peace. The Treaty of Guadalupe Hidalgo, negotiated by a State Department clerk without the authority of the president but submitted by Polk anyway, was approved by the Senate, though opposed by Benton and Webster, who questioned its legality. The president dismissed Benton's opposition as vanity because "Old Bullion" had not been consulted. But the treaty did confirm Benton's wisdom in urging military explorations and occupations of Alta California and Nuevo Mexico, which the treaty authorized the United States to annex. The Oregon and Mexican agreements confirmed the nation's "Manifest Destiny" to control all the territory west of the Louisiana Purchase to the Pacific from Puget Sound to San Diego, including the Mexican lands between Texas and California. But the new territories intensified the debate over slavery and created a family crisis for Benton that was to worsen his relations with Polk Democrats.[19]

John Charles Frémont, "the Pathfinder," had eloped with Benton's daughter Jessie Ann in 1841. Much to Old Bullion's consternation, the Byronesque Frémont, twenty-eight, secretly married the beautiful Jessie, seventeen, at the Washington home of Senator and Mrs. John J. Crittenden of Kentucky. After first throwing Frémont out of his house, Senator Benton relented and invited the couple to move into his home. Becoming almost an adopted son to the senator, and inspired by his expansionist views, Frémont led an expedition to Oregon and Fort Vancouver in 1843. Sharing Benton's dream of acquiring the whole West, Frémont then explored the "Great Basin" between the Rockies and the Sierras, eventually crossing into Sacramento Valley.

In a later expedition on the eve of the Mexican war, Lieutenant Colonel Frémont inspired the "Bear Flag" revolt of June 23, 1846, in Sacramento. He combined his irregular troops with Commodore Robert Stockton's naval forces and General Stephen Kearney's army regiment to defeat Mexican forces in California. Stockton then appointed Frémont civil governor of California, but a dispute broke out between Stockton and Kearny, with Frémont supporting Stockton. When Frémont refused to switch allegiance upon orders from Washington, Kearney had him arrested and returned first to Washington and then New York to await court-martial. Benton, headstrong in defense of his son-in-law as he had been with brother Jesse, insisted on a military trial, much to the dismay of President Polk. When a panel of regular officers (West Point graduates) found Frémont guilty of mutiny and disobedience, Polk pardoned him; but Frémont resigned his commission—a hero to much of the country. Both Benton's vision and Frémont's exploits made it easy for the United States to annex the California and New Mexico territories by treaty. But Calhoun interpreted the dream of Manifest Destiny in a different, more explosive way.[20]

On August 8, 1846, an obscure Pennsylvania Democrat, David Wilmot, saw his amendment to an appropriations bill for the Mexican War passed by the House. The "Wilmot Proviso" stated that, for any territory acquired from Mexico by the United States, "neither slavery nor involuntary servitude shall ever exist in any part of said territory." The proviso was attached to appropriation bills by the House; but the Senate, the last bastion of power for the southern states, rejected it. Moreover, Calhoun was given an opportunity to dramatize the plight of the South. In reaction to the House passage of a "Three Million Bill" for the war, amended with the proviso, Calhoun in 1847 presented his "resolutions" in defense of the southern position on slavery. He argued that the South was a minority everywhere but in the Senate and that "the day the balance between the two sections . . . is destroyed, is a day that will not be far removed from revolution, anarchy, civil war, and widespread disaster. The balance of the system is in the slaveholding states. They are the conservative portion." Though he supported the expedience of the Missouri Compromise, Calhoun argued that its principle was subversive of the Union. He then offered resolutions that the territories are "the joint and common property" of the several states of the Union, that Congress cannot deprive any state of equal rights in the territories, that Congress may not bar citizens owning slaves from migrating to the territories, and that the people of a territory are free to draft their own constitution except for the requirement of a republican government.

Benton immediately rose in protest against disrupting "the necessary business of the session to vote on such a string of abstractions." He labeled the resolutions "firebrands" of disunion; and four days later, with the entire cabinet seated in the gallery, he delivered his "first Calhouniac." He proposed to "skin Calhoun," who had been:

> wrong in 1819, in giving away Texas—wrong in 1836, in his sudden and hot haste to get her back—wrong in all his machinations for bringing on the Texas question of 1844—wrong in breaking up the armistice and peace negotiations between Mexico and Texas—wrong in secretly sending the army and navy to fight Mexico while we were at peace with her . . . wrong in writing to Mexico that he took Texas in view of all possible consequences, meaning war—wrong in offering Mexico . . . ten millions of dollars to hush up the war which he had created—wrong now in refusing Mr. Polk three millions to aid in getting out of the war which he made—wrong in throwing the blame of this war of his own making upon the shoulders of Mr. Polk—wrong in his

retreat and occupation line of policy ... and more wrong now than ever, in that string of resolutions which he has laid on the table.[21]

From 1847 to 1850, the country followed the Benton–Calhoun debates over slavery in the same way the national press covered the Lincoln–Douglas debates of 1858. The triumph of many of Calhoun's ideas in the Democratic Party assured immediate victory in the 1850s but inevitably guaranteed the disunion Benton so feared.

For a year, the Senate debated a bill establishing a territorial government in Oregon with an antislavery constitution, opposed by Calhoun and his supporters. Finally, the Oregon bill was passed in 1848, while Calhoun argued against Benton's call for pragmatism and compromise. Admitting Oregon without slavery, claimed the fanatical Calhoun, would "convert all the southern population into slaves; and he would never consent to entail that disgrace on his posterity. ... The separation of the North and the South is completed. ... This is not a question of territorial government, but a question involving the continuance of the Union." Despite Calhoun's absurd position on Oregon, only one southern senator criticized him, Benton's old friend Sam Houston of Texas. He asked: "Would it [the South] raise troops to cut off emigrants to Oregon, because they were going there without negroes?"[22]

In the presidential election of 1848, Benton supported Lewis Cass, the Democratic Party nominee, even though his old friend Martin Van Buren was the antislavery, Free-Soil Party nominee. But Benton realized that his moderate, virtually silent, position on slavery could not hold the middle ground in a state like Missouri. The Missouri General Assembly passed a series of resolutions supporting Calhoun's position on territorial slavery and instructing the state's senators to do so as well. The resolutions were a direct challenge to Benton's reelection in 1850. He was also excluded from a secret caucus of southern members of Congress that produced the "Southern Address," which was filled with complaints of northern aggression and with predictions of race warfare. Benton denounced the movement as treasonous.

Aware of his uphill battle for reelection, Benton accepted the challenge from the legislators and appealed over their heads:

> The General Assembly ... adopted certain resolutions ... and gave me instructions to obey them. From this command I appeal to the people of Missouri ... and if they confirm the instructions, I shall give them an opportunity to find a Senator to carry their will into effect, as I cannot do anything to dissolve this Union, or to array one-half of it against the other. ... I do not admit a dissolution of the Union to be a remedy, to be prescribed by statesmen, for the diseases of the body politic, any more than I admit death, or

suicide, to be a remedy to be prescribed by physicians for the diseases of the natural body. Cure, and not kill, is the only remedy which my mind can contemplate in either case.

But his appeal split the Missouri Democratic Party; and in a speech at Jefferson City in 1849, he discussed the broader implications of the slavery question for liberty and democracy everywhere. Admitting that he was "born to the inheritance of slaves," he argued that slavery was safe wherever it then existed but the important question was the preservation of the Union: "Once called the model republic by our friends, we are now so called in derision by our foes; and the slavery . . . dissensions quoted as the proofs of the impracticable form of government which we have adopted. I cannot engage in such discussions, nor do anything to depress the cause of struggling freedom throughout Europe [in the revolutions of 1848]. Nor can I disparage the work, or abuse the gift of our ancestors." "Old Bullion" was inching toward condemnation of slavery, and being pushed there by Calhoun.

In a public letter, Calhoun joined in the campaign to defeat Benton. The South Carolinian accused the Missourian of opening the territories to "the use and enjoyment of all that rabble of foreigners which he enumerates with such zest as the efficient means of our exclusion." Calhoun warned southern sympathizers of the traitorous leopards with identifiable spots: "a strong profession of attachment to the Union, and condemnation of what is called the violence and ultraism of the South."

Anti-Benton Democrats in Missouri blasted him for his abolitionism and arrogance in disobeying the legislature. Benton shot back: "I shall crush my enemies as an elephant crushes piss-ants under his tread." But he knew he had an uphill battle as ten of Missouri's sixteen Democratic newspapers were anti-Benton. His pro-South colleague from Missouri, Senator David R. Atchison, told Calhoun that Benton had "as good a chance to be made Pope, as to be elected Senator."

Events in Missouri made Benton's fate obvious, as he refused to compromise his principles. When, in early 1850, a group of anti-Benton Democrats realized that in defeating him they were assuring a Whig victory, Benton rejected their peace overtures with the observation that he "would sooner sit in council with the six thousand dead . . . of cholera in St. Louis [during the recent outbreak] than go into convention with such a gang of scamps." In the Missouri General Assembly elections in 1850, sixty-four Whigs were chosen, along with fifty-five Benton Democrats, and thirty-seven anti-Benton, pro-Calhoun Democrats. At least, Benton was proud to note that "disunionism" lost, though he expected to be replaced in the Senate.

"Old Bullion," however, still played a prominent role in the Senate debates over the "Compromise of 1850," as his opposition to slavery strengthened. The drama began in December 1849, as Calhoun joined the Democratic caucus and with the aid of Atchison of Missouri and a new senator, Henry S. Foote of Mississippi, succeeded by one vote in removing Benton's name from every committee except Foreign Affairs, from which he promptly resigned. Early in the new year, the slowly dying Calhoun could muster enough strength for only a few appearances in the Senate. Benton did not take advantage of his ailing enemy, remarking: "Benton will not speak today, for when God Almighty lays hands on a man, Benton takes his off."

The failing Calhoun was replaced by Foote in confronting Benton. The senator from Mississippi attempted to extract the highest price from the North and West for admitting California as a free state. He wanted all five bills under consideration included in an "omnibus bill," to be voted on together, up or down. Benton countered with his insistence that the admission of California as a free state be voted on separately, together with separate votes on the other four bills.

Calhoun died on March 31. In the Senate, Benton refused to deliver a eulogy, remaining silent as Calhoun had upon the death of John Quincy Adams. When Webster pleaded with Benton to speak, "Old Bullion" replied: "He is not dead, sir—he is not dead. There may be no vitality in his body, but there is in his doctrines. . . . My people cannot distinguish between a man and his principles—between a traitor and treason. They cannot eulogize the one and denounce the other."

Not only were Calhoun's principles vital; they were virulent. On April 17, Benton denounced the "Southern Address," based on Calhoun's principles, for throwing the country "into a flame." Rising and defending the "holy work" of Calhoun, Senator Foote, who for several weeks had been trying to provoke Benton into a duel, saw the Missourian moving down the aisle toward him. Foote suddenly retreated to his desk, pulled out a pistol, and cocked it. Breaking loose from the grip of another senator, Benton strode toward Foote and shouted: "I have no pistols! Let him fire! Stand out of the way! Let the assassin fire!" Benton stood tall and calm in the uproar, and Foote handed the revolver to a colleague, who hid it in his desk.

As the debate over Clay's omnibus bill raged on, Benton finally abandoned his silence on the "evil" of slavery and delivered his strongest attack yet on June 10, 1850. "The incurability of the evil is the greatest objection to the extension of slavery," he said. "It is wrong . . . to inflict an evil which can be cured: how much more to inflict one that is incurable, and against the will of the people who are to endure it forever! . . . It is a question of races, involving consequences which go to the destruction of one or the other. . . . It seems to be above human wisdom. But there is a wisdom above human! and to that we must look. In the meantime, not extend the evil."[23]

Benton was vindicated when, during the summer of 1850, the Senate approved each of the then five omnibus bills separately. He described the scene: "At that moment the cats and dogs that had been tied together by their tails for four months, scratching and biting, being loose again, every one of them ran off to his own hole and was quiet." Benton voted for three but opposed the Texas–New Mexico boundary bill as being too generous to Texas. He abstained on the Fugitive Slave Act, which he argued was so complex that it would be impossible to enforce.

When Benton left the Senate in 1850, everyone expected a Whig victory in the Missouri assembly elections, which probably doomed his reelection by the legislature the following January. But he took comfort in the overwhelming defeat of the Calhoun Democrats and proclaimed to a large crowd in St. Louis on November 9: "I have sometimes had to act against the preconceived opinions, and first impressions of my constituents. . . . I value solid popularity—the esteem of good men, for good actions. I despise the bubble popularity that is won without merit and lost without crime." In January 1851, by a bare majority of the Missouri legislature on the fortieth ballot, a Whig replaced Thomas Hart Benton as senator from Missouri.

"Old Bullion" began his memoirs, *Thirty Years' View,* but remained active in politics. At the age of seventy, he was elected for one term to the House in 1852, where, as its oldest member, he opposed the Kansas–Nebraska bill in 1854 as "a deception and a cheat" and a cover for southern expansionist aims in Cuba and northern Mexico. But the "colonel" was defeated in his reelection bid for the House.[24]

Benton remained a loyal Democrat supporting the party's presidential nominees, Franklin Pierce in 1852 and James Buchanan in 1856, though he opposed their policies of appeasing the South. He even supported Buchanan against the newly formed Republican Party's standard-bearer, his beloved son-in-law, John Charles Frémont, because Buchanan was a national, not sectional, candidate.

Benton continued writing his memoirs until his death on April 10, 1858. He even found time to write a 192-page historical and legal examination of the *Dred Scott* decision of the Supreme Court in 1857. He wrote that the worst aspect of the decision was that the *obiter dicta* of the majority reopened the controversy. That majority had argued that the Constitution protected slaves as property in all territories and that the Missouri Compromise, already repealed, had been unconstitutional since its passage. The unnecessary opinion of the majority, instead of settling the question, had "become a new question, more virulent than the former."[25]

The confrontations in the Senate, both legislative and rhetorical, between Thomas Hart Benton and his adversary, John "Cataline" Calhoun, were struggles over the direction of the Democratic Party and the nation. Calhoun won the one, and Benton the other. Beginning with President Polk and continuing through Pierce and Buchanan, the party catered to Calhoun's prejudices. Benton's old Jacksonian alliance of western and southern farmers and northern workingmen split on the slavery question. Manifest Destiny under Polk only intensified the struggle. And Stephen Douglas, who dominated the Democrats in the Senate during the 1850s, let the party drift far from Benton's Union-anchored position. Appeasement of the South, fired up by Calhoun's rhetoric, only delayed the Civil War.

Benton, with all his personal flaws, was virtuous in trying to "cure" an ailing Union that suffered from an "incurable evil." Like the nation, he was trapped in a moral contradiction. Blinded and shorn of his senatorial rank by Calhoun's philistines, this border-state Samson weakened the pillars of the slavery temple. But its destruction came only after his death and as the result of a bloody war to preserve the Union that he would have fought but wanted to avoid.

With "an ego twice the size of his physique," while Webster and Clay "passed their zenith and fell," Benton "kept rising all the time." More important to him than becoming president was his place in history, of which he always seemed to be conscious since being expelled from Chapel Hill for petty thievery at sixteen. The "colonel" had his body scrubbed down each day with a rough horsehair brush, and when asked why, replied: "The Roman gladiators did it, sir." Mindful of his Plutarch, Thomas Hart Benton grew in courage and virtue.[26]

3

Lincoln's Prime Minister

William Pitt Fessenden vs. Charles Sumner (1850–1865)

Lying in an unmarked grave in Portland, Maine, are the mortal remains of one of the most important figures of the American Civil War, Senator William Pitt Fessenden. Historians have generally ignored or distorted his role during the Civil War and, especially, the Reconstruction. But no such fate has befallen the famous crusader against slavery, Senator Charles Sumner: his toga-clad bust, opposite Lincoln's, greets visitors in the grand entrance hall to the U.S. Senate gallery, and his serene, majestic presence watches over Harvard Square.

Pitt Fessenden, as he was known, five years the senior of Charles Sumner, entered the U.S. Senate from Maine in 1854, in time for the critical debates over the establishment of the Kansas and Nebraska territories. Though Fessenden had served from 1841 to 1843 in the House of Representatives as a Whig supporter of Henry Clay's American System, Sumner was better known since his debut as a Free-Soil senator from Massachusetts in 1851 with a stirring attack on the Fugitive Slave Act. Sumner opposed the "Webster Whigs," who supported the Compromise of 1850. Though elected as a "Conscience Whig," Fessenden quickly aligned himself with the newly formed Republican Party, as did Sumner. Scarcely a week after Hannibal Hamlin of Maine presented his new colleague to the Senate, Fessenden joined the national debate over slavery. James S. Pike, a correspondent for Horace Greeley's *New York Tribune,* described Fessenden's speech as one of the "first blows of the Civil War."[1]

During the all-night session of March 3, the "*noche triste* of our history" in the words of his friend Henry Wadsworth Longfellow, Pitt Fessenden delivered the last speech against the bill that repealed the Missouri Compromise of 1820, providing that slavery would "forever" be excluded from all territory north of the 36°30′ parallel of the Louisiana Purchase. According to the bill, proposed by Senator Stephen A. Douglas of Illinois, the territories of Kansas and Nebraska would be organized as "slave" or "free" in elections conducted by the settlers of each territory. If the Senate voted to break the covenant of the Missouri Compromise, warned Fessenden, and "if there is excitement, if there is fanaticism . . . in the free States from this time forward, you will just cast your eyes back to those who made it, started it, and gave occasion for it." When Fessenden suggested that the Southern threat of secession was laughable, Senator Andrew Butler of South Carolina interjected: "No, sir, if your doctrine is carried out, if such sentiments as yours prevail, I want a dissolution right away." Retorted Fessenden: "As has been said before, do not delay it on my account." And this phrase became a popular slogan in the North.[2]

Two years later, as a civil war raged in Kansas, Sumner delivered his famous "Crime against Kansas" speech, attacking the same Andrew Butler for being a "Don Quixote who had chosen a mistress to whom he made his vows, and who . . . though polluted in the sight of the world, is chaste in his sight—I mean, the harlot, slavery." The following day, Butler's nephew, Congressman Preston Brooks, walked into the Senate chamber and, with a gutta-percha cane, repeatedly struck Sumner over the head and back, beating him almost to death. "Bleeding Sumner" and "Bleeding Kansas" energized the extremists of both the North and the South. "Martyr" Sumner slowly recuperated over the next four years, fighting psychogenic neurosis and physical disability outside the Senate—with his seat kept open by a sympathetic Massachusetts legislature. In the meantime, Fessenden, sharing Sumner's principles but not his tactics, grew in stature in the leadership of the Republican Party. By the time Sumner returned to the Senate as a national symbol, the embodiment of abolitionism, Fessenden had become the recognized leader in the Senate, from 1861 until 1865, when he clearly became the second most powerful man in the country, chairman of the Joint Committee on Reconstruction.

Fessenden and Sumner, who were so close ideologically, but so far apart temperamentally and tactically, came from very similar but psychologically different backgrounds. Both had to confront the problem of illegitimacy. Sumner failed to reveal in his autobiography that his father, Charles Pinkney Sumner, a lawyer, was born illegitimate; and Fessenden himself was a child of love, of an affair of his father when an undergraduate at Dartmouth.

Both men were virtuous, but they differed in virtue. Fessenden's was a constant, in handling the national finances, in dealing with the death of a son in the war, and in justice for the Native Americans. Sumner's was all-consuming, in supporting the rights of African Americans. Their differences did not come to a head until late in the war, or after the assassination of Lincoln. Fessenden's life from 1854 until 1868, though largely unknown, was central to American history at that time and in some ways on a more heroic scale than Lincoln's.

Many factors beyond origin of birth contributed to Sumner's unbridled individuality and Fessenden's more controlled and critical sense of himself. Were it not for his illegitimacy, and awareness of how the issue damaged the candidacy of the first Republican nominee, John Charles Frémont, in 1856, Fessenden might have sought the presidency in 1860 with a claim as good as Lincoln's. Reared by loving grandparents, Sarah and the Reverend William Fessenden, a Harvard graduate, for his first seven years, and then by his natural father, the abolitionist Samuel Fessenden, noted for his humanity and tolerance, Pitt Fessenden as a child and young man knew warmth and affection in a strict Puritan but cultivated atmosphere. He grew up emotionally secure enough, but still defensive about his lineage when, upon turning twenty-one, he received his first letter from his natural mother, Ruth Greene. After consulting his father about the "secret," he decided not to meet or communicate with her.[3]

Sumner, on the other hand, developed a "natural coldness" from his struggling lawyer father, who rarely smiled, and his "distant" seamstress mother. Keenly conscious of being born north of the line that divided the "bob" from the "nabob" side of Beacon Hill, "Gawky Sumner" was sent to school wearing "cheap sky-blue satinet clothes." The shy, awkward student at Boston Latin and Harvard would develop into a self-made and powerful political loner as an adult. Sumner's political autobiography would ignore not only his undemonstrative parents but also his eight brothers and sisters, especially his twin sister, Matilda, who died at the age of twenty-one, almost unnoticed by Charles.[4]

Pitt Fessenden was also the eldest son, with eight younger half-brothers and a half-sister, and a demanding stepmother, Deborah Chandler. Though also a frail and serious boy, Fessenden, unlike Sumner at Harvard, excelled both as a scholar in classics and as an "excellent debater" and was described as "warm in his friendships" but "bitter and uncompromising in his hatreds." He was popular among his peers at Bowdoin, including the Longfellow brothers, Franklin Pierce, Nathaniel Hawthorne, and the first African American college graduate, John B. Russwurm. But the seventeen-year-old Pitt also had a rebellious streak, as evidenced in his receiving his degree in absentia after being expelled for "the irregularity of eating and drinking at Wardsworth's Tavern without permission."

The young Fessenden did get a boost up from his famous and influential godfather, Daniel Webster, who never let his godson forget the twenty-mile ride through sleet and snow to attend his christening. And Pitt's relationship with the "Godlike Daniel" helped him in his early legal and political career. But even here, Fessenden was his own man. He summed up a trip west with Webster in 1837: "Mr. Webster would never gain popularity by personal intercourse—to strangers he appeared repellent. So far as gaining friends was concerned, Mr. Webster might well, if not better, have stayed at home and left his fame and public service to speak for him." Though a great debater himself, the laconic Fessenden developed by the time he had become a Senate leader a strong dislike of "the gabbling propensity," a Sumner specialty.

Fessenden's life would be haunted by more suffering than even those of Sumner and Lincoln. In early 1829, after a long courtship, Fessenden became engaged to Elizabeth Longfellow, a favorite sister of his poet–friend of Bowdoin days, but she died six months later. The anguished young lawyer tried to lose himself in his work, "deriving absolute enjoyment from nothing but a new 'suit' and a long account of fees with a balance in my favor." Even his marriage three years later to Ellen Deering, daughter of one of Portland's wealthiest merchants, proved difficult within a year as she became a semi-invalid after the birth of their first son, James. Pitt and Ellen had three more sons, William, Francis, and Samuel, and finally a daughter, Mary, who died of scarlet fever in early childhood. In 1857, shortly after Fessenden had achieved national prominence and celebrated his silver wedding anniversary, Ellen died. Broken in health himself from recurring bouts of malaria from 1854 on, and from a mild case of smallpox in 1866, William Pitt Fessenden during the last decade of his life was tested as much as any nationally prominent figure.[5]

Carl Sandburg wrote that Fessenden by 1864 had "three boys who had gone into the army": Sam, who was killed in the "Second Battle of Bull Run"; Frank, who had been severely wounded and lost a leg; and Jim, who had been ordered by General David Hunter to command and train the first African American regiment in May 1862, only to have it disbanded by Lincoln. In Sandburg's view, Fessenden understandably "could have joined the Vindictives." Instead, during the summer and fall of 1864, he served as Lincoln's secretary of the treasury and a kind of prime minister, to aid in the president's reelection. Back in the Senate during the crazed years after Lincoln's assassination, Fessenden became a trusted symbol of stability to the country, as he demonstrated, in Sandburg's words, that "he was his own man," deflating "Sumner's pompous heroics" with "casual and unexpected points bearing on what was immediately practical."[6]

Pitt Fessenden was one of the most impressive figures in Washington during the 1850s—the very embodiment of senatorial dignity. Impeccably dressed in long black jacket with velvet lapels and a starched stick-up collar gathered by a tie of fine black silk, he was generally regarded as the best-dressed member of the Senate. With a classically handsome face, Fessenden was very conscious, as he wrote to his father, of the way "people are taken with good looks." It "will not do for men in high positions to fall below the ordinary standard." Fessenden's quick, precise manner of walking rein-forced his image of a leader, and his reserved manner and piercing eyes, to his opponents, reflected an intense disdain. Although critics considered him irascible during increasing periods of ill health, those closest to him saw great goodwill and generosity. Fessenden's friends in the Senate, during an era of declining public morality, were all known for their integrity: Solomon Foot of Vermont, Hamilton Fish of New York, Lyman Trumbull of Illinois, and James Grimes of Iowa.

Slavery and civil war in Kansas dominated Fessenden's political and personal life through the 1850s. In June 1856, in Washington, he received word from Portland that his youngest son, Sam, a fifteen-year-old, had run away to fight for freedom in Kansas. Only months later, after Sam had joined a group of Free-Soilers, the boy was taken prisoner by "border ruffians" and put aboard a boat to Illinois, where Judge Lyman Trumbull, Fessenden's later Senate ally, arranged for Sam's return to Portland. A few years later, after Sam was killed at the Second Battle of Manassas, the senator liked to read to friends the boy's account of his Kansas adventure.

In February 1858, Fessenden delivered probably the "best speech on the Republican side" against the admission of Kansas under its proslavery Lecompton Constitution. In praising the speech, Horace White, a correspondent for the *Chicago Tribune,* said of Fessenden, "a more consummate debater or more knightly character and presence has not graced the Senate chamber in my time, if ever." Stephen Douglas, recalling the great speakers of his era in the Senate, called Fessenden "the readiest and ablest debater."[7]

Advocates of slavery and their Northern Democratic allies still had the upper hand in 1858 as the bill passed the Senate and in amended form became law, providing for an open and fair vote on the Lecompton Constitution by all eligible residents of Kansas. If the ratification failed, the admission of Kansas as a state would be indefinitely postponed. But if the Lecompton Constitution were approved, Kansas would be immediately admitted to the Union as a slave state and awarded grants of public lands.

The Republicans denounced the terms of the Lecompton Act of April 30,

1858, as a bribe, and Fessenden commented: "The whole thing is disgraceful to all concerned. The South has lost all claim to honor, and the Democratic North never had any." But Fessenden foresaw the legislation as a Pyrrhic victory since the "deliverance" of the people of Kansas was "in their own hands." And on August 2, Kansans by more than six to one rejected the Lecompton Constitution.

In the midterm elections of 1858, in reaction to "Bleeding Kansas," the Republicans swept the North, including President James Buchanan's home state of Pennsylvania, though Stephen Douglas was reelected to the Senate by the Illinois legislature in his contest with Lincoln. Fessenden, the ex-Whig, and Hannibal Hamlin, the ex-Democrat, had presented a unified Republican campaign in Maine. And in December 1858, Fessenden received word in Washington that Republican members in the Maine legislature had unanimously reelected him to a full six-year term in the U.S. Senate.

During 1859, the nation was moving inexorably toward the "irrepressible conflict" that Senator William Seward had predicted. And John Brown's raid on Harper's Ferry in October, in an effort to instigate a slave insurrection, further fanned the flames, as did the hanging of the martyr Brown on December 2. In the Senate, Fessenden, in a spirited defense of the Republican Party against Stephen Douglas's charge of complicity in the Harper's Ferry raid, wondered about the real threat: that Southerners would consider the election of a Republican president in 1860 cause for dissolving the Union.

Plagued by poor health when planning would have been necessary, Senator Fessenden went trout fishing in Maine during the summer of 1859 and opposed all efforts to get himself elected president. In December, he wrote to his cousin Lizzy from Washington: "They say here that my chances are much better than those of anybody else. But do not be alarmed. I am not deceived, or elated in the least. Positively I do not wish for it, and tell everybody that no one can do me so much injury in any way as by mentioning my name, and I believe that people are satisfied of my sincerity."

But when Maine Republicans met in convention in March 1860 in Augusta to elect delegates to the national convention, the mention of Fessenden's name set off an enthusiastic demonstration. "It was difficult in the convention to keep a resolution specifically recommending you from being offered," wrote the young future presidential aspirant James G. Blaine, chairman of the State Republican Committee, "and it was only upon the assurance that you would not desire it that the movement was suppressed."

How strong Fessenden's candidacy might have proved in Chicago is debatable, but he probably could have won majority support from the New

England delegates. And Blaine reported that, of all those mentioned, Fessenden was the only one completely acceptable to the crucial Pennsylvania delegation.

In May, the Republican National Convention in Chicago nominated Abe Lincoln of Illinois on the third ballot. Lincoln's views on slavery were more moderate and compromising than Fessenden's. But the senator was pleased with Lincoln's selection of a running mate, Senator Hannibal Hamlin, a rival for control of Maine's Republicans.

As much as his health would permit, Fessenden campaigned for the Lincoln–Hamlin ticket and was delighted that it swept the September election in Maine. And as Maine went, so did the North in November. Lincoln's election precipitated a national crisis; and Fessenden returned to Congress as one of its most powerful men when he was elected chairman of the Senate Finance Committee, which then included appropriations. In effect, he was Senate majority leader.

During the secession winter between Lincoln's election and his inauguration, Fessenden wrote to his friend Hamilton Fish that "the people of the South are led captive by ignorance and pride. They must be left to learn their own weakness, and then the cure will be speedy and certain." Although he was chosen one of Maine's delegates to the unofficial Peace Convention held at Willard's Hotel in Washington during February, he refused to attend. He also voted against Senator John J. Crittenden's compromise, a peace resolution calling for recognition of slavery in the territories south of 36°30′. In the meantime, beginning with South Carolina on December 20 and ending with Texas on February 1, eleven Southern states had seceded from the Union; and Senator Jefferson Davis of Mississippi was elected provisional president of the Confederacy by a "convention" or "provisional Congress" meeting at Montgomery, Alabama. On March 4, Lincoln was inaugurated as president of the United States, asserting that no state "can lawfully get out of the Union" but pledging that there would be no violence "unless it be forced upon the national authority."

Fessenden wrote to his son William: "I am told that I have the reputation of being the most determined adversary of compromise in the ranks of the Republican Party." And on the Senate floor in mid-March 1861, during a debate, Stephen Douglas lost his temper, directing vicious "epithets" at Fessenden, unrecorded but described as "better adapted to a pothouse than the Senate Chamber." References were made to settling the question "elsewhere" according to the "code of honor," but both parties backed down.[8]

In the spring of 1861, Senator Fessenden was disturbed at the poor quality of the new cabinet: Senator William Seward of New York as secretary of state and especially the notoriously corrupt Senator Simon Cameron of Pennsylvania as secretary of war. Cameron, Fessenden had warned Lincoln, was "utterly incompetent"; and after nine months of maladministration, Cameron was "put on ice" as minister to Russia.

South Carolina's firing on Fort Sumter on April 12, 1861, occurred before the newly elected Thirty-seventh Congress had convened in a special session called for July 4. But with the Southern assault, the president, using the "war powers" he possessed as commander in chief, called out the militias of various states, proclaimed a blockade of Southern ports, and suspended the writ of habeas corpus in certain vital areas such as the border state of Maryland. Fessenden wrote Senator James Grimes of Iowa: "I confess that were I in Lincoln's place a small scruple would not detain me from doing what was needful." When senatorial colleagues criticized usurpation of power by the executive, Fessenden endorsed Lincoln's action "without crossing a t or dotting an i."[9]

In 1861, Senator Fessenden played his most important role in financing the war effort. He first of all amended the Morrill Act, passed during the waning days of Buchanan's presidency, to provide for a substantial increase in tariff receipts. In fact, with the Southerners gone, tariffs under Fessenden's leadership were raised from an average of 19 percent in 1857 to 47 percent by the Act of 1864. To the opposition of Senator Charles Sumner, who feared offending European nations, especially the United Kingdom, Fessenden tartly replied: "I am willing to take all the risk of the righteous indignation of people abroad who think they do not make quite so much money out of us as they ought." Fessenden remained a true classical liberal in wanting to finance the war on a pay-as-you-go basis but was in a minority in Congress. He personally and tenaciously ushered through Congress the three-year, 7.30 percent treasury notes, the popular "seven-thirties" that were important in financing the war.

Unlike many others, Fessenden did not panic after the Confederate rout of Union troops at Bull Run in July 1861, noting that he was too old to run and that no one knew the direction in which to run. He was upset at the self-appointed generals in Congress, such as Senator Benjamin Wade of Ohio, and hoped the defeat would teach everyone a "lesson" in the need for "greater activity" and senators especially "that they had better attend to their appropriate duties."

Fessenden was never one to forget family duties. When unable to attend his youngest son Sam's graduation from Bowdoin, he sent instructions to his older brother William: "You must provide for Sam's bills. He has written with regard to an entertainment, and I am willing he should have a reasonable one, but not that he should provide a large quantity of liquors and have a spree. You may look out for it, but on a scale as economical as is consistent with the necessary gentility."

The impetuous Sam would soon join his older brothers James and Frank in accepting commissions in the Union army. Fessenden wrote Frank in the fall of 1861 that he hoped "to meet you all again before I die, and in better times for the country" and "that each should do his duty in the sphere of action assigned to him, and wait patiently for the developments of time."

Northern morale received a temporary boost on August 30, 1861, with General John Charles Frémont's celebrated "confiscation order." Frémont placed his military district in Missouri under martial law and ordered the confiscation of all property belonging to persons resisting the authority of the U.S. government, including slaves, who should be considered free. Fessenden wrote to his friend James Pike, minister at The Hague, that Frémont's emancipation "proclamation" was having an "electric effect upon all parts of the country." But Fessenden's elation was short-lived: President Lincoln ordered Frémont to rescind his order and, when defied, removed him from command. Fessenden wrote to Senator James Grimes of Iowa that the president's dismissal of Frémont was "cruel" and "inexcusable" and that, by Lincoln's nullification of the emancipation order, "the President has lost ground amazingly."

Washington at the time buzzed about Mrs. Frémont's confrontation with Lincoln. Jessie Benton Frémont, a chip off "Old Bullion," traveled two days and two nights by train from Missouri to meet the president. Upon checking in at Willard's Hotel, she was given a message, commanding her to come to the White House immediately. Covered with dust from the trip, without a chance to bathe, the spunky Jessie met President Lincoln in the Red Room at 9:00 P.M., September 10. As she recorded, Lincoln condescendingly greeted her: "You are quite a female politician." The president confessed to his secretary that Mrs. Frémont "taxed me so violently" that he barely kept his temper. Lincoln denounced Frémont's order and told his wife: "The General should never have dragged the Negro into the war. It is a war for a great national object and the Negro has nothing to do with it."[10]

Because of such sentiments, congressional Republicans were unhappy with Lincoln. In the second session of the Thirty-seventh Congress, opening on December 2, 1861, Fessenden became a moderating force between the Republican leadership in Congress and the president. He generally supported the congressional leadership and wrote home that the president "has lost all hold upon Congress, though no one doubts his personal integrity." Fessenden was especially upset with Lincoln's refusal to permit escaped or captured slaves to fight in the Union army. In April 1862, as chairman of the Senate Finance Committee, Fessenden joined the Committee on the

Conduct of the War in a meeting with the new secretary of war Edwin Stanton, who had replaced the incompetent Cameron. Fessenden expressed concern about the president's timid policy on fugitive slaves. Why should the army descend to slave catching and return fugitive blacks to their owners?[11]

But Fessenden worried about the Confiscation Bill. He strongly supported the emancipation of slaves of everyone supporting the rebellion, as he favored the use of African American troops and was one of the strongest supporters of the bill to abolish slavery in the District of Columbia. But he worked to tone down the first bill that would render all property within rebellious states liable to confiscation. Fessenden voted for the second Confiscation Bill but favored carrying the policy "to just that extent, and no further, that I judge the good of the country requires." As he worried that Lincoln would veto the bill, he thought that "it would have been better not to legislate upon the subject of confiscation at all."

Fearing the impact of such a vote, Fessenden decided to discuss the bill with the president personally. Noting Lincoln's objections, particularly the extension of forfeiture "beyond the lives of the guilty parties," Fessenden convinced Congress to pass an explanatory resolution modifying the bill according to the president's objections. But Senator Ben Wade would denounce Fessenden for "mousing around" the White House.

In 1862, as chairman of the Senate Finance Committee, in a bill providing for new "five-twenty" treasury bonds, Fessenden convinced his colleagues that the interest should be paid in specie. But he failed to persuade the Senate to delete the "greenback" clause, which would permit payment of customs duties in "legal tender." He would privately complain that Secretary of the Treasury Salmon P. Chase "lacks both system and courage, sometimes."[12]

Fessenden also steered the Internal Revenue Bill through the Senate, despite the opposition of many colleagues. It increased slightly income tax rates and spread duties to a wider variety of items.

During the summer of 1862, Fessenden was more personally affected by the war than most of the prominent Republicans. During April, his son Captain Frank Fessenden had a bullet shatter his arm at the Battle of Shiloh. In May, another son, Captain James Fessenden, on the staff of General David Hunter, was placed in charge of training the "First Regiment of the Carolina Volunteers," later disbanded by Lincoln, which was the first regiment of freed slaves mustered into the Union army.

Then his youngest, the rambunctious Sam, an artillery lieutenant in General John Pope's Army of the Potomac, was killed on August 30, 1862, at the Second Battle of Bull Run. Fessenden wrote from Portland to his friend Senator Grimes of Iowa: "He lived about thirty-six hours, manifesting through all . . . the most heroic calmness and self-possession." The Senate leader wanted to retrieve his son's body from behind enemy lines but was finally persuaded to let his nephew do so under a flag of truce. Eventually, the boy's body was exhumed and returned to be buried in Portland's Evergreen Cemetery next to his mother and baby sister. Fessenden told his Iowa friend: "His loss has affected me most severely, and the fact that two others of my sons are exposed to the same fate renders me unquiet and unhappy—but I have nothing for it but patience & submission."[13]

In November 1862, the senator returned to Washington, where he was joined by his brothers Tom and Sam, both of whom the Maine voters had sent to the House of Representatives. On his trip back by train, Pitt Fessenden was met and accompanied by several senatorial colleagues, and they discussed recent events. He was opposed to Lincoln's proclamation suspending the writ of habeas corpus in loyal states where no insurrection existed, he privately told his colleagues, though shortly afterward, he would publicly defend the president's arbitrary arrests. He also privately expressed surprise at Lincoln's preliminary Emancipation Proclamation (probably because of Lincoln's earlier dismissal of Frémont), which he called a *"brutem fulmen"* that was "very unfortunately worded" and that "did not and could not affect the status of a single Negro."[14]

Fessenden found Congress in an ugly mood, especially after the horrible slaughter of Union soldiers at Fredericksburg on December 13, 1862. Several days later, Republican senators determined to seek a shake-up of Lincoln's cabinet, with the exception of Secretary of War Stanton and Secretary of the Treasury Chase. Chase had been one of the chief critics of the president's failure to consult his cabinet. But Lincoln would outmaneuver his congressional critics.

Fessenden kept a detailed account of the Senate Republican efforts to remove Seward from the cabinet. A nine-man committee was received by President Lincoln on the evening of December 17, "with his usual urbanity." But Ben Wade, the first speaker, created a charged atmosphere. He said the conduct of the war "was left in the hands of men who had no sympathy with it or the cause." Commenting "on the recent elections in the West," Wade imputed "the defeat of the Republicans to the fact that the President had placed the direction of our military affairs in the hands of bitter and malignant Democrats."

After Senators Grimes and Jacob Howard expressed their lack of confidence in Secretary of State Seward, Fessenden spoke. He praised "the patriotism and integrity of the President." Though disclaiming any desire "to dictate to him with regard to his Cabinet," he politely did just that: "A belief existed in the community that the Cabinet were not consulted as a council—in fact, that many important measures were decided upon not only without consultation, but without the knowledge of its members." Committee members believed, said Fessenden, "that the Secretary of State was not in accord with the majority of the Cabinet and exerted an injurious influence upon the conduct of the war." He also argued that it "was singularly unfortunate that almost every officer known as an anti-slavery man had been disgraced," such as Generals Frémont and David Hunter. And he warned Lincoln to protect his administration from the Democrats and General George McClellan.[15]

Charles Sumner continued the attack on Seward. He claimed that the secretary of state "had subjected himself to ridicule in diplomatic circles at home and abroad" and that he spoke of Congress "repeatedly with disrespect in the presence of foreign ministers" and had written "offensive dispatches."

At a second meeting two evenings later, Fessenden led the discussion with the president and raised the broader issue of parliamentary responsibility, or the inherent conflict in the Constitution between executive and legislative privileges and responsibilities. He suggested that Seward's resignation be accepted: he had "lost my confidence before he became Secretary of State, and had I been consulted I should not have advised his appointment." Lincoln claimed not to have had the opportunity to consult Fessenden, who then reminded the president that through Senator Lyman Trumbull of Illinois he had advised the president-elect "that before forming your Cabinet you should come to Washington where you could advise with Senators. I am sorry you did not do so." Fessenden then inquired: "Do you wish us to advise with our fellow-senators on the point suggested?" "I think not," replied the president, and the five-and-one-half hour meeting broke up at 1:00 A.M.

Over the weekend, Fessenden learned that the president had outmaneuvered the Senate Republican leadership by rejecting the proffered resignations of both Secretaries Chase, a radical favorite, and Seward. Though Lincoln had replaced McClellan with Ambrose Burnside, who would soon be replaced by Joseph Hooker, as commander of the Army of the Potomac, the president was not about to accept Fessenden's concept of parliamentary responsibility, implicit in the forced resignation of Secretary of State Seward.[16]

By late 1862, Fessenden referred in correspondence to the "anomalous character" of Lincoln. It puzzled Carl Sandburg that a man like Fessenden who "had clean hands and a rare sense of justice in politics, owning himself with a decency, with a record quite spotless" should "misread Lincoln." But did Fessenden misjudge the president at that time, or was Lincoln in the process of learning from his own mistakes? When John Murray Forbes, the

Boston abolitionist, wrote that he wanted Fessenden in the cabinet, the senator lamented: "No friend of mine should ever wish to see me there. . . . You cannot change the President's character or conduct, unfortunately; he remained long enough at Springfield, surrounded by toadies and office-seekers, to persuade himself that he was specially chosen by the Almighty for this crisis, and well chosen. This conceit has never yet been beaten out of him, and until it is, no human wisdom can be of much avail. I see nothing for it but to let the ship of state drift along, hoping that the current of public opinion may bring it safely into port."[17]

Fessenden's opinion of Lincoln and his administration reached low ebb when he wrote his cousin Lizzy in January 1863:

> Nobody seems to think of the country these days. Many of our poor soldiers have not had a dime for months. Civil, isn't it? I would be content to borrow & mortgage my house, if that would help them. Nobody can blame them for deserting. I am heartsick when I think of the misnoble mismanagement in our army. In what is called the "Convalescent Corps," thousands are almost without shelter, & miserably provided with food—all through the utter stupidity of our officers—for there have been ample means provided. If I was Secretary of War, wouldn't heads fall? The simple truth is, there never was such a shambling, half & half set of incapables collected in one government before, since the world began. I saw a letter this morning written in good English by the King of Siam to Admiral Foote, which had more good sense in it, & a better comprehension of our troubles, I do verily believe, than *Abe* has had from the beginning—But it's of no use to scold.[18]

Publicly, however, Fessenden remained a loyal Senate leader and chairman of the Finance Committee as he supported the National Currency Act of February 1863. He feared that the "national banknotes" would destroy the state banks, but he loyally supported Chase's efforts at centralized banking, which included the more comprehensive National Banking Act of 1864.

Through 1863 and 1864, Fessenden demonstrated a rare sense of justice, certainly keener than Lincoln's. Alone among his senatorial colleagues, he opposed "one little bill" that its sponsor, Senator James Lane of Kansas, stated "will excite no discussion." It provided for "the extinction of Indian titles in Kansas and the removal of the Indians from said State." While professing to be no expert in arguing against the unanimous opinion of the Committee on Indian Affairs, Fessenden did object to the philosophy of the bill—that "all the rights and all the justice . . . are to be reserved exclusively for the whites." He asked: "Suppose you remove them to the Indian territory, how long will it be before the whites encroach on them there? How long will it be before . . . the feeble little remnant must go still further into the wilderness?" And he summed up his philosophy: "If any man chooses to come into my neighborhood and settle, and by his improvements increase the value of the land which I occupy, it does not follow that he has a right to take that land from me or compel me to sell it to him; and I think the same rule holds with reference to colored people, whether they are of African descent or native Indians."

Fessenden exposed the anti-Indian racism of Lincoln's policy of removal and even suggested using bayonets against law-breaking whites to protect the Indians. Lincoln's policy required, the Maine senator said, "that the white man should steal from the Indian; and if he cannot do it in any other way, he is to cut his throat; and if he is not strong enough to do this, the Government of the United States is to help him!"[19]

Fessenden also attacked the War Department's overly liberal policy of exemption from the Conscription Act of March 1863 and of increasing the bounties for "volunteers" way above the agreed-upon $300, to as much as $800. Recruiting of the poor, especially Irish and German immigrants, was being done in "a very clumsy manner."[20]

The Maine senator had long advocated the enlistment of freedmen into the U.S. Army. And his oldest son, Captain James, was the only member of General David Hunter's staff willing to train the first recruits—former slaves in South Carolina. One company of these recruits was deployed in the quartermaster's department and later became the nucleus of the Massachusetts regiment enlisted and organized by Colonel T.W. Higginson. Captain James Fessenden had written to his father about this first "regiment of colored men" that "the fine appearance and good behavior of the men are a source of wonder to everybody."[21]

No wonder, then, that Fessenden was upset by the bitter attacks of Boston abolitionists such as Wendell Phillips and William Lloyd Garrison in early 1864 when he opposed a blanket retroactive pay raise for all 60,000 African American soldiers, supported by Sumner. While, as chair of the Finance Committee, he was dealing with a huge deficit, Sumner's supporters, such as the *Boston Commonwealth,* accused "Fessenden and other Conservatives" of "bigotry, jealousy, and copperheadism." This issue has even falsely shaped his reputation among modern historians with their examination, casual at best, of the charge. Fessenden claimed that he had advocated, before Sumner, as early as 1862, "that the black troops thus raised ought to be put upon an equality in all respects with the white." He argued that for members of the two Massachusetts black regiments, who had been promised equal pay by Governor John Andrew, contrary to Secretary of War Stanton's order, and for the one Kansas and the two South Carolinian black regiments made similar promises, special bills should be introduced, which he would support. Though he backed a compromise, retroactive equality in pay to the beginning of 1864, including bonuses if possible (though there was considerable inequity there), he pointed out the different conditions among the 60,000 black soldiers, such as those who had been slaves on the Mississippi, with wives and children also to be provided for by the federal government. As he suspected, the issue of retroactive equality for African American soldiers opened a Pandora's box of problems the country was about to face in Reconstruction.[22]

Fessenden was a neo-Hamiltonian conservative on fiscal matters and a radical supporter of civil rights. His fiscal integrity forced him to question the right of Congress to promote Ulysses S. Grant to the special rank of lieutenant general with a pay raise, though the senator finally gave in to Secretary Stanton's plea that the promotion was needed for morale purposes in the army. Fessenden also criticized workers' unions as "simply reducing them all to the same level." He opposed an eight-hour day for federal workers, along with Sumner, in almost modern, antibureaucratic rhetoric: "From the laborers in the Government employ you do not get more than two thirds as much work as you do from those in private employ as it stands now." Though his public persona was not adaptable to the myth of the self-made man that settled so easily on Lincoln, Fessenden spoke for the virtues of work and honesty that have come to be associated with the figure of Lincoln.[23]

When Senator Henry Wilson of Massachusetts introduced a resolution to expel Senator Garrett Davis of Kentucky for disloyalty, Fessenden stated that he would vote neither to expel nor to censure the senator. Though "garrulous Garrett" had said "many violent and unreasonable things about the administration," Fessenden argued: "It was easy to imagine a state of things in any country when its government had become so obnoxious to the people that it was the duty of a senator to rise in his place and say, 'I call upon the people to resist this outrageous exercise of authority.'" After Fessenden's remarks, Wilson withdrew his resolution.

Fessenden also confronted Senator Zachariah Chandler, a founder of the Republican Party and spoilsman of Reconstruction years, whose statue represents Michigan in the United States Capitol. In June 1864, Fessenden opposed Chandler's bill to grant a private company the use of a U.S. ship and $50,000 a year for ten years to build a telegraph line across British and Russian territories in the Pacific Northwest and then across the Bering Strait to connect with a Russian line across Siberia. Fessenden asked for the contracts, remarking: "There was nothing before the Senate to give them information." After the measure was so amended that Fessenden could vote for it, Chandler protested that the proposal had effectively been killed. A bitter enemy of Fessenden during Reconstruction, Zach Chandler, an expansionist and imperialist, was usually interested in making a fast buck.[24]

During early 1864, Fessenden was pressed to oppose Lincoln's renomination at the "Union Party" Convention in June in Baltimore. But he wrote home: "Our great men are busy in trying to make themselves Prest. Abe, however, has the inside track, and as things look now, his renomination and reelection are sure. My friend Chase is nowhere, but he doesn't see it."[25]

Fessenden's views on Lincoln had mellowed throughout 1863, especially after the successes of Gettysburg and Vicksburg. He then would grow closer to the president in 1864 when he joined the cabinet. At the same time, for many reasons discussed in the next chapter, Sumner and Fessenden grew further apart in 1864 and 1865.

After Lincoln was renominated on the Union Party ticket, he selected a "war Democrat," Senator Andrew Johnson of Tennessee, to replace Hannibal Hamlin of Maine as his running mate. The president was anxious to present a strong administration to the electorate in November to challenge General George McClellan, the expected Democratic nominee. And so when Lincoln accepted Chase's resignation on June 30, 1864, he decided to appoint as secretary of the treasury the prominent war Democrat, ex-Governor David Tod of Ohio.

Tod, however, refused the appointment on grounds of ill health, and Lincoln cajoled, if not forced, Fessenden to accept. Though twice attempting to decline, once in a formal letter, Fessenden reluctantly accepted and was immediately confirmed by the Senate, as long-term government bonds jumped two and one-half points on Wall Street. Though he did not want the office, which "may result in the destruction of all the reputation I have gained, ... I do not feel like complaining when I think of Frank's amputated limb." Colonel Frank Fessenden had recently lost a leg at the battle of Montell's Bluffs.[26]

Fessenden served a few days more than eight months as secretary of the treasury. His main job was to stand out as a beacon of integrity within the administration and to the country, and Lincoln was delighted with the almost universal support for Fessenden.

But Fessenden's selection supports his earlier skepticism about the president's decision making. Lincoln expressed surprise to his secretary, John Hay, "that this appointment of Fessenden is so popular," especially since "no one ever mentioned his name to me for that place." But after "thinking over the matter," the president thought of three reasons for the selection's popularity: "First, he knows the ropes thoroughly; as chairman of the Senate committee on finance he knows as much of this special subject as Mr. Chase. Second, he is a man possessing a national reputation and the confidence of the country. Third, he is a radical—without the petulant and vicious fretfulness of many radicals."[27]

Even Chase thought Fessenden was the most admired man in the country, and Benjamin Brown French, superintendent of public buildings and friend of Lincoln, would comment in his diary on July 3, 1864: "The best man in the U.S. . . . was nominated and at once confirmed by the Senate. He, at first, declined to accept the place in consequence of his worn out health, but so urgent has been the pressure upon him from all parts of the loyal states that, I believe[,] he has decided, as a patriot and a sterling man as he is, to accept it. I look upon his acceptance as the financial salvation of the country, for his eminent ability, his untiring industry, his perfect integrity, his high character in every respect, point him out as the man, and I believe the only man[,] that can save us in these times, from ruin."[28]

During the eight months Fessenden served as secretary of the treasury, Nathan Farwell replaced him in the Senate on an interim appointment. In effect, Fessenden had become Lincoln's prime minister to ensure the president's reelection. Fessenden's policy was essentially to keep the ship of state on an even keel, as it slowly approached the safe harbor of victory and reunion.

Fessenden was a supporter of hard currency. But when he took office on July 5, gold was selling at $270 an ounce, which meant that $4,000 in gold would purchase more than $10,000 in U.S. government bonds. Since most of the U.S. bonds bore interest payments of 6 percent in specie, the government was actually paying an effective, real interest rate of 16 percent. Fessenden, the pragmatist, consequently decided to rely on the popularly proven seven-thirties, payable at 7.3 percent in paper.

As Fessenden was developing a reputation for honesty in cleaning out corruption in the treasury, he considered hiring the Philadelphia financier Jay Cooke to market bonds the way Secretary Chase had done. Instead, Fessenden decided to market the seven-thirties through the new national banking system. But the demand was weak during the autumn of that presidential election year, even for gold-bearing bonds issued that September. Fessenden wrote home in late August: "All will depend very much on the results of the elections. If we carry them, the war is substantially over. If not, all is over with us."

But a few days before the election, Fessenden thought it then safe to ask Cooke to buy $10 million worth of five-twenty bonds issued October 1, which had become a glut on the market and New York bankers had refused. Cooke immediately bought 3 million and asked for an option on the remainder, to be purchased after a visit to Wall Street. With this daring move by Cooke, coupled with Lincoln's reelection, Fessenden's "bond drive" proved successful. Cooke's patriotism and shrewdness proven, the treasury secretary finally bargained with Cooke and Company to become a general agent for the treasury in the sale of government bonds. As General Grant's forces were wearing down General Robert E. Lee's, bond purchases soared; and Fessenden told Cooke's brother Henry that "he wasn't afraid now that there would be any lack of money to pay off the army." In fact, supplying Cooke and Company with sufficient bonds had suddenly become the problem.[29]

On March 3, 1865, after obtaining congressional authorization for $600 million in three-year treasury notes, Secretary Fessenden resigned his post in favor of his comptroller of the currency, Hugh McCulloch. The secretary would return to the Senate on March 4 to the plaudits of Horace Greeley's *New York Tribune:* Fessenden was "unassuming, conscientious, just, wise, democratic. . . . It is these qualities of simplicity and integrity that have saved his administration of the Treasury in the most critical epoch of our Finances. . . . A just History of the war or the Union will give him a place beside the great Generals who have won the Union victories." And a scholarly economic study of the period portrays Fessenden's administration as "marked by efficiency and sagacity."[30]

Fessenden's reelection to the Senate by the Maine legislature in January 1865 was not a foregone conclusion. He had a strong competitor in Hannibal Hamlin. And Hamlin forces were led by a former Fessenden supporter and political bellwether, young Congressman James G. Blaine.

When Chief Justice Roger B. Taney died on October 12, 1864, Blaine urged Hamlin to write Fessenden "pricking his ambition for the place" as "by far the most desirable capstone in his political edifice." But Fessenden heard from Lincoln that Chase was under consideration for the position. Since he "was satisfied Mr. Chase would accept," he "could not now, honorably consent that any movement should be made" in his behalf.[31]

A shrewd politician, Fessenden, with humor and deftness, informed his influential friends in Maine and President Lincoln: "My very able successor, Mr. Farwell [a friend and supporter of Hamlin], is so devoted to my interests that he would undoubtedly desire me to remain Secretary of the Treasury—Failing that, he would like to have me go to France, & has offered me his aid and influence for that eminent position—Failing both of these, he would undoubtedly be willing that I should go to the Devil, & give me a seat in the Cabinet there—*provided* I will get out of Hamlin's way for the Senate. . . . At any rate, the question is one which requires my concurrence. My wishes are for my old place, and none other, as my friends very well know."[32]

Turning down all bargains and making no promises, Fessenden's "Treasury Garden" strategy worked, and he was overwhelmingly elected to his old seat.

A few weeks later, with the Senate in recess, Fessenden traveled from Portland to New York. He was addressing a public meeting at the Customs House on April 15, when word arrived of the assassination of Lincoln and the wounding of Seward—possibly as part of a rebel plot. The senator recalled seeing the worn-out president recently and saying: "Mr. President, the people of the United States are praying that God will spare your life to see the end of this rebellion." And he recalled Lincoln's reply: "Mr. Fessenden, it may be that I should not live to see it, and sometimes I think I shall not; but if I were taken away there are those who would perform my duties better." Then, though usually tactful but now overwrought in the conspiratorial air, the Senator told his audience: "We will hang Jeff Davis!" But William Pitt Fessenden would not abandon his "rare sense of justice" during the Reconstruction of the Union.[33]

4

"Worthy of Plutarch"

Fessenden vs. Sumner (1865–1870)

The Thirty-ninth Congress, elected in late 1864, convened in its first session under a new president, Andrew Johnson, on December 4, 1865. And Pitt Fessenden was immediately elected chairman of the Joint Committee on Reconstruction, composed of fifteen members of Congress—six senators and nine congressmen. One historian has written: "No other Committee of Congress ever wielded the power of the Joint Committee on Reconstruction or left so permanent an imprint on the country's history." Fessenden was clearly the second most powerful person in the nation.

Historians have exaggerated the differences between the committee's "conservative" members, led by Fessenden, and its "radical" members, headed by the Speaker of the House, Thaddeus Stevens. In this manner, Fessenden has been wrongly labeled; he was in some ways a more principled radical than any of the others. This was evident in the drafting of the Fourteenth Amendment, as Stevens admitted. Fessenden was comfortable in supporting honesty and hard work and in advocating civil rights for all races, and eventually both sexes. But this virtuous man saw his positions twisted for political gain. Fessenden's fall from power in 1866 shaped the impeachment trial of President Johnson and the history of the Reconstruction.

Many of the controversies can be traced to the jealousy of Sumner, who was piqued at not being a member of the Joint Committee of fifteen. The two men had been old friends from the days they frequently met at Senator Hamilton Fish's home in 1856, Sumner, a handsome bachelor, and Fessenden, a widower and father of four sons. The two men were then on close terms—"my dear Sumner" and "my dear Fessenden," and they were often seen walking arm-in-arm into the Senate.[1]

But when Sumner returned to the Senate three and one-half years after his brutal beating, their relationship changed. In a letter to Fish in December 1859, Fessenden worried about the effects of the caning on Sumner: "He calls himself well, but there is a change in him which strikes me unpleasantly, but which is more easily felt than described. There is a lack of his old alertness, which, perhaps, may be accounted for on other grounds than bodily infirmity."[2]

Increasingly throughout the Civil War, Sumner suffered from what the radical Republican Congressman George W. Julian called "the big head, . . . [which] threatens to become a very offensive disease with him." When Sumner's old friend Julia Ward Howe, composer of the "Battle Hymn of the Republic," visited him in Washington in the spring of 1864, she noted that he had attained a new level of "self centeredness." When asked whether he had seen Edwin Booth perform, Sumner replied, "Why, n-no, madam— I, long since, ceased to take any interest in individuals!" And the quick-witted Julia retorted: "You have made great progress, Sir. God has not yet gone so far—at least according to the last accounts."[3]

Sumner's frequent claims to moral superiority appeared insufferable to Fessenden, who witnessed the Bostonian's compromising or contradictory principles. He held up the organization of Montana as a territory on the issue of African American suffrage. When told that there were virtually no blacks there, he replied: "If there were but one, that would be enough to justify my opposition." Yet he could argue that there was no need to guarantee black voting in Northern states because the disfranchisement of blacks was "on so small a scale that it is not perilous to the Republic."[4]

Differences between the two men publicly surfaced in 1864. Fessenden would stress the need for practicality; Sumner ran to rhetoric. As Fessenden was shepherding the National Banking Bill through the Senate, Sumner objected to a minor provision affording the states the power to tax certain assets. He elaborated effusively on John Marshall's comments in *McCulloch* (1819), pontificating: "If I err in this conclusion, I err on the side of my country and in a patriotic purpose. . . . This is not the time to think of anything less than our whole country." Fessenden replied that he did not object to having Senate business interrupted by Senator Sumner's "running commentary upon a decision of the Supreme court . . . with which those of us who are lawyers might be supposed to be tolerably familiar, in connection with a little poetry." But the *McCulloch* case had "no earthly application as a matter of law to the question now before us." Quipped Fessenden: "[I]t is not to be assumed . . . we must sit at the feet of the

Honorable Senator from Massachusetts to learn what is practical in matters of legislation, especially in matters relating to finance."[5]

A Polish observer of the American Congress, Adam Gurowski, scoffed at Sumner's "learned appeals to Shakespeare on the question of a mint for Oregon or Philadelphia." He also scorned the senator's "doctor-like . . . sentences about finances and political economy," which exposed him for "his arrogant assumptions and superficiality." Sumner even went off on such tangents as numerological explanations. In an article about seven law journals published in America, he devoted twelve pages to occult properties of the number "seven."[6]

Amid the growing animosity between the two senators, Harvard University awarded Pitt Fessenden an honorary LL.D. in 1864, which must have irked Charles Sumner. Though the wounded Sumner had received a similar honor in 1859, he probably harbored memories of the way Fessenden's godfather, Daniel Webster, had killed Sumner's appointment in 1845 as Joseph Story's successor to the Dane Professorship at Harvard Law School. Furthermore, Charles Francis Adams, an old Sumner adversary, received an honorary LL.D. along with the Maine senator, and it was no secret that Fessenden and Adams were favorites of the Boston Brahmin establishment, so much at odds with Sumner and the Garrisonian abolitionists.

The feud intensified at the nominating convention in Baltimore of the Union Party—in essence, the Republican Party reinforced with some war Democrats. Many of the New England delegates believed reports that the Massachusetts delegation withheld its support for the renomination of Hannibal Hamlin as vice president at the urging of the senior senator from Massachusetts. Sumner supposedly wanted Hamlin to return to Maine to be elected to the Senate, replacing Fessenden. Lincoln, it was thought, would choose David Dickinson, a war Democrat from New York, as his running mate and replace William Seward, also from New York, as secretary of state. To the chagrin of Sumner, Lincoln selected Senator Andrew Johnson, a war Democrat from Tennessee.[7]

Through the election of 1864 and victory at Appomattox, Lincoln was successful at controlling Sumner. At that time, Sumner privately remarked: "Lincoln's election would be a disaster, but [George] McClellan's damnation." But Congressman Shelby M. Cullom of Illinois dismissed the effectiveness of Sumner's bluster: "Mr. Lincoln was the only man living who ever managed Charles Sumner, or could use him for his purpose." And the president was happy to have the senator keep Mary Todd entertained.[8]

In early March 1865, Sumner was "acting like a madman," Richard H. Dana wrote to Charles Francis Adams. Yet on March 6, Senator Sumner was invited to escort Mrs. Lincoln to the inaugural ball. "You may imagine," remarked the easily flattered Sumner to a friend, "the kind of wonder which was excited when, with Mrs. Lincoln on my arm, I made my way through the throng and placed her in her selected seat." Mary Todd frequently sent Sumner little notes and flowers and admired him, to the degree she hated Seward.[9]

By December 1865, Fessenden's election to the chair of the Joint Committee on Reconstruction, while Sumner was not even a member, guaranteed a permanent rupture in relations between the two men. And the break occurred during the debate over the Fourteenth Amendment, in which Fessenden's role has been overlooked or distorted.

The same month, Sumner introduced a draft bill of the Fourteenth Amendment that would be virtually identical to the one reported to the Senate by the Joint Committee in January 1866. Sumner's "amendment" was designed to neutralize the increase in population of Confederate states when fully counting freedmen. Sumner proposed to make representation proportional to the number of voters, not to the total population. His draft would force the Southern states to enfranchise blacks or lose a proportionate number of seats in Congress. But it also meant that states could disfranchise African Americans if they were willing to pay the political price of a reduced number of representatives. Unfortunately for Sumner's political fortunes, his amendment would also cut down the number of congressmen from Massachusetts, which had a "disportionate" number of women (who could not vote) and unnaturalized aliens (who would no longer be counted).

Massachusetts politicians denounced the plan, which would reduce their numbers and influence. The popular, four-term governor, John A. Andrew, in his valedictory address on January 5, 1866, criticized Sumner's plan as "a delusion and a snare." And pundits speculated that Andrew would make a strong opponent for Sumner in the 1868 senatorial race.

When the committee's draft amendment was proposed on January 20, 1866, it provided for apportionment of representatives according to total population but added that "wherever the elective franchise shall be denied or abridged in any State on account of race or color, all persons of such race or color shall be excluded from the basis of representation." This proposal accomplished what Sumner had originally intended, but without any political cost to Massachusetts.

But Sumner could still be accused of permitting the disfranchisement of freedmen. Already, Massachusetts newspapers, such as the *Springfield Republican,* were accusing him of "dodging the negro suffrage question." So he decided to do more than remove the objectionable section by amendment. To keep from being out-demagogued by Andrew, Sumner decided to oppose the committee's draft of the Fourteenth Amendment in such strong language that everyone would forget that he had the previous month sponsored a virtually identical proposal. On February 5, Sumner opened the debate with a two-day, five-hour oration entitled "The Equal Rights of All," with which he told Fessenden he would "put his foot on [the amendment] and crush it."[10]

Sumner labeled the committee proposal "uncertain, loose, cracked and rickety," an "abomination," "the very Koh-i-noor of blackness," and "the most utterly reprehensible" measure ever considered by Congress. His speech prevented the proposed amendment's securing the necessary two-thirds vote. Thaddeus Stevens was outraged by Sumner's "puerile and pedantic criticism" and remarked that the "Amendment," already approved by two-thirds of the House, had been killed by "the united forces of self-righteous Republicans and unrighteous Copperheads."[11]

Sumner's oration rallied abolitionists throughout the nation. Writing to Speaker Stevens, Wendell Phillips denounced the amendment as a "fatal and total surrender." Woman suffrage advocates also supported Sumner's opposition to the amendment. Susan B. Anthony congratulated him on his "repeated protest against that proposed Amendment." "You stand in the Senate," she wrote, "almost the lone man to vindicate the absolute Right." But racism was also evident among some of the middle-class feminist leaders. Elizabeth Cady Stanton worried about "the negro's hour" in a letter to Phillips. "Is there not danger that [the male Negro], once intrenched in all his inalienable rights, may be an added power to hold us at bay? Why should the African prove more just and generous than his Saxon compeers?" she asked. Without the suffrage and other civil rights, Southern black women would find that "their emancipation is but another form of slavery." Stanton concluded: "In fact, it is better to be the slave of an educated white man, than that of a degraded, ignorant black one."[12]

Sumner was clearly the radical man of the hour, or so he appeared to those who were unaware of his demagoguing. He privately boasted to a friend, who was expected to show the letter to Governor Andrew: "I am glad to know that Andrew agrees with me in opposing the Amendment." But Fessenden was about to expose the hubris of Sumner, whose speech and demeanor displayed virtue but masked political expediency.

Fessenden's proposed draft of the Fourteenth Amendment has been completely overlooked by "Reconstruction" historians. On January 20, two propositions were placed before the Joint Committee. The "Blaine amendment," which was Stevens's proposal, was approved 11 to 3 and then defeated on the floor after Sumner's speech. The rejected "Fessenden amendment" was simpler, more direct, and more radical. It would have made the Fifteenth Amendment unnecessary. It clearly stated: "Representatives and direct taxes shall be apportioned among the several States within this Union, according to the respective numbers of citizens of the United States in each State; and *all provisions in the Constitution or laws of any State, whereby any distinction is made in political or civil rights or privileges, on account of race, creed or color, shall be inoperative and void*" [my italics]. When Fessenden reported the "Blaine amendment," adopted by the committee, to both Houses of Congress, he stated that although he would support the decision of the committee, he preferred his proposition, which "abolished all distinctions on account of race, creed, or color." Fessenden's proposal, which included black suffrage, was the most radical before the committee; and the majority, including Stevens, opposed it. Passage of the clearly worded "Fessenden amendment" would probably have been a more effective and rational basis for the Reconstruction of the South.[13]

The day after Sumner delivered his speech, Fessenden brilliantly challenged him "to answer me why and how he can denounce one measure in the strongest possible terms . . . while he himself offers another [unenforceable resolution] which is founded upon the same idea, and can only accomplish the same results." Fessenden even sounded like a feminist. Noting how Sumner repeatedly talked about taxation without representation, the Maine senator said to him in their colloquy on the Senate floor: "I should like to have him tell me why every female that is taxed ought not to vote." Though Sumner proclaimed, for black males, "A moral principle cannot be compromised," he had to admit that, for women, the suffrage was "not judicious at this moment." Fessenden also pointed to the educational requirement in the Massachusetts Constitution: "A man must read or he cannot vote." How would that apply to the freedmen? Fessenden said he hated "caste exclusion" as much as Sumner and then asked, "[W]hat are the objections to putting into the Constitution at once a provision doing away with all distinctions of this kind?" But the majority on the Joint Committee, which he chaired, said Fessenden, supported their draft with one question in mind, "What can pass?"

To Sumner's claim of moral superiority, Fessenden replied: "My constituents did not send me here to philosophize. They sent me here to act, and to find out, if I could, what is best for the good of the whole, and to do it, and they are not so shortsighted as to resolve that if they cannot do what they would, therefore they will do nothing."[14]

Sumner's playing to the gallery was too much for the ailing Fessenden, who was suffering severe headaches and about to get sicker. Especially distasteful to him was Sumner's "malice" and use of "epithets" that were "deserving of reprehension," such as "bad mutton," "disgusting ordure, loathsome stench." Was Sumner fair in calling the draft amendment a "compromise of human rights, dishonoring the name of the Republic?" Fessenden asked.

But the maladroit Andrew Johnson "saved Sumner from political ostracism," in the words of the senator's principal biographer. The president vetoed the extension of the Freedmen's Bureau and the Civil Rights Act, while the Senate quarreled over the wording of the proposed Fourteenth Amendment. The hostile reaction on Capitol Hill to Sumner's oration encouraged the president to veto the Freedmen's Bill on February 19, even though almost all the Republicans in Congress supported it. President Johnson's veto of the Civil Rights Bill on March 27 brought the final break between him and the overwhelming majority of House and Senate Republicans.

Fessenden vividly described the charged atmosphere. The president, he wrote, "has broken his faith, betrayed his trust, and must sink from detestation into contempt. . . . I see nothing ahead but a long wearisome struggle for three years, and in the meantime great domestic convulsions, and an entire cessation of the work of reform—perhaps a return to power of the Country's worst enemies—Northern Copperheads." Secretary of State Seward had "abandoned all his principles, and fallen beneath contempt," but the senator felt "more compassion in his case, for his appearance & conversation have sometimes clearly indicated a rapidly increasing failure of intellect. If he lives five years longer, he will become a mere driveller!" And "perhaps I shall be in the same condition," Fessenden concluded, "for these times are well calculated to drive one mad." Seward told the *Nation* that he had no more concern for Negroes than Hottentots and that the civil rights of blacks should be left to the Southern states.[15]

Though the obtuse president had ruined Fessenden's position of conciliator, the senator could still demonstrate a practical (or critics might say Machiavellian) side in the vote on seating John P. Stockton of New Jersey as a Democratic senator. With a rare touch of hubris—realizing that "it is all important now that we should have two-thirds in each branch" to override vetoes, Fessenden found a legal flaw in the election of Stockton by a deadlocked New Jersey legislature. Fessenden maintained that "the joint meeting [of both houses of the New Jersey legislature], in changing the rules [providing for a majority, not a plurality vote] contrary to all established prior law and without referring the result back to the legislature, had not acted legally as a legislature in accordance with the Constitution."[16]

The Democrat Stockton was denied a seat in the Senate by a 23–20 vote. And it was by the margin of a single vote that the Senate on April 6 overrode the veto of the Civil Rights Bill. Fessenden's impatient leadership in the Stockton case—he had to lose his temper at his friend Lyman Trumbull—was crucial in saving the civil rights program. Convinced of Stockton's "villainy" in the intensifying partisan atmosphere, Fessenden confessed: "I never will consent to take in a man from one of the Confederate States [as a congressman or senator], until we have some security for the future. Andy's conduct has rendered this course a necessity."[17]

The political spotlight, however, was now focused on two men who were very much alike, Andrew Johnson and Charles Sumner. Once the president made up his mind, he was every bit as unyielding as the Massachusetts senator. Like Sumner, Johnson felt like an outsider. He possessed little political sensitivity and no moderation, and his actions played into the hands of his congressional enemies.[18]

In his veto of the Civil Rights Bill, Johnson maintained that it would not be "sound policy" to make African Americans citizens while the eleven states of the Confederacy were unrepresented in Congress. In passing the Civil Rights Act over the president's veto, most of the Republican senators worried that the courts might rule the act unconstitutional. In their view, legislating the Fourteenth Amendment was urgent.[19]

In mid- and late April, the Joint Committee on Reconstruction continued to amend its draft, both Thaddeus Stevens and Pitt Fessenden accepting an amendment by former Congressman Robert Dale Owen, son of the English utopian socialist, to grant freedmen suffrage on July 4, 1876. But Fessenden's health then suddenly deteriorated. He came down with the varioloid, a mild case of smallpox, and was forced to miss meetings in late April and May. Since Stevens did not want to bring the committee's amendment to the floor without Fessenden present to defend it, opponents of black suffrage grew stronger during the delay; and disfranchisement was still included, with Sumner's approval.

After continuing delays, in the last week of May, Sumner still wanted to collect more evidence on the possible effects of the "amendment." Fessenden retorted: "If we adopted the advice of the Senator from Massachusetts to wait until we got every particle that by any possibility might throw light on the subject, we should wait until the next century perhaps." Then, in a sudden *volte-face,* Sumner denied any formal opposition to the "amendment" and apologized: "Most probably I am in error; but I have performed my duty, and in a humble way satisfied myself by making this declaration." On June 8, 1866, the Senate ratified the Fourteenth Amendment, with the support of Sumner and three others who had earlier opposed it. Sumner abandoned his intellectually muddled opposition to disfranchisement in the "representation clause," once his grandiloquent support of black suffrage had calmed criticism back in Massachusetts.[20]

In the meantime, President Johnson announced his opposition to the

Fourteenth Amendment. During the second half of 1866, the legislatures of ten of the eleven ex-Confederate states refused to ratify it. But the Republicans made big gains in the North during the fall 1866 congressional elections. Their campaign document was the "Fessenden Report of the Joint Committee on Reconstruction." The approximately thirty-page report bore the clear mark of Fessenden's pen and reflected his thinking on the Reconstruction of the Southern states: "Slavery, by building up a ruling and dominant class, had produced a spirit of oligarchy adverse to republican institutions, which finally inaugurated civil war. The tendency of continuing the domination of such a class, by leaving it in the exclusive possession of political power, would be to encourage the same spirit, and lead to a similar result." But he acknowledged constitutional problems—"whether Congress had power, even under the amended Constitution, to prescribe the qualifications of voters in a State, or could act directly on the subject." Leaving "the whole question with the people of each State, holding out to all the advantage of increased political power as an inducement to allow all to participate in its exercise . . . would be in its nature gentle and persuasive." He "hoped, at no distant day," for "an equal participation of all, without distinction, in all the rights and privileges of citizenship, thus affording a full and adequate protection to all classes of citizens, since all would have, through the ballot-box, the power of self-protection."[21]

Events such as the New Orleans riot of July 30, 1866, made Fessenden's "gentle and persuasive" constitutional approach hard to maintain. Local white policemen there violently broke up an assembly of Unionists and killed about forty persons, mostly blacks. Ten policemen were "wounded slightly." The meeting was a "rump convention" of thirty to forty delegates of the Louisiana State constitutional convention of 1864. They planned, quorum or no quorum, to disfranchise ex-Confederates and enact African American suffrage. President Johnson quickly asked his attorney general to order General Philip Sheridan to use "sufficient force to sustain the civil authority in suppressing all illegal or unlawful assemblies, who usurp or assume to exercise any power or authority without first having obtained the consent of the people of the State."

The riot assumed national significance when Johnson's private secretary leaked Sheridan's report to the president to the *New York Times* but censored a crucial part. Sheridan had planned to arrest the head men "if the proceedings of the convention were calculated to disturb the tranquility of the department." But he argued there was "no case for action until they committed the overt act." And then, in the censored part, unreported in the *New York Times* dispatch, Sheridan stated: "In the meantime, official duty called me to Texas, and the mayor of . . . [New Orleans], during my absence, suppressed the convention by use of their police force, and in so doing attacked the members of the convention and a party of two hundred negroes, and with fire-arms, clubs, and knives, in a manner so unnecessary and atrocious as to compel me to say that it was murder."[22]

General Sheridan was incensed at the "breach of military honor" in censoring the report. And such a stalwart supporter of Johnson as Henry Ward Beecher expressed shock over the White House action and the president's failure to take the right side. Johnson, in a speech in St. Louis on September 8, ignored the bloodshed and instead denounced the New Orleans radicals and radical members of Congress.

By the time the lame-duck Thirty-ninth Congress reconvened in December 1866 (a more radical Fortieth Congress had already been elected in November), Fessenden found his nonvindictive attitude increasingly undermined. Power in the Senate shifted from him to Benjamin Wade of Ohio and his chief ally, Charles Sumner. In the House, Speaker Thaddeus Stevens confessed: "I was a Conservative in the last session of this Congress, but I mean to be a Radical henceforth."

The new political lines were drawn on March 4, 1867. The new Senate of the Fortieth Congress met, for the first time in history, nine months early, to prevent President Johnson from usurping power. Normally, there would have been an interim, between the end of the Thirty-ninth Congress in the first week of March and the customary convening of the new Fortieth in the first week of December, thirteen months after its election. The new Senate met in an angry, vengeful atmosphere that the president had helped to create. And some of the Republican senators were conniving to replace him with one of their own.

Three days earlier, by a vote of 22 to 7, the Republican caucus of the new Senate had elected Benjamin Franklin Wade over William Pitt Fessenden president pro tempore of the Senate and next in line to succeed to the presidency, should Andrew Johnson die or be convicted in an impeachment trial. Fessenden, who resigned as chair of the Finance Committee in favor of John Sherman, was ostracized to Foreign Relations, chaired by Charles Sumner. The only role left to Fessenden now was that of constitutional conscience, while the Wade–Sumner coalition led a majority of Senate Republicans, who did not value his virtue and scruples.

At this time, the upright Fessenden rebuked Ben Wade and made a point that historians would be well advised to heed. He attacked the Ohioan's distortion of his position on suffrage for freedmen. Fessenden did not oppose the Fourteenth Amendment, only its failure to mention race or color, and the Blaine amendment to it, which gave Southern states the opportunity to deny the franchise should they want to lose a proportionate part of their representation. Fessenden's rejected version would have granted the suffrage and made the Fifteenth Amendment unnecessary. He then taunted Senator Wade and future historians: "If gentlemen who glory in the name of radical are not quite so radical on that subject as I am, that is all the difference between us. And now, for being too much of a radical, I am to be lectured in this side-hand way by the honorable Senator from Ohio."[23]

Charles Sumner's life had also changed dramatically. In the summer of 1866, he had become engaged to the young widow Alice Mason Hooper, one of the capital's beauties, who was twenty years his junior. But the autumn marriage failed in less than a year as "that woman" separated from the fifty-five-year-old senator, while he accused her of repeated unfaithfulness, violence, and being "a devil, self-willed and infernal."[24]

Personal factors, then, intensified Sumner's animosity toward his archrival Fessenden when the Bostonian pressed for the impeachment of President Johnson. In letters home to Portland, Fessenden complained privately of Sumner's pettiness; but while Fessenden was recuperating, trout fishing in Maine, Sumner, in late August 1867, went public in a press interview. He called Fessenden "Captain of the Obstructives," claiming he was dragging down efforts to reconstruct the South. "All the slave-masters in the Senate never wounded me as did this colleague from New England," complained Sumner, attacking the Maine senator as "an evil influence in the Senate."

About the same time, on the Senate floor, Zachariah Chandler of Michigan, a founder of the Republican Party, who would become a "spoilsman" of the Ulysses S. Grant administration and mastermind of the "theft" of the election of 1876, denounced Fessenden. Chandler tagged "the conservative Senator from Maine" and his kind as "hybrids" and political "perverts."

Fessenden countered these attacks in his straightforward way: "I shall leave my public record to take care of itself." He also noted that he was influenced not by confidence in Andrew Johnson but by "a want of confidence . . . in those who would assume to direct what they have not the capacity to direct."[25]

On the eve of the presidential contest between U.S. Grant and Horatio Seymour in November 1868, in a letter to his friend Freeman Morse, American consul in London, Fessenden wrote that he got "the name of conservative by advising against the reconstruction acts," for which he had reluctantly voted. He believed that once "we had proposed the Fourteenth Amendment, the rebel States had rejected it and we had provided military protection for our friends, enough was done by Congress towards reconstruction, and we had better leave the matter where it was until the people of those States asked for admission in proper form." He thought "our furious radical friends" were politically naive in plotting to "secure the votes of all those States through the aid of the negroes." Fessenden still advocated "gentle" persuasion. It was his realistic opinion that the Confederate states, "once recognized" after ratifying the Fourteenth Amendment, would have "the wealth and intelligence of the State" rule them, "and we had better let them stay out until after this election." Almost anticipating the disputed Rutherford B. Hayes–Samuel J. Tilden election of 1876, he feared that the Democratic nominee, the former Governor of New York Horatio Seymour, might win enough electoral votes so that the unreconstructed states of Virginia, Mississippi, and Texas could potentially elect him president. This, he feared, would set off a national crisis.[26]

Winning by 300,000 popular votes in 1868, Grant presumably received most of the votes of the estimated 700,000 "Negro" voters. According to one historian of the Republican Party, the radical element, or Wade–Sumner supporters, in the Republican Party assumed in African American enfranchisement "the establishment in the South of a great body of voters anxious to advance Republican aims." There "safe fiefdoms" could be established for the radical wing of the party. In "Equal Rights of All," Charles Sumner told his colleagues that only through the African American "can you redress the balance of our political system and assure the safety of patriot citizens. Only through him can you save the national debt from the inevitable repudiation which awaits it when recent rebels in conjunction with Northern allies [Democrats] once more bear sway. He is our best guarantee. Use him." But Sumner's ideals were quickly abandoned by his party; a federally enforced radicalism turned to enforced expansionism and imperialism, as Republican aims quickly changed. Southern blacks were not only used but abused in the "Compromise of 1877."[27]

In many ways, Fessenden's tiny amount of fame rests upon the anticlimactic impeachment trial of President Andrew Johnson in 1868. Fessenden would be the most prominent of the "seven" Republican recusants who joined twelve Democrats in preventing the conviction and removal from office of the president by a vote of 35–19. Johnson was already a lame duck. The Senate adjourned for ten days in the middle of the voting while Republicans convened in Chicago to nominate U.S. Grant for president. But Fessenden would be consistent in opposing anything that might abuse the Constitution as he wrote home: "I prefer tar and feathers to lifelong regret."[28]

Fessenden's written opinion is a masterpiece of constitutional reasoning and writing. It focuses largely on the First Article of impeachment, which charges the president with attempting to remove Edwin M. Stanton from the office of secretary of war in violation of the law and of the Constitution of the United States.

The disputed law was the Tenure of Office Act, passed March 2, 1867. It prohibited the president from removing officials appointed with the advice of the Senate without senatorial approval. Though Fessenden had voted against the act as unwise and improper, he had also voted against upholding Johnson's veto because he believed the law was constitutional.[29]

Johnson's cabinet by 1867 was comprised of loyal appointees except for the holdover from Lincoln's cabinet, Edwin M. Stanton, who had close ties with congressional Republicans and had resisted the president's desire that he resign. On August 5, 1867, the president received two bits of information. One proved that Judge Advocate Joseph Holt, under Stanton's control, had withheld a petition for clemency to the president for Mrs. Mary Surratt, the first woman executed by the federal government, for her complicity in the assassination of Abraham Lincoln. The other was a letter from a former U.S. spy in Jefferson Davis's office. The man had obtained a pardon for perjury from Holt, as a quid pro quo for cooking up evidence that Johnson was involved in the assassination plot against Lincoln. Being Holt's superior, Stanton was officially responsible, in Johnson's view. On August 12, the president suspended Stanton and appointed General Grant secretary *ad interim* for six months until the next session of Congress. The president then reinstated Stanton on January 13, 1868, only to decide on a constitutional test by again dismissing him on February 21, in defiance of the Tenure of Office Act. Three days later, the House of Representatives quickly impeached the president on eleven charges, and the stage was set for the trial before the Senate to begin on March 30, Chief Justice Salmon P. Chase presiding.

Sumner, at the "trial," passionately maintained that the impeachment was "a political proceeding before a political body with a political purpose." Sumner, therefore, saw no problem in Senator Ben Wade's voting on the question, which, if approved, would make him president. Nor was there any problem for Sumner in seating two new Republican senators from the reconstructed state of Arkansas, in the middle of the trial—an effort that failed. In Fessenden's words, Sumner continued to play, "Heads I win; tails you lose." He was completely confident of the verdict, amid rumors that Wade planned to appoint him secretary of state, which he appeared to believe, according to a letter to the Duchess of Argyll.[30]

Sumner's official opinion supporting impeachment was full of intemperate language. He called Johnson "the attorney of Slavery, the usurper of legislative power, the violator of law, the patron of rebels, the helping hand of rebellion, the kicker from office of good citizens, the open bung-hole of the Treasury, the architect of the Whiskey Ring, the stumbling-block of all good laws by wanton vetoes and criminal hinderances." He denounced the "technicalities" and "quibbles" of those opposing impeachment, which he compared to "parasitic insects, like 'vermin generated in a lion's mane,' " which were "so innumerable and numerous that to deal with them as they skip about, one must have the patience of the Italian peasant, who catches and kills one by one the diminutive animals that infest his person." The senator proclaimed Johnson "guilty of all, and infinitely more." And "very like Robespierre," Sumner concluded that "the people are as competent to decide as the Senate. They are the multitudinous jury. . . . In nothing can we escape their judgement. . . . They are above the Senate and will re-judge its justice."[31]

The simplistic and highly romanticized account of the trial in John F. Kennedy's *Profiles in Courage* gave a minor figure, Senator Edmund Ross of Kansas, credit for rescuing the president. But it was Fessenden's reasoning that carried six other Republican votes, preventing conviction. His speeches and official written "opinion" reflected his lifelong integrity and brilliant constitutional expertise.

Senator Ross had already tipped his hand, when he voted with the Democrats and Johnson's supporters to agree to the president's removal of Stanton on January 13, 1868. Fessenden, on the other hand, "was among Stanton's most vigorous defenders"; and in executive session on January 14, in Stanton's words, Fessenden "electrified the Senate," defending him against unjust charges of "being responsible for the suffering of Union soldiers while prisoners of war." Stanton wrote to Fessenden that his speech "delivered me from revilers and persecutors who sought to destroy my good name and has covered them with confusion." In casting a vote against impeachment, Fessenden most disliked "the necessity of grieving Mr. Stanton." It was Fessenden's vote that contemporary observers, including General Grant, knew was truly undecided and crucial. A friend of Fessenden, Senator Justin Morrill of Vermont, feared the political repercussions of voting against impeachment and in a "pathetic" letter on May 10 pressured Fessenden to vote for conviction: "As an idol of a very large portion of our people, you would be knocked off your pedestal. . . . and it would sour the rest of your life." "You cannot afford to be buried with Andrew Johnson," warned Morrill.[32]

Fessenden argued that the president's power of removal existed "among the implied powers of the Constitution." He traced the history of that power, referred to specifically in the 1789 acts establishing the State, War, and Treasury departments. In fact, John Adams, "when the Senate was in session," removed Timothy Pickering from the office of secretary of state "without asking the advice and consent of the Senate" and nominated John Marshall on the same day.

The Maine senator further maintained that Andrew Johnson, like his predecessors John Tyler and Millard Fillmore, was sworn in, with a specific term, as president, not acting president. Mr. Stanton held office after the death of President Lincoln "at the pleasure of President Johnson, by his permission, up to the passage of the act of March 2, 1867, and might have been removed by him at anytime." Stanton, as secretary of war, was not covered by the Tenure of Office Act "unless he can be considered as having been appointed by Mr. Johnson." Thus, Johnson "had a right to remove him" and "cannot be held guilty under the first article." In fact, even if Stanton was covered by the act, "the act done by the President did not remove him, and he is still Secretary of War. It was, at most, an attempt on the part of the President which he might well believe he had a right to make." The evidence "fails to show any design on the part of the President to effect his purpose by force or violence." Fessenden continued: "To depose the constitutional chief magistrate of a great nation, elected by the people, on grounds so slight, would, in my judgment, be abuse of the power conferred upon the Senate, which could not be justified to the country or the world."

By Fessenden's reasoning, Articles 2 through 9 and Article 11 failed by the rejection of Article 1. And Article 10, based on extracts from Johnson's speeches, failed because of conflict with the First Amendment. Though some of the speeches were "highly objectionable in style, and unbecoming a President of the United States," they were not "menacing towards Congress or to the laws of the country." To consider them "a high misdemeanor" would be unjustified and contrary to "the importance of liberty of speech to a free people" because the First Amendment states: "Congress shall make no law . . . abridging the freedom of speech."

Fessenden concluded his written opinion with an obvious rebuttal of Sumner's line of reasoning that "popular opinion demands the conviction of the President":

> I reply that he is not now on trial before the people, but before the Senate. . . . The people have not heard the evidence as we have heard it. The responsibility is not on them, but upon us. They have not taken an oath to "do impartial justice according to the Constitution and the laws." I have taken that oath. I cannot render judgment upon their convictions, nor can they transfer to themselves my punishment, if I violate my own. And I should consider myself undeserving the confidence of that just and intelligent people who imposed upon me this great responsibility, and unworthy a place among honorable men, if for any fear of public reprobation, and for the sake of securing

popular favor, I should disregard the convictions of my judgment and my conscience. The consequences which may follow either from conviction or acquittal are not for me, with my convictions, to consider. The future is in the hands of Him who made and governs the universe, and fear that He will not govern it wisely and well would not excuse me for a violation of His law.[33]

The denouement came on Saturday, May 16, at 12:00 noon, when the Senate convened to vote on the Eleventh Article of impeachment. The galleries were packed—every ticket highly prized and sought after—as members of the House entered into the mobbed chamber. But Chief Justice Chase, presiding, insisted on absolute silence and strict order.

The prosecution began the voting on the Eleventh Article, a somewhat broader version of the First and dependent on it, as their best chance of conviction.

The secretary of the Senate called the role in alphabetical order, and Fessenden's name was the first of the "doubtful" Republicans. "Mr. Senator Fessenden, how say you? Is the respondent, Andrew Johnson, President of the United States, guilty or not guilty of the high misdemeanor as charged in the article?" In a clear and even voice, Fessenden replied: "Not guilty."

Senator Edmund Ross commented on the crucial role of Fessenden, who "had the unquestioned confidence of his partisan colleagues." Because of his "long experience in public life" and "his great ability as a legislator," but especially because of "his exalted personal character," Fessenden had won "the admiration of all his associates regardless of political affiliations." Though "foreseeing that his vote would probably end a long career of conspicuous public usefulness, there was no sign of hesitancy or weakness as he pronounced his verdict."[34]

The chief justice announced the vote as thirty-five "guilty" and nineteen "not guilty." The conviction of the president had failed by one vote, and the Senate as a court of impeachment adjourned until Tuesday, May 26, at 12:00 noon. Senator Fessenden, ashen-faced, walked through the Capitol amid jeers, as someone in the crowd shouted: "Fessenden! You villainous traitor!" He kept walking and proceeded to his F Street home, where he collapsed, sobbing, upon a couch. Though "all imaginable abuse has been heaped upon me," he was convinced that "the mass of the people do not understand the question."[35]

During the next ten days, the Republicans convened in Chicago and nominated General U.S. Grant for president, and more pressure was put on Fessenden to change his vote. There had even been threats to his life. But both he and the Senate, upon reconvening May 26, voted the same way on Articles 2 and 3. The "court" then adjourned *sine die* and would never vote on the remaining articles. The trial was over, and Andrew Johnson would remain as president for another nine months, until General Grant was sworn in as the eighteenth president on March 4, 1869.

At least since the fall of 1866, rumors abounded that Ben Wade's friends, especially Zach Chandler, were plotting to make him president. Even John Bigelow, serving in France as American minister, heard this as early as October 1866. Huge Republican victories in the November congressional elections would guarantee Wade's election as Senate president, so that he would be next in line to succeed Johnson in the White House upon his conviction in an impeachment trial. "President" Wade could then appoint enough supporters to the Supreme Court and the federal judiciary to ensure his program for Reconstruction.

On the other hand, the election of the reputed radical Wade as president pro tem may have made Johnson's conviction more difficult, as Thaddeus Stevens realized. If so, Fessenden's vote not only prevented President Johnson's conviction, but the senator's defeat in the Senate president's contest also guaranteed Johnson's serving the remainder of his presidential term. Would Johnson have been convicted and removed from office with Fessenden next in line? Perhaps so, but, unlike Wade, not with the aid of his own vote.

Less than a month after the final impeachment vote, Sumner was abandoned by most of his friends in a vote on appropriations for an examiner of claims in the State Department; Fessenden came to his defense. The examiner was George Bemis, a distinguished expert on the diplomacy of neutrality. The incident occurred when the United States was beginning to press the "*Alabama* claims" against Great Britain; and Fessenden again exhibited his virtue, as he sprang to Sumner's defense. Writing about the episode, Fessenden told his friend Senator James W. Grimes: "Every day he gets some hard rubs in the Senate all round. Yesterday I was obliged to defend him, as he was badly treated." Roscoe Conkling denounced the way Sumner would "rise here and, *ex cathedra,* express opinions." Sumner's amendment was approved by a vote of 22 to 14, supported by Fessenden and Ross. The "nays" included not only Conkling but also Wade, Chandler, Sherman, and one "recusant" Republican against impeachment, Lyman Trumbull. The next day, Sumner joined Fessenden in opposing an eight-hour day for federal government workers. Supporting the measure were Wade, Chandler, and Ross. Such mixed voting patterns reveal a confusing portrait of the so-called radical Republicans, not the clear ideological picture painted by many Reconstruction historians.[36]

Fessenden and Sumner served together for the last time in the spring of

1869. Fessenden privately supported Sumner for the office of secretary of state in the Grant administration, but Hamilton Fish was selected. The Maine senator heard of growing opposition to his reelection in 1870; and Sumner, recently reelected, "had little more to say about President Johnson, reconstruction, or the freedman" and started "giving close attention to bills wanted by Massachusetts merchants and shippers."[37]

William Pitt Fessenden, tending his garden in Portland, died of a "ruptured lower intestine" on September 8, 1869. And the tributes poured in from across the country. The *Chicago Tribune* remarked that "for years he had been the model senator of the United States." Almost everyone testified, like Senator H.L. Dawes of Massachusetts, to his speaking and debating skills: "He wielded a Damascus blade that was never broken and seldom parried."[38]

Charles Sumner suffered more humiliation in the Senate. In his opposition to Grant's desire to annex Santo Domingo, he refused even to speak to the president or to Secretary of State Fish, who succeeded in having him removed as chairman of the Senate Foreign Relations Committee in 1871. The Republican Party was quickly abandoning the ideals of both Fessenden and Sumner.

Lonely, and rumored to be drug-addicted, Charles Sumner died of a heart attack in Washington on March 11, 1874. His body lay in state in the Capitol, and his funeral in Boston was the biggest in its history, with thousands of blacks participating. When the funeral procession on Beacon Hill caused a huge traffic jam, his former wife, Alice Hooper, looked down at the coffin, turned to a friend, and quipped: "That is just like Charles; he never did show tact."[39]

Fessenden was a hero to some of the outstanding figures of the next generation. Maine Congressman Thomas Reed, Speaker of the House, remembered the senator's addressing the citizens of Portland, Maine, shortly after his controversial impeachment vote: "Although all the world might falter, you knew that calm face would be steadfast. To him had happened the rare good fortune of having the courage and character which matched a great opportunity. Few men have been so brave, and fewer still successful." Almost thirty years after Fessenden's death, Andrew D. White, the first president of the American Historical Association, wanted to erect a statue "to commemorate his great example. . . . It was an example of Spartan fortitude, of Roman heroism worthy to be chronicled by Plutarch."[40]

Writing in the 1890s, after the Republican Party had abandoned Southern blacks to Jim Crow and the Ku Klux Klan, the highly respected Senator Justin Morrill evaluated the two New England senators. He was the member of the Joint Committee on Reconstruction who had pressured Fessenden to vote for impeachment. More than twenty-five years later, Morrill praised him as a "practical conservative" and called Sumner "more sentimental and radical." The Republican Party had become respectably conservative by 1893 and had a distorted view of the Civil War and Reconstruction.[41]

Reflecting this view was the racist history of James Ford Rhodes, which tarnished Fessenden's reputation among later generations. Radical historians from W.E.B. Du Bois to Eric Foner have misunderstood Fessenden, whose racial radicalism and constitutional conservatism were quite compatible, whether he was legislating for Native Americans or African Americans. He cannot be so neatly categorized as "consistent conservative," nor can Sumner as "radical." Integrity and temperament cannot be quantified or labeled.

Conservative and *radical* were derisive terms used by opponents during the Civil War and Reconstruction. They are not helpful in understanding what actually happened, and their use by so-called radical historians provides a good example of historiographical hubris. Fessenden has become a victim of present-mindedness, or what might be called "political correctness." Eric Foner singled out what was perhaps the only line ever uttered by Fessenden that might be construed as racist. It was taken out of context in a question put to Sumner by Fessenden in a discussion of African American suffrage. Fessenden, having a year earlier witnessed Sumner's delaying tactics on the Fourteenth Amendment, asked whether he was linking the ballot with the possession of "a piece of land." Sumner was calling for homesteads for freedmen in terms similar to Thaddeus Stevens's bill in the House, providing for forty acres each from confiscated Confederate land. In their interchange on the Senate floor, Sumner denied that possession of land was essential for a republican form of government but thought that it would "complete the work of the ballot." After Senator Grimes asked: "Have we not done that under the homestead law?" Sumner said he wanted land where the freedmen "are residing." Fessenden then interjected: "That is more than we do for white men." To which Sumner replied: "White men have never been in slavery." In a fascinating way, this exchange might be considered an early debate over modern-day "affirmative action." But the issue was even more controversial then and, as everyone knew, had no chance of becoming law. To build a radical, ideological view out of such selected quotations distorts history. The crazy quilt of the Reconstruction was woven out of "mixed motives" into patterns of "mixed moral consequence." Fessenden's support for racial justice is clear, and he deserves the encomium of Justin Morrill's biographer, who called the Maine senator "the noblest of the defenders of the Constitution."[42]

Rival Sumner's eulogy on Fessenden helps us to understand why so many historians have misjudged him. Admitting that sparks fell between them but testifying to his "perfect integrity and austerest virtue," Sumner evaluated the Maine senator: "As Mr. Fessenden rarely spoke except for business, what he said was restrained in its influence, but it was most effective in this chamber. Here was his empire and his undisputed throne." Moreover, this was accomplished, as Lyman Trumbull put it, with Fessenden's "utterly abhorring all show, pretension, and humbug."[43]

In eulogizing his friend Senator Solomon Foot of Vermont in 1866, Fessenden viewed the judgment of history with typical Down East modesty. Fessenden contemplated "the load of injustice" that a senator, "if he would retain his integrity, . . . must learn to bear unmoved." He would be "sustained only by reflection that time may do him justice, or if not, that . . . even his name among men, should be of little account to him when weighed in the balance against the welfare of a people."[44]

III

The Rise and Fall of the Senate Oligarchy (1870–1940)

No other senator was as representative of the values of his age as the omnipresent John Sherman of Ohio, whose career ran from the Civil War to the Spanish-American War. But no senator wasted his time and influence as much running for president, at least three times seriously: his campaign manager in 1880, James Garfield, won the Republican nomination and election. Known as "the Ohio Icicle," Sherman did not have the charisma to win the highest office; nor did his cousin George Frisbie Hoar, an eccentric-looking Pickwick from Massachusetts. But although cousin John had a keen eye for profit and career advancement during the Civil War and the Gilded Age, "Frisbie" Hoar served twenty-seven years in the Senate as a symbol of the old-fashioned values of the Founding Fathers, among them his grandfather Roger Sherman.

With a strong commitment to progress in history in an English Whig sense, Hoar fought lonely battles in the Senate, supporting woman suffrage, the rights of Chinese immigrants, and the protection of African American voting rights in the South. With the failure of the latter in 1890, blacks were to be abandoned until World War II and the civil rights movement of the 1950s. At the end of his life, Hoar eloquently opposed the annexation of the Philippines, but the nation endorsed the "new imperialism" of William McKinley, Teddy Roosevelt, and Hoar's Massachusetts colleague Henry Cabot Lodge.

Weakened politically after three campaigns for the presidency, John Sherman in the 1890s publicly remained nominal leader of the Senate Republicans. But as Hoar became a party of one among the Republicans, so did Sherman, who saw any power he possessed fade away. Behind the scenes, insiders witnessed the growing power of Senator Nelson Aldrich of Rhode Island, who was to become the chief oligarch or "boss" of the Senate. A Rhode Island grocery clerk turned multimillionaire, Aldrich became the most powerful member of the Senate by 1900, quietly working as a member of the Finance Committee for thirty years. This parvenu grandfather of Vice President Nelson A. Rockefeller reveled in the power he had to run the Senate, often from the porch of his estate in Newport, Rhode Island. Second only to Presidents McKinley, Roosevelt, and William Howard Taft in power, he viewed the Senate as a body representing the various corporate interests in the country. Along with Cabot Lodge, he helped to push McKinley into the Spanish-American War. Aldrich epitomized a corporation-dominated Republican Party that tacitly supported a segregated nation while enthusiastically endorsing an imperialistic foreign policy with racist implications. But he only made a real negative difference when, in 1909, he forced the Payne–Aldrich protective tariff on his party and the country and stirred up a rebellion of reform-minded western progressive Republicans.

The Senate oligarchy reached the pinnacle of its power between 1900 and 1920 at the very time it was increasingly threatened by the populism of the progressive movement. But the enactment of the Seventeenth Amendment, calling for the direct election of senators, did not change the Senate overnight into a democratic institution. In fact, the last of the oligarchs, Henry Cabot Lodge, aided by the progressive Republicans, shaped the nation's history at a crucial point immediately after World War I. Senator from Massachusetts from 1893 to 1924, Lodge served as a loyal lieutenant to Aldrich until his retirement in 1911. Lodge then became the leading Senate Republican when the party split of 1912 led to Democratic control of both the Senate and the House for the next six years. The khaki elections of 1918 returned both houses to Republican control and made Lodge second only to President Woodrow Wilson in power. During the next two years, Lodge and the Senate demonstrated the power of a fading oligarchy against a self-destructive imperial presidency.

Lodge worshipped at the altar of his Federalist Cabot ancestors and wrote biographies of his great-grandfather George Cabot, senator from Massachusetts from 1791 to 1796, and Alexander Hamilton. But his Lodge forbearers' export interests, such as those in the China trade, shaped his worldview. During the Spanish-American War, he strongly supported national realpolitik abroad. His personal enmity with fellow Ph.D. Woodrow Wilson helped to defeat the ratification of the Treaty of Versailles. Lodge's concern for a united Republican Party led him to placate the "irreconcilable" Republicans, who opposed any compromise on the treaty and threatened to bolt the party in the presidential election of 1920. The last oligarch led the Senate in the exercise of its negative, constitutional power, but a new progressive yet isolationist Senate was beginning to take shape.

The son of Irish immigrant parents, Thomas James Walsh of Montana entered the Senate in 1913 as a staunch Wilsonian Democrat. He was allied with the western progressives, but during the war hysteria of 1918, when up for reelection, he drafted the draconian Sedition Act. The extreme measures taken during the "Red scare" of 1919, however, caused the safely reelected senator to reexamine his position on free speech and to challenge the policies of the Justice Department under Wilson's Attorney General A. Mitchell Palmer and his assistant J. Edgar Hoover. But most important, Walsh, using the "lamp of experience" in the Whig tradition, broke with Wilson and came close to achieving a compromise with Lodge to ratify the Treaty of Versailles.

Tom Walsh served as a beacon of integrity in the Senate during the twenties when he exposed the Teapot Dome scandal. In 1928, he halfheartedly ran for president as an Irish Catholic, rural, dry alternative to Governor Al Smith of New York. Had Walsh been the Democratic nominee, would his Catholicism have been a major issue? Or was Smith's poorly educated, urban-Tammany background more of an issue for rural, Protestant America?

William Edgar Borah served in the Senate from 1907 to 1940 as Idaho's second most famous export. One of the great Republican progressives, he was the chief advocate of the Seventeenth Amendment. But he was more skeptical than most progressives of big government, opposing Wilson's Federal Trade Commission, which he thought would be controlled by the great corporations. With his huge physical presence, he penned Cabot Lodge in the corner of the "irreconcilables," opposing the Treaty of Versailles. Succeeding him as chair of the Foreign Relations Committee in 1924, Borah became the architect of the Kellogg–Briand Pact outlawing war. Throughout the thirties, he was one of the nation's leading isolationists. After Hitler's invasion of Poland in September 1939, Borah coined the term "phony war" to describe the lull after Britain declared war but before actual hostilities broke out in the West. He did not live to see the Nazi invasion of the Low Countries the following spring.

George William Norris's reputation, unlike Borah's, remains unsullied. A national poll of historians in 1957 selected Norris as the greatest U.S. senator. His forty years in Congress, thirty in the Senate, comprise a brilliant record. He fought to democratize the House, and his filibuster helped to postpone the nation's entry into World War I. He also championed civil liberties during the patriotic hysteria sweeping the nation from 1917 to 1919.

The twenties found Norris trying to implement his progressive Republicanism. He was father of the Tennessee Valley Authority, opposed by Herbert Hoover, but championed by Franklin Delano Roosevelt (FDR), who called Norris "the very perfect, gentle knight of American progressive ideals."

But the thirties were Norris's decade, as he became one of the most influential senators, though his party was out of power. Unlike Borah, he proposed to use the federal government to clear away the "spider's web of Wall St." ensnaring small businesses and average Americans. While most of the western progressive Republicans were eclipsed by the New Deal, Norris, increasingly independent, became one of FDR's strongest supporters, even on Supreme Court reform. Unlike most of the western Republicans, who were isolationists, he did not underestimate the threat of Hitler.

With a simple faith in democracy akin to Hoar's, Norris tried to extend it to southern blacks in his final year in the Senate. But they would have to wait until 1964. Defeated by Nebraska voters in 1942, Norris retired and refused to take a penny from the federal pension fund. A symbol of integrity to the nation, Norris was the best and one of the last of the vanishing breed of progressive.

World War II created an imperial presidency as the legislative branch became almost an appendage to the executive. The rule of a Senate oligarchy died of populism, depression, and World War II.

5

"Try Justice"

George Frisbie Hoar vs. John Sherman
(1870–1900)

George Frisbie Hoar entered national politics in 1869, during the first year of the Ulysses S. Grant administration, as a freshman congressman. His kinsman, John Sherman, had been a presence on the Washington scene since his election to the House in 1854. In the intervening years, Sherman had served six years in the House and was almost elected Speaker in 1859, before his move to the upper chamber from Ohio in 1861. In March 1867, Sherman was selected chairman of the Senate Finance Committee to replace Pitt Fessenden, who had ample but limited faith in the abilities of the Ohioan. He voted in 1868 to convict Andrew Johnson of subverting the constitutional powers of the Senate.

"The story of his public life and service is, as it were, the history of the country for half a century," remarked President William McKinley upon the death of Sherman in 1900. His cousin and colleague, Hoar, called Sherman "the very embodiment of the character and temper of his time" and one of those men "who represent the limitations as well as the accomplishments of the people around them." But the mugwump E.L. Godkin summed up Sherman as "the most active wobbler in public life."[1]

Opponents also criticized Hoar for being too attached, like Sherman, to the Republican Party. According to Hoar's autobiography, "one very self-satisfied critic," William Lloyd Garrison, compared Hoar with his Massachusetts colleague Henry Cabot Lodge, by observing "that Mr. Lodge has no conscience, while I have a conscience but never obey it."[2]

Frisbie Hoar entered the Senate in 1877, just as John Sherman was leaving to become President Rutherford B. Hayes's secretary of the treasury. But the two would serve as colleagues when Sherman returned in 1881 until President McKinley appointed him secretary of state in 1897. Hoar was reelected to the Senate four times, serving until his death in 1904.

Though both men were party loyalists in presidential elections, Hoar pursued a more independent course, especially in matters of human rights. His optimistic view of human progress, based on the sanctity of the Declaration of Independence and the U.S. Constitution, provided a marked contrast to Sherman's innate pessimism.

In urging his older brother, William Tecumseh, to accept a position in the field at the outbreak of the Civil War, John Sherman predicted: "The men who have confidence in [the Union] and do their full duty by it may reap whatever there is of honor and profit in public life." Much later, in 1884, Senator Sherman, in a letter to the wealthy former Senator William Sprague of Rhode Island, reflected the social Darwinist philosophy of the self-made men of the times: "The tendency of all civilization is to make the rich richer and the poor poorer, with sudden fluctuations and changes in life beyond the control of prudence and care, but these have always existed and always will exist in any society where property is protected." Sherman concluded: "He would be a wise man who would change this course of civilization, and a very bold one to try to do it."[3]

Boldness in defense of principle was not one of Sherman's attributes, but it was one of Hoar's. In an era of strong anti-immigrant feeling, he supported "the external principles" of the Declaration of Independence and opposed discrimination against the African American, the Native American, the Chinese immigrant, and the Boston Irishman. He told the Massachusetts General Court in 1901: "Freedom, self-government, justice, the welfare of humanity are still the tests by which we mark the progress of the nation and the race." He summed up his faith: "I believe that the Mora! Law and the Golden Rule are for nations as well as individuals."

Hoar, unlike Sherman, was strongly influenced by filiopietistic sentiments. He could not understand Sherman's "lack of romance and feeling" in not contributing to the restoration of the family tomb in England. John Sherman's father grew up in Connecticut, a distant relation of Hoar's maternal grandfather, Roger Sherman, signatory of the Declaration of Independence and author of the Connecticut Compromise in the U.S. Constitution. Hoar was fond of recalling that Patrick Henry ranked Roger Sherman with George Mason as the two greatest statesmen he had known. Hoar was also proud of his great-grandfather John Hoar and his grandfather Samuel Hoar, who helped to drive the British back at Concord Bridge, April 19, 1775.[4]

Sherman's father had migrated from Connecticut to become a founding father of the Western Reserve in Ohio. John was one of eleven children, with unpleasant childhood memories at the age of six of the death of his father, Ohio Supreme Court Judge Charles R. Sherman. From eight to twelve, the boy lived with Ohio relatives under an unsympathetic roof; and though abandoning a college education, by twenty-one he was a substantial real estate owner and practicing lawyer in Mansfield. There he courted the daughter of a judge, Margaret Stewart, to whom he was married for more than fifty years.

Hoar had one older brother, Ebenezer Rockwood, who became Grant's first attorney general. Frisbie, as he was known to his friends, graduated from Harvard College and Law School and opened his law office in Worcester, Massachusetts. While Sherman was generally religious, strongly influenced by the piety of his mother, Hoar grew up in Concord during the height of transcendentalism. Like Ralph Waldo Emerson, he combined a dutiful Puritanism with an optimistic, transcendental Unitarianism. Both Hoar and Emerson championed individual responsibility and orderly social progress, equating individual morality with the common good.

Before the Civil War, Sherman had been a Whig convert to Republicanism. Hoar watched his admired old brother, "E.R.," coin the phrase "Conscience Whig" on the slavery question and then joined the Free-Soil Party. It was especially strong in Worcester and opposed the "Webster Whigs," supporting the Compromise of 1850. Like his hero of the 1850s Charles Sumner, Hoar especially hated the Fugitive Slave Law.

Both Sherman and Hoar became "half-breed" Republicans in opposition to the "stalwarts," such as Roscoe Conkling of New York and Zach Chandler of Michigan. The half-breeds believed, perhaps naively, in combining social harmony with industrial expansion. They also supported civil service reform, which Conkling referred to as the "snivel service." The stalwarts more narrowly supported the "spoils" and patronage of the Grant administration.

Though the senatorial careers of Hoar and Sherman were ideologically similar, they also reflected their home states. The Massachusetts General Court remained solidly Republican during Hoar's twenty-seven years in the Senate. He was also given considerable independence by Massachusetts politicians as the acknowledged heir of Charles Sumner. Furthermore, Hoar was not troubled by presidential ambitions, as was Sherman, at least three times.

John Sherman represented Ohio, "the mother of presidents," a politically divided swing state throughout American history. During Sherman's forty-three years in Washington, Ohioans elected four Democratic governors and thrice sent Sherman a Democratic colleague in the Senate. In Ohio, with its polyglot population and diverse economy, only compromisers could survive. It contained southerners from south of the Ohio River, easterners in the Western Reserve, new immigrants in the cities, and flourishing farms—

its strength—in the countryside. The cautious Sherman took frequent trips home "to look after his fences," which was coined into the political expression "mending fences."

Temperament also determined the two men's careers. Sherman's cool eyes signified an analytical detachment that so impressed businessmen but not rank-and-file politicians, who tagged him "the Ohio Icicle." In his contests for the presidency in 1880, 1884, and 1888, he was unable to win the united support of his home-state Republicans. The well-known but politically weakened candidate was the ideal figurehead to chair the Senate Republican caucus while others, such as Nelson Aldrich, were to exercise real power for the corporations.

Hoar had no grandiose ambitions. He remained steadfastly loyal to the Republican Party but grew increasingly outspoken. Like his English hero the Liberal Prime Minister W.E. Gladstone, Hoar became the grand old man of a party. As he grew older, he developed into a rather rotund, lovable Mr. Pickwick, from whom a certain amount of eccentricity was expected.

Attacked by the mugwumps for being too partisan, Hoar took great delight in distinguishing the minute differences between himself and the independent-minded New Englanders, who equated his party loyalty with hypocrisy. They were mostly academic and literary reformers who valued political independence above party regularity. Hoar denounced them as men with "white and clean hands" who never did "any strenuous work on the honest side" when moral issues were involved. Instead, they wrote disparagingly of the United States "in excellent English in magazine articles, in orations before literary societies, or at the Commencements of schools for young ladies." A member of the Harvard Board of Overseers, Hoar once denounced a group of Harvard professors as "these gentle hermits of Cambridge," who degraded "the public life of the Commonwealth by teaching our educated youth to be ashamed of their history."[5]

Hoar was elected to the House of Representatives in 1868. Like Sherman, he supported the impeachment of Andrew Johnson as both constitutional and necessary. But over the years Hoar was more consistently supportive of the rights of southern blacks than Sherman and more fearful of the return to power in the South of the "lily-white" Democrats, the "Bourbons." Though Hoar strongly supported the "Force Acts" in opposition to the Black Codes and the Ku Klux Klan in the South, by 1871 he was convinced that military force alone would not reform the South. Only a national system of general education could permanently change racial conditions in the South and the country. Hoar was a gentler version of his youthful hero Sumner and on occasion was attacked by some of his Garrisonian allies the way they had attacked Fessenden.[6]

Hoar's loyalty to President Grant was tested when the president summarily fired E.R. Hoar as attorney general, after stalwarts in the Senate defeated his nomination for the Supreme Court. Though Frisbie supported Grant's reelection in 1872, he blamed his brother's rejection on such stalwarts as Congressman Ben Butler of Massachusetts. And growing opposition to Butler helped Frisbie Hoar get elected to the Senate in January 1877. When he failed to seek reelection to the House during his fourth term in 1876, friends and supporters began a movement to elect him to the Senate to replace George Boutwell, who had been elected in 1873 to serve for the remaining four years of the term of Senator Henry Wilson, who had become Grant's vice president. Boutwell and Butler had served as "managers" of Andrew Johnson's impeachment in the House, and Boutwell as Grant's secretary of the treasury from 1869 to 1873. Associated with the Republican stalwarts, Boutwell was tarred, like Butler, with corruption. Senator Boutwell had voted against the impeachment of Grant's corrupt secretary of war, William Belknap, accused of the sale of a lucrative post on an Indian reservation. Hoar, however, had submitted the indictment in the House. For these reasons, liberal and moderate Republicans united behind Hoar, as a symbol of integrity, to give him a majority of both houses of the Massachusetts General Court to elect him senator.

During the election crisis that stretched from November 1876 to March 1877, Hoar was appointed to the Electoral Commission, which awarded the disputed electoral votes of South Carolina, Florida, and Louisiana to the Republican nominee, Governor Hayes of Ohio. This would elect him president by one electoral vote over Democratic Governor Samuel J. Tilden of New York, who had won by more than 250,000 popular votes. Aware of the disfranchisement of blacks, Hoar, the virtuous Republican, approved the "theft" or "compromise," in his own view, on partisan but moral grounds.

Montgomery Blair, Thomas Hart Benton's old associate and President Abraham Lincoln's postmaster general, saw in the "Compromise of 1877" a realignment of the party politics of Andrew Jackson's time. Blair argued that the southern acquiescence in Hayes's "defeat" of Tilden had "a precedent in the alliance of [John C.] Calhoun and the Nullifiers with Mr. [Henry] Clay to overthrow Jackson and [Martin] Van Buren after the defeat of nullification. . . . The jobbers and monopolists of the North made common cause with the Southern oligarchy." In fact, Thomas A. Scott, president of the Pennsylvania Railroad, won support for Hayes, who pledged greater federal support for the Texas and Pacific Railroad, of which Scott was also president. Tom Scott's railroad played the role in the seventies that Nicholas Biddle's bank had played in the thirties. And as the heirs of the old Whigs gained control of the Democratic Party in the South, the Whiggish element under Hayes took control of the Republican Party in the North and abandoned the Reconstruction of the South. The party of emancipation and freedmen's rights abandoned southern blacks to their former masters. As the old "radical" Republican journal the *National Republican* remarked in an editorial, the freedman was permitted to "divert himself for a time with the bauble of suffrage" but had been persuaded "to relinquish the artificial right to vote for the natural right to live, and to make his peace with his old master as the highest right to be subserved."[7]

Senator John Sherman had been the first to support Hayes for the nomination at the Republican National Convention in Cincinnati in June 1876. And he was rewarded with the position of secretary of the treasury. Though both Hoar and Sherman were "reformist" half-breed Republicans, like President Hayes, Sherman reverted naturally to his Whig temperament of the 1850s, as he courted southern Whigs in his later bids for the presidency. Hoar remained, in temperament, a Free-Soiler.[8]

Under the "New Departure" of "His Fraudulency," President Rutherford B. Hayes, the country experienced both "reunion and reaction." Gone were Grant and greed and the opulent parties, such as one given by Zach Chandler that featured a confectionery replica of the imperial court in Beijing. Hoar approved of the prohibitionist White House parties given by Mrs. Hayes, "Lemonade Lucy." And Hoar's sophisticated cousin William M. Evarts, who had defended Andrew Johnson during his impeachment trial, became secretary of state. The political pendulum had swung to the opposite extreme of 1868. But reunion was achieved upon the backs of the southern freedmen when Hayes, after a month in office, withdrew the last federal troops from the South and witnessed the collapse of the last two "carpetbag" governments in South Carolina and Louisiana. As James McPherson put it, the "freedom and equality of the Negro" were to a great extent based "on the military and political exigencies of war and reconstruction." Also, the North's "conversion to emancipation and equal rights was primarily a conversion of expediency rather than one of conviction. . . . A policy based on 'military necessity' may be abandoned when the necessity disappears, and this is what happened in the 1870's."[9]

Hoar's support for the 1877 compromise was short-lived. In the 1878 congressional elections, the southern Bourbon Democrats triumphed, and Hoar found their policies objectionable. He denounced obstructionist Democratic tactics in the House and opposed a Mexican War pension for the "unrepentent" Jefferson Davis. Hoar also called for greater African American representation at West Point and opposed an annual quota of black cadets. In 1880, he supported the sentiments of Senator Blanche K. Bruce of Mississippi, the last African American to serve in the Senate until 1967, who denounced the alleged attack on the lone black cadet at West Point in April 1880. Noting the Senate's efforts "to pass a bill which will more effectually civilize and Christianize the Indians," Bruce admonished his fellow members: "I think the Senate would do well if it would devote a little time to the civilization of West Point." Hoar went further but was overly optimistic: "[T]his American Republic, with its four million colored citizens equal before the Constitution and the law, will grind that institution to powder unless this abuse is cured." The president did appoint General Oliver O. Howard, former chief of the Freedmen's Bureau, as the new superintendent of West Point, but the pious abolitionist presided over an all-white academy, as the controversial black failed natural philosophy and flunked out. Only thirteen African Americans were admitted to West Point during the five decades after the Civil War, with three graduating, while Annapolis did not admit a single black midshipman.[10]

As secretary of the treasury, John Sherman generally pursued a hard-currency policy. While civil service reform was becoming a major issue, Sherman conducted himself as "a responsible spoilsman." In administering the treasury, Sherman did have a keen eye for talent. Charles S. Peirce, on the staff of the U.S. Coast Survey, conducted mathematical and astronomical investigations and, in the January 1878 *Popular Science Monthly,* introduced a theory of philosophy that became known as pragmatism. Lester Frank Ward, working in the Statistics Office, was writing *Dynamic Sociology,* published in 1883, and arguing that the government should be responsible for the people's welfare and should work to abolish poverty.[11]

But Sherman, with a "the poor will always be with you" attitude, courted the wealthy, urbane elite and acted as a leading member of the Gilded Age aristocracy. According to a report in the *Cleveland Leader* in 1882, there were seventeen senators with a net worth of more than $600 million. The same Tom Scott of the Pennsylvania Railroad who engineered the Compromise of 1877 had taken Sherman in 1872, "along with a few gentlemen connected with the Texas and Pacific," as guests on his private train to the West Coast. It was the senator's first trip to California, where he found Los Angeles "a typical Mexican town of great interest" and better suited as a terminus for the Texas and Pacific Railroad than San Diego. Sherman also loved trips to Europe, especially Paris, where in 1867 he wined and dined with the likes of Emperor Napoleon III and Eugenie, Tsar Alexander II, the Prince of Wales, and Chancellor Bismarck. In a trip to Yellowstone Park in 1881, he took the romantic landscape painter Alfred Bierstadt with him and was repaid with a painting of "Old Faithful." Like the financial potentates of Wall Street, Sherman built an impressive town house on K Street in

Washington, which was a tasteful mini-chateau of granite facade and re-
cessed columns, with finely carved wainscoting in the hallway, staircase,
and library. John Sherman fit in to the oligarchic Senate of the late nineteenth century like beautiful wood paneling.[12]

Though he admired cousin John's performance at treasury, Hoar discour-
aged friends from organizing Massachusetts delegates for Sherman in the
presidential campaign of 1880, for fear of alienating supporters of James G.
Blaine and Grant. The 1880 Republican National Convention in Chicago
became a dragged-out contest between the stalwarts and the half-breeds,
with the Blaine forces controlling the balance of power. The stalwarts ma-
neuvered to enforce the "unit rule," which provided that a state cast all of its
votes for the candidate of the majority in the delegation. Such a rule would
have ensured Grant's nomination on the first ballot. But the forces of
Blaine, Grant's chief opponent, united with the half-breeds to defeat the
"unit rule" and to elect Frisbie Hoar as temporary chair and then permanent
chairman of the convention. In that position, Hoar, though impartial, played
a crucial role.

The convention deadlocked through thirty-four ballots, with the Blaine
forces preventing Grant from getting the nomination. But on the sixth day,
there was a swing to Ohio Congressman James Garfield, Hoar's secret
candidate. Garfield had nominated Sherman in a stirring speech, praising
his twenty-five years of national office "with no flaw in his armor, no stain
on his shield." But as votes switched in his favor, Congressman Garfield, on
a point of order, protested to the chair: "No man has a right, without the
consent of the person voted for, to announce that person's name, and vote
for him, in this convention." Hoar immediately cut him off: "The gentleman
from Ohio is not stating a question of order." Then, with the aid of Blaine
votes, Garfield was nominated on the thirty-sixth ballot. But with fateful
consequences: as a sop to the stalwarts, Roscoe Conkling's friend Chester
Arthur was nominated for vice president. In the view of Hoar's brother
Rockwood, it was "a mere plagiarism from that Roman Emperor who made
his horse consul."[13]

Upon Garfield's election, Hoar's name was rumored for the post of
secretary of state. But politics dictated the selection of James G. Blaine,
who would become leader of the half-breeds through the 1880s, shaping the
Republican Party's support for the new industrialism. After the shooting
and lingering death of President Garfield in September 1881, Hoar delivered a famous eulogy that was a cry of despair for half-breeds. But Chester
Arthur proved to be no real threat to them. He failed in a clumsy attempt to
defeat Hoar's reelection to the Senate in January 1883. And the Pendleton

Act, which established the principle of the nonpolitical selection of the middle and lower echelon of government employees, represented a victory for the half-breeds in memory of Garfield, who was killed by a disappointed office-seeker.

In 1881, Hoar turned fifty-four and was already looking like an old man, with a round figure and pink-cheeked face, wearing gold-rimmed spectacles, with hair "as white as Boston beans are before baking." His very appearance was more senatorial than presidential, in contrast to John Sherman's handsome, elegant presidential manner. Totally at ease with his eccentricities, Hoar for many years addressed his wife Ruth (Miller) as "Carrisima Pussycatta."[14]

Beginning in 1868, Hoar served actively in the New England Woman Suffrage Association. He told the Massachusetts legislature: "I have failed to think of a single reason which I can give why you or I should have the right of suffrage which does not include women." And by 1880, he had won the appointment in the Senate of a Standing Committee on Woman's Rights. He possessed a rather chivalrous view of women as "the natural opponent[s] of corruption" and argued on practical grounds that Republicans should court women voters as a counterbalance to the large number of Irish immigrants joining the Democrats.

Hoar was also the only member of Congress to vote against both the Chinese Exclusion Act of 1882 and a more moderate version in 1902. He told the Senate: "I believe that everything in the way of Chinese exclusion can be accomplished by reasonable, practical and wise measures which will not involve the principle of striking at labor, and will not involve the principle of striking at any class of human beings merely because of race, without regard to the personal and individual worth of the man struck at." He stressed that "all races, all colors, all nationalities contain persons entitled to be recognized everywhere they go on the face of the earth as the equals of every other man."[15]

It is questionable whether the presidential elections of 1884, 1888, and 1892 had much lasting significance. To Hoar, the Republican nominee had to be supported at all costs against the mugwumps, especially in 1884, when they attacked James G. Blaine, "the continental liar from the state of Maine." Perhaps because both the Massachusetts mugwumps and Frisbie Hoar claimed to wear the idealistic mantle of Charles Sumner and were so close ideologically, they fought so bitterly over the appearance of morality in politics.

At a time when the Congress was growing more powerful at the expense of the presidency, Hoar tilted toward the executive, even if the incumbent president was a Democrat. Breaking with his Senate Republican colleagues,

Hoar proposed the complete repeal of the original Tenure of Office Act of 1867, which was the basis for the impeachment charges against President Andrew Johnson. Hoar's bill, signed by President Grover Cleveland in 1887, provided that Congress abandon its claim to control the presidential prerogative to suspend or remove officials in the executive branch.

For Hoar, however, the Republican Party was still the Party of Lincoln and Sumner, and the Democrats had compromised the rights of the African Americans in the South. And in 1888, presidential candidate Benjamin Harrison proposed a federal election law to lessen corruption everywhere, as he wrote privately that "these vile southern methods are spreading their contagion, like the yellow fever, into our northern states."[16]

Hoar and Senator John Coit Spooner of Wisconsin introduced an "election bill" to the Senate in April 1890 but permitted Congressman Henry Cabot Lodge to originate the bill from his House Special Committee on Elections. It provided for bipartisan boards of elections to canvass irregularities in disputed House and Senate elections. A board's majority could certify a candidate; and on appeal, the federal circuit court would decide. There were also provisions for jury selection and federal enforcement of the law, which white southern Democrats feared could lead to implementing the Fifteenth Amendment and eliminating loopholes in state voting laws. For both Hoar and Lodge, the bill exposed the moral hypocrisy of the mugwumps, who were embarrassed by their southern Democratic allies. Lodge especially enjoyed using the bill against the editor of the *Nation,* E.L. Godkin, his "first Wilson."[17]

The bill was filibustered to death in the Senate, and not just southern Democrats opposed it. Western silver-state Republicans, who were unsatisfied with the Sherman Silver Purchase Act, formed an alliance with Democratic opponents of the election bill. City machine bosses did not want federal inspectors canvassing their wards, and conservative labor leaders feared any use of troops. Northern businessmen also feared southern boycotts of their products. In anger, Senator Hoar snapped: "Rather than have constitutional government overthrown and be governed by minorities for the sake of protecting their southern investments, the people of Massachusetts would prefer to have their factories burned and live on codfish and 50 cents a day."

To the southern Democrats, Hoar vainly pleaded: "You have tried everything else, try justice." And his lonely voice resounds to the present: "The error, the fundamental error, of the Democratic Party of the South, in dealing with this problem, is in their assumption that race hatred is the dominant passion of the human soul; that it is stronger than love of country, stronger than the principle of equality, stronger than Christianity, stronger than justice."[18]

John Sherman also supported the election bill. But he remarked that the Senate and the American people were more interested in "money matters than in election bills." And he worked to protect his own investments, winning appropriations to widen and improve Washington's 16th Street to make his real estate more accessible.

The so-called Force Bill was the Republicans' last effort to secure African American voting in the South. And in 1894, the Democrats, under President Cleveland, repealed all existing federal laws calling for election supervision. While African Americans were sacrificed by the Republicans upon the altar of big business, a racist Democratic Party catered to southern white populists. Hoar, however, would never accept the need for segregation or black disfranchisement.[19]

The defeat of the election bill in 1891 marked a turning point in Hoar's efforts to lead the Senate Republicans. Increasingly, representatives of the new industrialism, such as Senator Nelson Aldrich of Rhode Island, would shape the policies of the Senate majority. A former grocery-store clerk, Aldrich rose to become chairman of the Finance Committee and "boss of the Senate." He rarely addressed the Senate but behind the scenes, especially on tariff matters, was a powerful spokesman for northeastern industrial and manufacturing interests. In his first interview with a reporter when elected to the Senate in 1881, he set his strategy for the next thirty years: "No, don't ask me any questions. . . . Let's talk about something else." In the words of his great-grandson, Nelson Aldrich "abhorred the people." An almost stereotypical symbol of the Gilded Age, he became a political power, the equal of Presidents McKinley, Theodore Roosevelt, and William Howard Taft. Grandfather of future Vice President Nelson Aldrich Rockefeller, Senator Aldrich was a parvenu with the values of the new aristocracy forging the industrial American empire. David Graham Phillips called the marriage of his daughter in 1901 to the only son of John D. Rockefeller an alliance between "the chief exploiter of the American people" and "the chief schemer in the service of their exploiters." In contrast, as grandson of Roger Sherman, Hoar was both a throwback to a simpler, Federalist era and a reminder of the abandonment of the ideals of the American Revolution.[20]

In 1890, Hoar and Senator George Edmunds of Vermont were the joint authors of the Sherman Antitrust Act. John Sherman had originally introduced the bill, but Hoar and Edmunds so significantly amended it that the Judiciary Committee presented a substitute to the full Senate. Hoar never solved the contradiction between his support for economic growth and his fear of industrial combination (or mergermania). The Sherman Antitrust Act had to be drafted with great skill, wrote a friend of Hoar's: "The draftsman is in need of the peculiar skill of the hunter who in shooting at the animal dimly seen in the fog is expected to hit it if it was a deer and miss it if it was a calf."[21]

Hoar's draft of the bill determined that the federal judiciary should implement the act to counter the special interests and lobbyists. He also favored a provision that would exempt labor unions from its provisions, but it was deleted from the final bill. His antitrust views appear naive today because he found it inconceivable that a portion of the business community could believe that "greed is good." Surely the great majority of manufacturers would follow policies that would lead to a better life for all Americans. But even in 1891, a wealthy, genteel reformer would mourn the fact that the elderly Justin Morrill, father of land-grant colleges, and Hoar were "almost the only men now in public life" who viewed public issues according to "the interests of the people." The same year, the venerable Senator George Edmunds retired after twenty-five years in the Senate and decried its decline.[22]

During the early 1890s Teddy Roosevelt viewed Hoar as the Cicero of the Senate, though by the turn of the century, T.R. would consider him a threat to the Republican Party. Both men thought they had high moral standards and were fiercely independent, though partisan Republicans. And both men considered Grover Cleveland anti-Negro and an enemy of real civil service reform. Cleveland himself reportedly found Hoar puzzling. The president remarked of the senator: "The recording angel is going to have a rough time of it with that old fellow. He has done so many good things and said so many spiteful things that I shouldn't know how to deal with him."[23]

Hoar believed that "demonstration of masses of the people has no lawful place; only the formally elected representatives of the people can speak for the sovereign will." In his view, the Pullman strikers struck not only against George Pullman and his company but against the American people, who comprised the great bulk of the laboring force.

But Hoar always remained supportive of tolerance, even against growing racial and religious bigotry. He was especially opposed to the resurgence of the Know-Nothing movement in the form of the American Protective Association (APA). In Massachusetts, the organization was aimed at the growing power of the Irish Catholics. Members of the APA called themselves "true Americans," who were concerned about the separation of church and state and especially about the growth of parochial schools. Though Hoar himself disliked parochial education because it disrupted the unity and harmony of a democracy, he deplored the attempt to revive "the animosities and feelings of the dark ages." And he compared the leaders of the Irish home rule movement to the American Founding Fathers.

In August 1895, Hoar was the first prominent Republican to confront the

APA. In reply to a letter from an angry Orangeman in Boston, T.C. Evans of the T.C. Evans Advertising Agency, who argued that a good Roman Catholic could not be a good American, Hoar issued a letter, published around the country, that was praised by the *Nation,* the *New York Times,* and Washington Gladden, advocate of the Social Gospel. Hoar argued pragmatically and eloquently:

> Your method would overthrow the common school system, would overthrow the Republican Party, and would end by massing together the Catholic voters, as proscription always does mass men together, to increase and strengthen that political power which you profess so much to dread. . . . The time has come to throw down the walls between Christians. . . . The American spirit, the spirit of the age, the spirit of liberty, the spirit of equality, especially what Roger Williams called soul liberty, is able to maintain herself in a fair field and in a free contest against all comers. Do not compel her to fight in a cellar. Do not compel her to breathe the damp malarial atmosphere of dark places. Especially let no member of the Republican Party, the last child of freedom, lend his aid to such an effort. The atmosphere of the Republic is the air of the mountain top and the sunlight and the open field. Her emblem is the eagle and not the bat.

Though Hoar preferred the House Speaker, "Tsar" Tom Reed, for the presidency in 1896, he enthusiastically supported William McKinley as the Republican nominee against William Jennings Bryan's Democratic populism, which was "a crazy attempt at revolution and a passionate crusade of dishonor." The victory of McKinley and the Republican Party, with the strong support of the urban voter, led to a clear Republican popular majority and control of the presidency for sixteen years.[24]

Hoar and McKinley were temperamentally alike, with their high-flown patriotic sentiments and support for high tariffs. But they would strongly differ on the new American imperialism that had been brewing for the previous decade. Was the Spanish-American War a war for humanity that the Civil War had become in Republican folklore? And could expansion and domination be justified in the same way?

But can Hoar be described as an anti-imperialist when he failed to oppose the annexation of Hawaii? He had been ambivalent about Hawaii ever since the pineapple magnate Sanford B. Dole and others had organized a revolt against Queen Liliuokalani in 1893. Hoar was not unhappy when President Cleveland withdrew the annexation treaty, submitted by President Benjamin Harrison in 1893.

Nor was he happy when the popular, newly elected President McKinley submitted a new treaty of annexation in 1897. After Hoar submitted a petition of more than 21,000 Hawaiian citizens opposing annexation in December 1897, the president asked his assistant secretary of the navy,

Theodore Roosevelt, and Captain Alfred Thayer Mahan to lobby Hoar. When Hoar was asked by the president whether the respected eighty-eight-year-old Justin Morrill should be urged to vote for annexation, Hoar replied that he was "very doubtful" if he would himself. He was bothered that supporters of the treaty were asserting that annexation of Hawaii was necessary "in order to help us get our share of China." McKinley stressed that Hawaii was needed for military security because Japan would seize the islands by force if the United States did not move first.

Borrowing from the John Tyler–John C. Calhoun method of annexing Texas, after the outbreak of war with Spain, President McKinley supported a joint resolution of both houses of Congress annexing Hawaii. And Hoar would vote for the resolution, while his old friend Justin Morrill was the only Republican voting "nay." The Vermont senator linked Hawaii with further imperialist ventures as a step toward the "expensive and furious" European "catch-as-catch-can naval hunt to seize ports and harbors, or any tidbits of the Chinese Empire." The elderly Morrill, who died a few months later, had delivered his last speech on imperialism.[25]

Teddy Roosevelt considered both Hoar and Morrill "men of a by-gone age." He wrote to Mahan that "we have in America among our educated men a kind of belated survivor of the little English movement among the Englishmen of thirty years back. They are provincials, and like all provincials, keep step with the previous generation of the metropolis." T.R. congratulated Senator Henry Cabot Lodge for converting one "provincial," Hoar, on Hawaiian annexation.[26]

But Hoar warned President McKinley that he was drawing the boundary of expansion at the Hawaiian Islands, as an isolated measure, because of existing American ties there and the threat of Japanese aggression. He insisted that, in the ongoing war with Spain, the United States should "acquire no territory," "annex no people," and "aspire to no empire or dominion." But the illogical implications of Hoar's speech were not lost upon Senator Richard Pettigrew of South Dakota, who commented: "The Senator from Massachusetts says that this is wrong; that it is a sin; that it is wicked; but the [Hawaiian] islands are so little that if we will forgive him for taking that country, he will sin no more; he will be virtuous and resist a larger crime if it involves a larger acquisition of territory."[27]

Hoar's position on the Philippines was clear-cut, though weakened with some of the mugwumps because of his vote on Hawaii. He did penance for calling Queen Liliuokalani a "barbarian Queen" when he sought a congressional pension for the deposed monarch.[28]

From the time rebellion against Spain broke out in Cuba in 1895, Hoar hoped for the peaceful establishment of Cuban home rule. But the sinking of the USS *Maine* in Havana harbor with the loss of 260 American lives on February 15, 1898, virtually made war with Spain inevitable, especially with the rise of "yellow journalism." After supporting the Teller Resolution, disclaiming any intention of annexing Cuba, Hoar voted for the joint congressional declaration of war against Spain.

During the remaining six years of his life, Hoar was caught in the contradiction of loyally supporting the McKinley and Roosevelt administrations while opposing or questioning their expansionist policies. McKinley even tried to head off Hoar's opposition to his Philippines policy by offering to the senator the prestigious post of ambassador to the Court of St. James, replacing Lincoln's secretary, John Hay, who had been appointed secretary of state. But Hoar declined the offer.

Hay replaced John Sherman as secretary of state when the old man resigned or was forced out by President McKinley one day after Congress had declared war on Spain in 1898. Sherman had been appointed in 1897, largely to make a Senate seat available for McKinley's *éminence grise,* Mark Hanna. The elderly Sherman was suffering from senility or what might today be diagnosed as Alzheimer's disease. For example, after Secretary Sherman assured the Japanese minister to Washington that the administration had no intention of annexing Hawaii, Sherman himself several days later signed the completed treaty and called the annexation "the destined culmination" of "the progressive policies and dependent associations of some seventy years." A symbol of an age and perennial presidential candidate, Sherman, like Daniel Webster, became a pathetic figure at the end of his career. One newspaper, which opposed his "demonetization of silver," found a morality tale in Sherman's demise. Observing that, in extreme old age, he had "nothing to console him save his money" and that one-twentieth of that "would answer all his present and future wants," the paper concluded: "His life ought to be a lasting lesson to ambitious young men."[29]

But Sherman, "the most active wobbler in public life," had warned Americans in his memoirs, published in 1895, against the "embarrassments" and "complications of foreign acquisitions." And by June 1898, the politically ruined and bitter Sherman publicly opposed the annexation of "any territory whatever, whether it be Cuba, Puerto Rico, Hawaii, or the Philippines."[30]

On February 6, 1899, the Senate, by a 57 to 27 vote (a 2-vote margin for two-thirds approval), ratified the Treaty of Paris, concluding the war with Spain and acquiring the Philippines and Puerto Rico as dependencies. Frisbie Hoar and Eugene Hale of Maine were the only Republicans to vote against it.

But Hoar was not about to bolt the Republican Party. The next morning, Henry Cabot Lodge cynically told Henry Adams, he found Hoar at the White House sitting next to President McKinley, "with arms about his neck," the "unctuous, affectionate, beaming, virtuous Hoar! . . . Only a few hours before, in the full belief that his single vote was going to defeat and ruin the administration, Hoar had voted against the Treaty, and there he was, slobbering the President with assurances of his admiration, pressing on him a visit to Massachusetts and distilling over him the oil of his sanctimony." In this new age of compulsive American imperialism, Hoar's party loyalty was more naive than sanctimonious.[31]

Hoar became nationally famous as an anti-imperialist, even being denounced as a traitor. But it was a new man on the national scene, Senator Albert Beveridge of Indiana, champion of the new American imperialism, whose "debate" with Hoar would dramatically frame the question. Beveridge was elected to the Senate by the Indiana legislature in January 1899 and left in May on a trip to the Philippines and the Far East. Even as early as 1890, the young lawyer had called for extending American dominion over Canada and Mexico, for acquisition of Cuba and Santo Domingo— "keys to the gulf, to the Mississippi, to the future Isthmus canal"—and for annexation of Hawaii and a string of coaling stations in the Pacific. In 1893, he warned a businessmen's group that the European powers were seizing "island and archipelago and new territory everywhere to make monopolies for their markets and fortresses for their flags."[32]

Washington anxiously awaited the maiden speech, set for January 9, 1900, of the boyish senator from Indiana after his return from the Far East. He had already introduced a resolution "declaring our purpose to retain the [Philippine] Islands permanently as the situation demands." But after consultation with party leaders, he deleted the word *permanently*.

The Senate galleries were jammed at noon on the ninth to hear this new star of turn-of-the-century young America. God, he proclaimed, "has marked the American people as His chosen Nation" to lead "in the regeneration of the world." In upholding Anglo-Saxon superiority, America had a "divine mission" to raise up "savage and senile peoples." Beveridge called upon the nation to retain control of the Philippines—"hold it fast and hold it forever." And he denounced the anti-imperialists, arguing that the Declaration of Independence should only be applied to civilized human beings who were capable of self-government. The Filipinos were "a barbarous race . . . [—] Orientals, Malays, instructed by Spaniards in the latter's worst estate."

As he concluded, Beveridge asked, "What shall history say of us?": "Shall it say that we renounced that holy trust, left the savage to his base condition, the wilderness to the reign of waste, deserted duty, abandoned glory, forgot our sordid profit even, because we feared our strength and read the charter of our powers with the doubter's eye and the quibbler's mind? Shall it say that, called by events to captain and command the proudest, ablest, purest race of history in history's noblest work, we declined that great commission?"[33]

Beveridge took his seat to thunderous applause from the gallery. But in a few moments, the aged Pickwickian of a bygone era requested the floor since he could not allow Beveridge's speech to go unanswered. The young senator's views were anathema to everything George Frisbie Hoar stood for. As he heard Beveridge's "eloquent description of wealth and glory and commerce and trade," Hoar said, he had listened in vain for those words Americans had uttered "in every solemn crisis of their history . . . the words Right, Justice, Duty, Freedom." He eloquently told Beveridge's admirers that "the God who made of one blood all the nations of the world had made all the nations of the world capable of being influenced by the same sentiments and the same motives, and that the love of liberty does not depend on the color of the skin, but . . . on humanity."

Many white Americans in 1900 had forgotten the principles of the American Revolution when applied to African Americans or other supposed "inferiors." The *Washington Post* editorialized that Americans "annexed these possessions in cold blood" and "intend to utilize them to our own profit." Representing the minority of anti-imperialists, the *Springfield Republican* called Beveridge "a young Attila come out of the West" and warned that "if his Americanism is now the true brand, then indeed is the Republic no more." William James wrote to Hoar from Germany: "Having puked up our ancient national soul after 5 minutes," Americans had become prisoners in "the chain of international hatreds," with "every atom of our moral prestige lost forever."[34]

Much to the chagrin of the mugwumps, Hoar supported McKinley's reelection, pointing out that William Jennings Bryan had cynically supported the Treaty of Paris. And after McKinley's assassination, Hoar met privately with President Theodore Roosevelt to urge "Teddy" to reidentify American foreign policy with the Declaration of Independence. Hoar wanted a pledge of full independence for the Filipinos, once peace and order had been established. Telling Hoar that the senator's every word was "engraved" on his memory, the president failed to act on his suggestion.

Roosevelt's Panama diplomacy presented Hoar with another challenge to party loyalty. He originally did not view a transisthmian canal through the Colombian province of Panama, negotiated peacefully, as a threat to the liberties of another people. But a surprisingly sudden "revolution" broke out in Panama after the Colombian Senate demanded a higher price for the land. After President Roosevelt quickly recognized Panamanian independence and ordered three naval vessels to prevent Colombian troops from violating the "neutrality" of Panama, Hoar offered a Resolution of Inquiry on December 9, 1903. He told the Senate that he was aware of American responsibilities for preserving the peace in the Caribbean. But he warned that our policy there must never be perverted into the actions of "a policeman who would manacle the intended victim of a robbery and then claim his pocketbook." Hoar, however, voted for the treaty with Panama. Again, he played the role of moralist and educator without threatening the born-again, imperial Republican Party.[35]

The Senate's "Nestor" served as its conscience until his death in 1904. An original half-breed Republican reformer, he was more sympathetic to unions than Garfield, more steadfast in his support of civil service reform and the rights of freedmen than John Sherman, and more independent and idealistic than George Edmunds and Justin Morrill.

Hoar always maintained that party loyalty and an independent conscience were not incompatible—an attitude that mugwumps could not accept. In his presidential address to the American Historical Association in 1895, he remarked: "I conceive that the man who conscientiously acts with his party is as truly independent in politics as the man who, according to Lord Dundreary's proverb, 'flocks by himself.'" He also reminded the historians of a comment from *The Federalist Papers:* "If every Athenian citizen had been a Socrates, every Athenian assembly would have been a mob." And Hoar chided the populist critics of representative government: "You can not separate the character of the people from the character of the men whom they deliberately, from year to year, and from generation to generation, elect to represent them."[36]

But in 1904, the character of America, which had come of age internationally, was represented by all the brashness of President Theodore Roosevelt. Realpolitik was in vogue in foreign policy, and the Senate had become an oligarchy, committed to serving corporate interests at home and abroad. Hoar was only too ready to challenge these new imperialists with the virtuous ideals of the Declaration of Independence, which Teddy Roosevelt thought better suited to a "by-gone age" and Henry Adams and Henry Cabot Lodge scorned as "sanctimony" from the "unctuous, affectionate, beaming, virtuous Hoar!"

Few of the progressives beginning to arrive on the national scene shared the breadth of humanity of Frisbie Hoar's vision. Theirs was a more parochial, midwestern one, in contrast to his more encompassing, perhaps more self-righteously simple, New England perspective. But who can deny the simple truth of his faith: "The Indian problem is not chiefly how to teach the Indian to be less savage in his treatment of the Saxon, but the Saxon to be less savage in his treatment of the Indian. The Chinese problem is not how to keep Chinese laborers out of California, but how to keep Chinese politics out of Congress. The Negro question will be settled when the education of the white man is complete."[37]

Robert A. Taft (*left*), senator from Ohio, 1939–53, conservative contrarian, with Arthur H. Vandenberg (*right*), senator from Michigan, 1928–51, architect of the North Atlantic alliance. *Harris & Ewing photo; Stock Montage, Chicago.*

Hubert H. Humphrey, senator from Minnesota, 1949–64, 1971–78, evangelist for the Great Society and victim of Vietnam. *Senate Historical Office (5189-10).*

Strom Thurmond, senator from South Carolina, 1954–56, 1956–96, inspired the Republican "Southern Strategy." *Office of Senator Strom Thurmond.*

William E. Borah, senator from Idaho, 1907–40, populist and apologist for appeasement. *Senate Historical Office (4 x 5 427)*

George W. Norris, senator from Nebraska, 1913–43, progressive Republican supporter of the New Deal. *Harris & Ewing photo. Senate Historical Office (5014-10).*

John Sherman, senator from Ohio, 1861–77, 1881–97, epitome of career politician and perennial candidate for president. *Senate Historical Office (66 x 13).*

George Frisbie Hoar, senator from Massachusetts, 1877–1904, philosopher of the Declaration of Independence. *Senate Historical Office (5458-15A).*

Henry Cabot Lodge, senator from Massachusetts, 1893–1924, Boston brahmin nemesis of Woodrow Wilson. *Senate Historical Office (5462-19).*

Thomas J. Walsh, senator from Montana, 1913–33, Irish Catholic, dry from the "Big Sky." *Senate Historical Office (5605-24).*

Charles Sumner, senator from Massachusetts, 1851–74, martyr of the antislavery movement. *Senate Historical Office (66 x 14).*

William Pitt Fessenden, senator from Maine, 1854–64, 1865–69, the Down East Lincoln. *Senate Historical Office (5391-15).*

James Monroe, senator from Virginia, 1790–94: from careerist senator to figure-head president. *Senate Historical Office (5491-9A)*.

Rufus King, senator from New York, 1789–96, 1813–25, first gladiator against slavery. *Senate Historical Office (5459-9)*.

Thomas Hart Benton, senator from Missouri, 1821–51: Samson and the temple of slavery. *Senate Historical Office (5358-4A)*.

John C. Calhoun, senator from South Carolina, 1832–43, 1845–50, fanatical apologist for slavery. *Mathew Brady photo. Prints and Photographs Division, Library of Congress (LC-USZ62-10556)*.

Margaret Chase Smith (*left*) senator from Maine, 1949–73, the first powerful female member of a male club, greets Madame Chiang Kai-shek (*right*). *Senate Historical Office (5985-41A).*

Robert F. Kennedy (*left*), counsel to Senate committee (later, senator from New York, 1965–68), and John F. Kennedy (*right*), senator from Massachusetts, 1953–60. *Senate Historical Office (5128-21A).*

J. William Fulbright (*left*), senator from Arkansas, 1945–74, and Wayne L. Morse (*right*), senator from Oregon, 1945–69, pictured here on the Foreign Relations Committee during the Vietnam debate. *Senate Historical Office (5985-38A).*

Eugene J. McCarthy, senator from Minnesota, 1959–71, Pied Piper of the antiwar movement. *Senate Historical Office (4 x 5 219).*

Michael J. Mansfield, senator from Montana, 1953–77, majority leader who quietly opposed escalation in Vietnam, but who refused to break with LBJ. *Senate Historical Office (5338-22).*

Samuel J. Ervin, senator from North Carolina, 1954–74, "King Richard" Nixon's constitutional nemesis during Watergate. *Senate Historical Office (4 x 5 8).*

6

The "Lamp of Experience" and "Bungalow Minds"

Henry Cabot Lodge vs. Thomas J. Walsh (1900–1920)

No other senators compared in this book came from such contrasting heritages as Thomas James Walsh and Henry Cabot Lodge. A son of Irish immigrants, Tom Walsh was born in Two Rivers, Wisconsin, where his father, Felix, was a lumberjack, tanner, and part-time clerk, and his mother, Bridget Comer, encouraged education and temperance. After his confirmation, young Tom took the pledge against drinking alcoholic beverages, mother Bridget even making special mincemeat without brandy for him. Much later, Tom Walsh received more than 100 votes for president at the Democratic National Convention in New York in 1924 as the Irish Catholic dry alternative to Al Smith.

Tom's father, Felix, read Irish history to his son and encouraged a life of public service. Tom heard about the efforts of his cousin Michael Davitt at land reform in Ireland. Walsh also recalled reading Henry George's *Progress and Poverty* "with profit." At the age of twenty, Tom Walsh began teaching public school but soon decided on a career in law, studying at the University of Wisconsin for a year. In a letter to his fiancée, Elinor McClements, in 1889, comparing the university at Madison with the elite institutions of the East, Walsh revealed his progressive temperament: "Don't you think it makes a vast difference what kind of air there is about a college? Whether it's laden with a large sympathy with all humanity or impregnated with a sort of we-are-the-elect idea."

After several years of practicing law in Wisconsin and with his brother,

Henry, in South Dakota, he arrived in Helena, Montana, in 1890, shortly after the state was admitted to the Union. There, at the outlet of two transcontinental railway systems, the Great Northern and Northern Pacific, Walsh established a lucrative law practice, winning many judgments for injured workers against big corporations but also representing Anaconda Copper in a "just cause."

Henry Cabot Lodge, born in Boston in 1850, was nine years the senior of Walsh and five years older than his *bête noire,* Thomas Woodrow Wilson. Cabot's paternal ancestors were relative newcomers: his grandfather Giles Lodge had arrived in Boston in 1791 after fleeing Santo Domingo, where he was a commercial agent during the great black uprising there. Giles and his son John, Cabot's father, grew wealthy in the China trade. But Cabot's maternal great-grandfather was George Cabot, United States senator and leading New England Federalist, a friend of George Washington, John Adams, and Rufus King.

Young Cabot was clearly one of "the elect." His first school was Mrs. Parkman's, for which he said he was "picked" from among the so-called proper Bostonians, such as the Bigelows, Cabots, Lees, and Parkmans. After a year in Europe with his family, Cabot entered Harvard in 1867, when Brahmin Boston, in the words of Van Wyck Brooks, was entering its "Indian Summer."

Cabot graduated from Harvard College in 1871, received his law degree there in 1874, and, after serving as Henry Adams's assistant on the *North American Review,* completed a dissertation on Anglo-Saxon land law under Professor Adams at Harvard, for the first Ph.D. in history awarded in the United States. Nine years later, his great nemesis Woodrow Wilson would be awarded a Ph.D. in history and political science at Johns Hopkins for a dissertation on congressional government.

Lodge, in 1876, plunged into Massachusetts Republican politics behind the scenes, while teaching American colonial history at his alma mater. But his principal interest lay in writing history, starting with the life of his great-grandfather George Cabot. Especially popular were his biographies in the American Statesmen Series, particularly *Alexander Hamilton* in 1882 and *Daniel Webster* in 1883. His exaggerated reverence for the old Puritan values, as exemplified in his filiopietistic accounts of the Federalist Party, foreshadowed his strong adherence to its heir, the Republican Party, in its battles with the "Jeffersonian" Democrats, especially Mr. Wilson. When George Bancroft warned Lodge about becoming too much of an apologist, he wrote back that although Jefferson was "the most consummate party leader of modern times," "as a statesman he was a failure, as all our history seems to me to show." Jefferson "appears to me insincere, and I am not ready to admit that the principles of which he was the apostle ... were sound. They are still on trial and their prospect of success seems to me at least uncertain."[1]

Lodge even discovered virtues in that rogue Federalist Timothy Pickering, one of those "successful men ... of intense prejudices and intense convictions," who though not "of so high a type as the broad and liberal-minded men," nevertheless "attain the greatest measure of immediate and practical success." With portents for his future political views, Lodge wrote approvingly of men like Pickering: "They appeal most strongly to the sympathies and passions of their fellow-men; for to the mass of humanity liberality is apt to look like indifferentism, and independence like unreliable eccentricity."[2]

Appropriately, Theodore Roosevelt, a good friend of Lodge, chose as his subject for the American Statesmen Series Thomas Hart Benton. Even in the 1880s, Teddy and Cabot were on a collision course converging in 1912.

Though disillusioned by defeat in a congressional race in 1884, with mugwump votes the margin of difference, Lodge was elected to the House of Representatives in 1886, where he was assigned the seat next to William McKinley—"a first-rate man ... [and] quite a friend of mine." And Lodge established a national reputation by guiding the Federal Elections Bill through the House in 1890. When Democratic Congressman William Stone of Missouri criticized it as a "Force Bill" and called Lodge the "Oscar Wilde of American statesmenship," he denounced the slur that a leader of Massachusetts was "effeminate": "It is the view which naturally is taken of a high civilization by a lower one. It is the view which would naturally be taken of the civilization of the public school by the civilization of the shotgun."[3]

When the "Force Bill" was defeated by southerners in the Senate, Lodge quickly dropped efforts to protect African American voting rights in the South. He had conspicuously established his credentials to be elected in 1893 to the Senate seat of Charles Sumner. For the next thirty-one years, Henry Cabot Lodge would represent the "high civilization" of Massachusetts in the upper house. But a senator from neighboring New York, Chauncey Depew, cast aspersions on this scion of Boston Brahmin culture, comparing Lodge's mind to the soil of New England, "naturally barren, but highly cultivated."[4]

Out in the intellectually barren Rocky Mountains, a young lawyer in the Jeffersonian tradition was making a reputation as a defense attorney for the poor. He became famous defending a railroad worker who had both legs severed above the knees by a Northern Pacific switch engine. Shortly after

Walsh won a court decision for his client, the railroad went into receivership and was sold to a new corporation, which repudiated the court judgment. But Walsh filed a new suit, contending that the foreclosure proceedings conducted by the prestigious New York law firm of Sullivan and Cromwell were irregular and that "in any event, the crippled man's award is a just one which the new Company is bound to pay." The new company compromised and settled out of court.[5]

Walsh also won a victory in 1895 that helped to protect stockholders' rights against big trusts. The bylaws of Standard Oil, incorporated under New Jersey laws, provided that only with the consent of the board of directors or the vote of preferred stockholders in regular session could the company's books be inspected. Walsh got the federal courts to rule that the spirit of the New Jersey law implied that every stockholder had the right at reasonable times to inspect the corporation's records.[6]

Montana at the turn of the century was little more than a fief of the Anaconda Copper Mining Company. "The Company" was originally a Butte silver mine bought by a shrewd Irish immigrant, Marcus Daly, on the hunch it contained copper. It was developed into the world's richest vein of copper, and in 1898, Daly negotiated with the Standard Oil Company one of the largest trusts in history, the Amalgamated Copper Company, which, in the next few years, bought out the opposition. When a Supreme Court decision in 1911 forced a paper reorganization, Amalgamated, the holding company, was dissolved into the Anaconda Copper Mining Company. But Anaconda still had a constrictorlike hold on the government, the press, and even the unions of Montana.

Amalgamated Copper Company, in Walsh's words, "intended to monopolize the production and sale of copper in this country, and was part of a comprehensive plan to ultimately dominate the world's copper market." And the corporation that "owned" the state of Montana offered Tom Walsh the position of general counsel. He refused, stating that he would take no retaining fee that bound him to defend any cause, whether good or bad, that Amalgamated assigned him. Though not a company man, Walsh was not a free agent until later in his career, and then not totally free.

In 1949, Senator James E. Murray recalled Walsh: "Probably there never was a lawyer in Montana before or since so recognized for his skill." And Murray described him as follows: "Walsh was a thin man, but wiry, pale-looking, and very efficient. He never fumbled with papers. He knew just where everything was. . . . In court he was very austere, clear, cold, precise, inspiring confidence. I guess I never saw a more earnest man. . . . His eyes were piercing, almost hypnotic in their effect. . . . He had life, vigor; he was alert and quick."

Walsh entered politics as a champion of the People's Power League in 1906, advocating initiative and referendum acts that would establish direct primary elections of U.S. senators. In 1910, though two-thirds of the Democratic majority in the Montana legislature supported Walsh for the U.S. Senate, Anaconda bribed enough legislators to block Walsh's election in the waning moments of the session. According to Walsh supporter and future Senator Burton K. Wheeler, a lobbyist offered him $2,000 for his vote at first but finally raised it to $9,000, informing the young legislator from Butte: "You can't lick the Company. You might as well join them." Walsh remarked: "The people of Montana were denied the right to send to the national Congress a senator of their choice because Standard Oil Magnates reserved for themselves the right to veto."[7]

But Walsh continued his campaigning for the next two years. And while the Seventeenth Amendment, calling for the direct election of U.S. senators, was being ratified by the requisite state legislatures during 1912 and 1913, Tom Walsh won the Democratic nomination for the U.S. Senate at the state Democratic convention and was unanimously elected senator by Montana's Thirteenth Legislative Assembly on January 15, 1913. He would serve in the Senate for the next twenty years. In his acceptance speech, he noted his lifelong affiliation with the Democratic Party because its principles "most certainly tend to justice to all men." But he was also a progressive: "I am not blind to the fact that party action is not infrequently the very antithesis of party principle." And he predicted that he would not be controlled by "set rules" or "governed by any party organization."[8]

Between 1909 and 1913, the Republican Party was shaken by a civil war between the progressives, such as Robert La Follette of Wisconsin, and the Conservatives, led by Henry Cabot Lodge of Massachusetts, political heir of Nelson Aldrich, who had retired in 1911 after thirty years. Lodge's interests focused largely on foreign affairs. Though not as publicly outspoken as Albert J. Beveridge, he was every bit as fervent in supporting American acquisition of Puerto Rico, the Philippines, and even Cuba. And he no longer wore the mantle of Sumner at home.

The imperialist Lodge passively supported the Republican Party's abandonment of African Americans as, for example, his good friend in the White House dishonorably discharged every soldier in three black companies in connection with the Brownsville, Texas, "riot" of 1906. Though not sharing the macho frontier mentality of Teddy, who went so far as to claim that the "most vicious cowboy has more moral principle than the average Indian," Cabot was not about to dispute Anglo-Saxon racial superiority theories at home or abroad. On the other hand, most of the progressive

Republicans were no more enlightened; and President Wilson, in practice, was to prove the worst racist in the White House since James Buchanan.[9]

Lodge's split with the progressive Republicans—including La Follette, Beveridge, and even old friend Teddy Roosevelt—began with the Payne–Aldrich Tariff of 1909. Backed by the new president, William Howard Taft, former governor of the Philippines and secretary of war, the tariff became a symbol of the growing rift in the Republican Party between the Old Guard, led by Senator Nelson Aldrich, coauthor of the tariff legislation, and the younger reformers. Critics of the tariff pointed out that it increased the profits of big businesses and trusts and that it did not significantly revise the tariff of 1897 downward, as the Republican Party platform had pledged in 1908.

Lodge supported the Payne–Aldrich Act because he believed in "protection" but not always consistently: he called for the importation of duty-free hides for Massachusetts shoemakers. During the Senate debates, the famous "Mr. Dooley" noted the senator's inconsistency, as the "Hinnery Cabin Lodge" who "pleaded f'r freedom f'r th' skins iv' cows" with words that "wud melt th' heart iv th' coldest mannyfacthrer iv button shoes."[10]

The major split occurred in 1912, when Cabot Lodge supported the reelection of Taft and many progressive Republicans backed the Bull Moose candidacy of Teddy Roosevelt. Ironically, Governor Woodrow Wilson of New Jersey criticized the populist outcry for direct legislation for the same reasons as Lodge had before 1911. But Lodge would break with T.R. in 1912 over the "reform" issue, while Wilson altered his views and rode the reform wave to the White House.

Lodge opposed the direct election of senators because, as he told the Yale Law School graduating class of 1902, the Senate would lose its "character and meaning" by being chosen in the same way, by the same constituency, as the House. But by 1911, he remarked in opposition: "I do not think it will bring a political milennium or be in the least ruinous." He also opposed the initiative and the referendum, but especially judicial recall. When Roosevelt began expressing sympathy for these measures, Lodge argued quite eloquently against the recall of judges: "To encourage resistance to the decisions of the courts tends to lead to a disregard of the law." And he told a Princeton audience that judicial recall would destroy justice itself because "there is nothing so essential, so vital to human rights and human liberty, as an independent court." As for the initiative and the compulsory referendum, Lodge pointed out that such direct democracy could lead to anarchy, and then tyranny, such as the French revolutions of 1848 and Louis Napoleon's use of the plebiscite. Lodge wrote to Roosevelt in 1912 that since "it is a good deal easier to elect a good representative than it is to pass a complicated law," he doubted that the voting public "have either the intelligence or character to legislate intelligently."[11]

In the presidential election of 1912, the Democrats, with Woodrow Wilson as their nominee, won with the help of the Bull Moose Party (mainly progressive Republicans) and Teddy Roosevelt, their nominee, who ran second. The Republicans and President Taft finished a poor third. Lodge himself during the Republican upheaval was reelected to the Senate in January 1911 by a majority of six votes.

Tom Walsh placed Woodrow Wilson's name in nomination at the Democratic National Convention in Baltimore in 1912, and he also helped to draft the party's platform. During his first term in the Senate, he remained a loyal Wilsonian Democrat and a good liberal capitalist. He supported the use of big government commissions, such as the Federal Trade Commission, to control and cooperate with big corporations. But who controlled whom? And perhaps with historical hindsight, some would portray this cooperation as a victory for conservatism.[12]

As a member of the Judiciary Committee, Walsh, long an advocate of women's rights, helped to draft the Woman Suffrage Amendment, eventually ratified as the Nineteenth Amendment in 1920. He supported the Federal Child Labor Amendment, which was never ratified, and also helped to draft that section of the Clayton Antitrust Act which protected farm organizations and labor unions from suit under the Sherman Antitrust Act.

In 1916, Tom Walsh led the prolonged fight for the confirmation of Louis D. Brandeis as the first Jewish associate justice of the Supreme Court. Walsh told the Senate: "The real crime of which this man is guilty is that he has exposed the inequities of men in high places of our financial systems. He has not stood in the awe of the majesty of wealth."[13]

From 1913 to 1919, Walsh generally stood in the shadow of the Republican progressives—William E. Borah, La Follette, and George W. Norris—as he supported the Democratic majority and President Wilson down the line, including a reluctant entry into World War I. And he especially differed with the Republican progressives on civil liberties when he sponsored a draconian amendment to the Espionage Act in 1918. But after being safely reelected during the "khaki" election of November 1918, Walsh blossomed into a civil libertarian and progressive statesman.

Walsh's conversion to libertarian is testament to his pragmatism and open-mindedness, but perhaps also to a sense of guilt about his conduct during the patriotic hysteria that swept Montana in 1917 and 1918 and caused him to ask for the resignation of his friend B.K. Wheeler as U.S.

attorney. It was an ideal time for "the Company" to use patriotism to stifle dissent, and Walsh learned that flag-waving was a good counteroffensive.

The period from 1917 to 1921 has been described as the years of "Montana's agony," with national ramifications. It was a special testing time for Tom Walsh, who also suffered a nervous breakdown after the death of his wife of twenty-eight years, Elinor McClements, on August 30, 1917. With his Senate seat on the line, Walsh at first failed miserably.

The "Big Sky" became a Savonarola Sky, lit up by the inquisitorial Montana Council of Defense. Antidraft riots and the Speculator Mine disaster, which killed 162 miners, fueled dissent against "the Company" and the war. And the only independent union to which the dissenters could turn was the radical Industrial Workers of the World (IWW), or Wobblies.

Frank Little, a member of the executive board of the IWW, was quoted by the *Anaconda Standard* telling the miners: "The IWW do not object to the war but the way they want to fight it. They should put the capitalists in the front trenches and if the Germans don't get them the IWW will. Then the IWW will clean the Germans." Shortly afterward, Little was found hanging from a railroad trestle in Butte, with the *Helena Independent* proclaiming: "There was but one comment in Helena, 'Good work: Let them continue to hang every IWW in the state.' " Even Vice President Thomas R. Marshall got in his two cents' worth, saying that "they hung an IWW leader in Butte and it had a very salutary effect." Such was the atmosphere in which Tom Walsh's appointee, B.K. Wheeler, the U.S. attorney for Montana, was working, as both men denounced the lynching and the language of Little. And both advocated tightening the Espionage Act.

Walsh was also a divided personality at this time of rising Irish American nationalism. For example, he sent a small statue of the 1803 Irish revolutionary Robert Emmet to the Butte Robert Emmet Literary Association, a radical front for the Clan-na-Gael, which supported the Irish revolt against England. He obviously hoped to keep its support, while endorsing Wilson's Anglophile foreign policy and crackdown on dissent. The state Council of Defense, in an inglorious moment, even called upon Captain Omar N. Bradley to use his army contingent to break up a St. Patrick's Day parade in Butte comprised of dissident miners, members of the Wobblies, and supporters of the Easter Rising in Ireland. Many of the 5,000 to 7,000 people shouted insults to "John Bull and Uncle Sam."[14]

The Montana legislature without dissent adopted a sedition act that was introduced by Tom Walsh as an amendment to the Federal Espionage Act of 1917 and became law as the Sedition Act of 1918. And it was the conservative Lodge who questioned its necessity, and the progressive Borah who toned down somewhat its draconian nature. The Walsh amendment called for fines of $10,000 and imprisonment up to twenty years for anyone who uttered or published "any disloyal, profane, scurrilous, or abusive language" about the U.S. government, the Constitution, the armed forces, their uniforms, or the flag; or used language to bring the same institutions and symbols into "contempt, scorn, contumely or disrepute." Senator Walsh made it clear that his amendment "makes it a crime to attempt to obstruct as well as actually to obstruct" the government. But Cabot Lodge at his constitutional best interjected: "This bill will not touch a single spy or a single German agent." "I think it will," shouted Lee Overman of North Carolina. Lodge continued: "The spies or agents do not go around uttering, publishing, and writing. The dangerous men keep quiet." Lodge also supported Borah's substitute amendment to Walsh's, which changed the word *calculated* to *intended*. As Lodge put it: "Any district attorney, on this word 'calculated,' could drag any man into court."[15]

A month before the 1918 election, in a teary scene, Walsh bowed to critics at home, calling for the scalp of B.K. Wheeler for being too soft on dissenters. The senator asked his friend to resign as district attorney. Although Walsh urged Wheeler to announce that he was resigning for the good of the Democratic Party, the feisty D.A. claimed his motive was "to satisfy the friends of T.J. Walsh who believed my retention in office would mean his defeat as candidate to succeed himself in the Senate."[16]

Upon being safely reelected in November 1918, Walsh slowly performed a *volte-face* on civil liberties. Perhaps political self-preservation had motivated him in 1917 and 1918. But in peacetime America, he even supported "bolshevik" Burt Wheeler in his unsuccessful race for governor in 1920.

During the "Red scare" of 1919–1920, initiated by Wilson's professing-Quaker Attorney General A. Mitchell Palmer and his assistant J. Edgar Hoover, Walsh, as a member of the Judiciary Committee, helped to squelch the national antibolshevik paranoia. He opposed the way the Espionage Act had become an "instrument of torture" used by the Department of Justice against thousands of pacifists and industrial dissenters. More than a thousand men and women had been sentenced to prison. Walsh attacked Palmer for his "unconstitutional methods of warfare" and observed: "It is only in times such as these that the guarantees of the Constitution as to personal rights are of practical use or value. In seasons of calm no one thinks of denying them."

It was Walsh in late 1920 who introduced a report criticizing Palmer's Justice Department, drafted by the National Popular Government League's committee of lawyers, which included Dean Roscoe Pound of Harvard Law School. Walsh asked that the report be referred to the Judiciary Committee. But fellow Democrat William Henry King of Utah complained that bolsheviks and seditionists were infiltrating the country and praised the "ability" and "integrity" of Attorney General Palmer. Walsh countered: "I do not think it is any answer at all to the charge that illegal things have been done to say that there are Bolshevists and anarchists in this country. If there are, they are entitled to whatever protection the law affords, even the most conscienceless and bloodthirsty murderer. They are all accorded certain rights under the law. It is no answer to charges of this character to say that the practices were directed against anarchists and Bolshevists."

Walsh became the "prosecuting attorney" of a special subcommittee of the Senate Judiciary Committee set up to investigate "Charges of Illegal Practices of the Department of Justice." In hearings held between January 19 and March 31, 1921, Walsh voiced concern about the apparent violations of the Fourth Amendment, which protects against arrest or search without a warrant. When questioned by Walsh at the hearing, Palmer, about to leave office, professed ignorance about the details of the raids and made this suggestion: "I can not tell you Senator, personally. If you would like to ask Mr. Hoover who was in charge of this matter, he can tell you." Hoover then stated that it was the job of local FBI agents to obtain the search warrants and that he was unaware of the number of warrants.

Though the Judiciary Committee after the hearings voted 7 to 4 to do nothing—with Walsh, Borah, Norris, and Henry Ashurst dissenting—Walsh continued to protest. While being praised and encouraged by the likes of Felix Frankfurter, Walsh regretted that the Senate "found lawlessness less reprehensible when perpetrated by the highest law offices of the Government than when the ignorant or misguided are guilty." Walsh reasoned simply: "Lawbreakers are lawbreakers . . . whether they hold official position or not, and a crime is a crime, by whomsoever committed."[17]

Walsh's greatest moment of statesmanship, however, came in the prolonged wrangle over the Treaty of Versailles. And this small, mild-mannered teetotaler almost succeeded in winning ratification. Walsh alone among Democratic senators in 1919 and 1920 stood out for "brilliance of mind." Though he was a "bloodhound for facts," he lacked the "personal force" of the aristocratic Cabot Lodge, "one of the cleverest and most resourceful parliamentarians in the history of the Senate."[18]

Lodge's previous twenty-five years in the Senate were a preparation for his preeminent position in American politics between 1918 and 1921. He had been the first prominent American to call for sending American troops to France. He was a great internationalist and had long distrusted mugwump reformers, such as Woodrow Wilson. These two Ph.D.'s and former professors of history and political science developed an intense dislike, if not hatred, for each other during Wilson's first term as president. And this animosity, enhanced by two enormous egos, helped to kill the treaty, with both men sharing the blame. But this personal political duel was also a confrontation between the leftover leader of an oligarchic Senate, on a decline after the ratification of the Seventeenth Amendment, and the champion of an imperial presidency in foreign affairs and national security.

The prior decade had not been kind personally to Lodge, perhaps accounting for a certain bitterness. The unexpected death of his older son, George Cabot Lodge, from food poisoning in 1909 was a wound that did not heal. "Bay," as he was known, according to Edith Wharton was a "young genius" of almost thirty-six, with an "adoring family." His mother, Anna, the senator's wife, never recovered from the loss and died in 1915. The senator did not remarry and privately bristled with anger when President Wilson remarried shortly after the death of his first wife.

Wilson's self-righteousness equaled Lodge's carefully cultivated cynicism. But the Princetonian president, an expert on congressional government, would demonstrate a practical ignorance of congressional manners that such "lowbrow" predecessors as McKinley had mastered. The Ohioan had included senators on the commission that negotiated the Treaty of Paris ending the Spanish-American War, but Wilson selected a five-member commission in 1918 that Lodge described as one to which Wilson had appointed himself four times along with the Anglophile "has-been" Henry White. (The other four were Woodrow Wilson, Secretary of State Robert Lansing, Wilson's alter ego Colonel Edward House, and General Tasker Bliss.) No senator was selected, though Tom Walsh had been frequently rumored for a position.[19]

President Wilson received a rather chilly bon voyage when he addressed a joint session of the "old" Sixty-fifth Congress on December 2, 1918, two days before he sailed to Europe. His contempt for certain "pygmy-minded" senators was evident: he thought the Senate would have to ratify a *fait accompli*. After the Spanish-American War, Dr. Wilson had written that the powers of the presidency were greatly increased when the nation plunged into international affairs. But the Treaty of Versailles went much further than earlier treaties and offered to become "the charter of a new world order." And the Republicans controlled both houses of the new Sixty-sixth Congress, with Henry Cabot Lodge the Republican leader of the Senate and chairman of its Foreign Relations Committee.[20]

The president returned from France for the first time in February 1919 to brief the Senate and the American people on the Peace Conference. The European "three" of the "Big Four" had vitiated his Fourteen Points in preparing a world unsafe for democracy. Though an American history and government Ph.D., Wilson was abysmally ignorant of European and world history. But he did extract from the other three leaders an agreement on a League of Nations. Upon returning, he held a grand state dinner for the Senate Foreign Relations Committee at the White House on February 26; but during a two-hour question period afterward, the president, according to Lodge, told them nothing. Two days later, on the Senate floor, Lodge called for "facts, details, and sharp, clear-cut definitions." He pleaded for "consideration, time, thought. . . . We cannot reach our objects by a world constitution hastily constructed in a few weeks in Paris in the midst of the excitement of a war not yet ended."

On March 4, 1919, just prior to the adjournment of the Sixty-fifth Congress, Lodge introduced a "round-robin" resolution with thirty-nine Republican signatories. Its purpose was to inform the president and his European conferees that the League "in the form now proposed" was unacceptable and that the League and the peace treaty must be decoupled for the latter to be approved by the Senate. But President Wilson was unpersuaded and cautioned as he sailed back to France that "you cannot dissect the Covenant from the Treaty without destroying the whole vital structure." He called the senators opposing him, "contemptible . . . narrow . . . selfish . . . poor little minds that never get anywhere but run round in a circle and think they are going somewhere."[21]

Back in France, Wilson secured some changes in the League Covenant that Lodge sought, and the treaty was signed at Versailles on June 28, 1919. But upon returning to the United States, the president had to present the treaty to a new Republican-controlled Senate and to a Foreign Relations Committee chaired by Lodge, with four new Republican members hostile to the League. And Wilson was in an uncompromising mood. Dr. Nicolas Murray Butler, president of Columbia University, had proposed certain tentative reservations acceptable to an "important group" of Republican senators and to both the French and the British foreign offices, when cabled by the French ambassador, Jules Jusserand. But when the ambassador went straight to the White House and presented the proposal, Jusserand was horrified at the president's grim reply: "Mr. Ambassador, I shall consent to nothing. *The Senate must take its medicine.*"[22]

President Wilson presented the treaty to the Senate in July; and on August 12, Lodge denounced the League of Nations on the Senate floor to the applause of marines sitting in the gallery: "I have never had but one allegiance—I can not divide it now. I have loved but one flag and I can not share that devotion and give affection to the mongrel banner invented for a league." Lodge was especially opposed to Article X of the treaty in which members of the League of Nations pledged to preserve against external aggression the political independence and territorial integrity of all member nations. Wilson responded by appealing to the country in a whistle-stop train trip coast to coast. He was at first greeted with apathy, but his later speeches met with greater enthusiasm. On his way home, he collapsed after a speech in Pueblo, Colorado, and was rushed back to Washington, where he suffered a stroke that paralyzed his left side.[23]

It was at this point that Tom Walsh began to play an important, though unsuccessful, role in attempting a compromise. In a letter to the acting minority leader in the Senate, Gilbert Hitchcock of Nebraska, dated November 18, 1919, Walsh pointed out that even though the Lodge reservations weakened Article X and American commitment to the League of Nations, three other articles gave substance to the new world organization. In a cover letter to Wilson, Hitchcock added that many Democrats shared the views of Walsh. But Hitchcock informed the president that even though these men did not think the Lodge reservations nullified the treaty, they would vote as the president directed for the sake of party regularity.[24]

The next day, the Senate took three votes. Substantial majorities voted to defeat the treaty: with the fourteen Lodge reservations, with only five of the reservations, and—a final vote—the treaty by itself. Most of the Democrats, including Walsh, voted with the "irreconcilables" to defeat the treaty with the Lodge reservations. But the fight was not over, as public support for a compromise increased. The president, however, issued a statement from his sickbed. He refused to allow the United States to join the League with the Lodge reservations and called on voters to make the 1920 presidential election a "great and solemn referendum."

One last attempt at compromise, however, took place between January 15 and 30, 1920, in a bipartisan conference of four Republican and five Democratic senators, including Lodge and Walsh. And on January 23, the conferees were near an agreement when Lodge compromised on Article X and the League.

But word leaked out. Senator Borah, as a leading irreconcilable, confronted Lodge and threatened a split in the Republican Party. Lodge would place party loyalty above the national interest. When the bipartisan committee next met on January 26, Lodge declared that he would make no concessions on his reservations relating to the Monroe Doctrine and Article X. And on January 30, the conference broke down completely.[25]

Tom Walsh would not give up, however, as support for a compromise grew in the Senate. He worried about a "Carthaginian peace" after reading and recommending John Maynard Keynes's new book *Economic Consequences of the Peace*. Before the final vote was taken on March 19, 1920, according to historian Thomas A. Bailey, Walsh, in his final arguments, made "one of the few really impressive speeches of the entire debate." He was confronted with two alternatives, both of which were "in a high degree distasteful": vote for the Wilson League again without reservations or vote for the Lodge reservations. Walsh found no grounds to hope that the treaty could be ratified "at any time in the future ... without reservations substantially like those now adopted by the Senate," since the Democrats could pick up five Senate seats at best in 1920. And the Covenant of the League of Nations was not "a vain thing without article 10": "Almost, if not quite all, that is or will be accomplished by article 10 is secured to the world by other provisions of the Covenant." Half a League was better than none, as Walsh, guided as he said by "the lamp of experience," pursued a practical course for his country, for his party, and for himself.[26]

When the clerk called the roll, three of the first four Democrats turned against Wilson and adopted Walsh's position, voting for the treaty with reservations. But after the clerk called the name of the highly respected Senator Charles Culberson of Texas, hesitating and with a perplexed look, he voted "nay." Later, he praised Walsh's speech and remarked, "You know, for a minute in there I didn't know how to vote."

The treaty with reservations was approved by a vote of 49 to 35 but lacked seven votes for the necessary two-thirds. The weak, vacillating minority leader, Hitchcock of Nebraska, voted "nay" along with the twenty-three staunch, uncompromising, predominantly southern, Wilsonians. Hitchcock would later call that vote "the mistake" of his life. And others, such as Senator J.C. Beckham of Kentucky, contended that Walsh's speech might have been decisive if delivered a few days earlier.

The politically timid Lodge worried more about a split in the Republican Party, similar to 1912's, than America's position in the world. Instead of encouraging the reasonable and flexible Democrats like Tom Walsh, Lodge caved in to the strong-willed Senator William Borah, who counted on "support" from the equally close-minded president. Former President William Howard Taft, who had sincerely supported the League of Nations but was rebuffed by both Wilson and Lodge privately, offered history's unflattering assessment. He wrote that both Lodge and Wilson "exalt their personal prestige and the saving of their ugly faces above the welfare of the country and the world."[27]

Cabot Lodge delivered the keynote speech at the Republican National Convention in Chicago. He made Wilsonism the issue of the 1920 campaign: "Mr. Wilson and his dynasty, his heirs and assigns, or anybody that is his, anybody who with bent knee has served his purpose, must be driven from control."[28]

The elegantly handsome Lodge presided over the convention, in the

words of H.L. Mencken, "from a sort of aloof intellectual balcony" with a
"general air of detachment." But Lodge occasionally descended into the
smoke-filled rooms to help select one of those "bungalow" minds as Republican presidential nominee, Senator Warren G. Harding of Ohio. The
irreconcilable Senator Borah did not bolt the party but scornfully remarked: "What I see here reminds me of the degenerate days of Rome
when they sold, on the auction block, the emperorship to the highest bidder." "Highbrowism" would be out of fashion in the return to "normalcy,"
but not even the erudite Lodge realized how cloddish the presidential-looking Harding really was. Tom Walsh was the man who would find out for
the country.[29]

Walsh was forced by the Democratic Party to go to its convention in San
Francisco, where he helped to draft the platform. On behalf of the League
of Women Voters, he introduced a clause calling for "the protection of
child-life through infancy and maternity care." He also witnessed the pathetic efforts of Wilson to win a third term, as the president granted interviews to select reporters and had photos taken of the nonparalyzed, right
side of his face. To Wilson, Walsh was by now a "traitor," though Walsh
supported Wilson's son-in-law, Senator William Gibbs McAdoo of California, for the Democratic nomination. Though a dry, Walsh campaigned for
the wet governor of Ohio, James Cox, whom the convention nominated
after forty-four ballots.

During the campaign, Tom Walsh backed Republican Elihu Root's advocacy of American participation in the World Court of International Justice
despite nonmembership in the League of Nations. But Senator Harding
wanted to remain out of both, and Walsh's plea for the "Root Commission"
went unheard in the heat of the 1920 presidential contest. Former Secretary
of State Elihu Root even led thirty other prominent Republicans to declare
their support for Harding on October 15. They argued that the election of
Harding would ensure American entry into the League, with reservations
protecting American sovereignty, because Harding did not really mean or
understand what he was saying in his speeches.[30]

For the last four years of his life, Cabot Lodge's cynicism continued to
color his judgment. During Harding's presidential campaign, Lodge reveled
in the Ohioan's "bloviations," writing Senator Harding that he had been "so
sickened over the egotism of Wilson that to listen to you was a refreshment
of the spirit." Lodge also dismissed Franklin D. Roosevelt, Governor Cox's
running mate, as "a well-meaning, nice young fellow, but light."

At the end of his life, Lodge moved further away from the racial equality
he had championed as an heir to Sumner. He voted for Japanese exclusion

in the Immigration Act of 1924, whereas President Calvin Coolidge opposed it. But the progressives were no better, and many of the Japanese were proclaiming their own racial superiority. George Norris called for "more stringent laws to bar the undesirable foreigner"; and Tom Walsh, who claimed he sought justice for African Americans, opposed a federal antilynching bill that he knew had no chance of surviving a southern Democratic filibuster.[31]

When former President Wilson died on February 3, 1924, at his home on S Street in Washington, Lodge, because of his seniority, was appointed a member of the special committee representing the Senate at the funeral. But Mrs. Wilson wrote him that he would be "unwelcome," and he honored her request. Later in 1924, Lodge himself would die in Cambridge and, as he wrote of Wilson a few months earlier, would "pass into the keeping of history, and there . . . will be justly judged."[32]

Meanwhile, Tom Walsh's reputation for political skill with integrity grew, in counterpoint to the ethical standards of the Jazz Age. Though remaining a loyal Democrat, he became increasingly identified with the progressives. By 1929, Mencken's *American Mercury* singled out only George Norris and Walsh as competent and militant progressives.[33]

It was another progressive, Robert La Follette, who helped make his friend Walsh famous. La Follette had begun a private investigation of the alleged corrupt deals resulting from the leasing of the oil rights on federal government land. After uncovering evidence of massive corruption, the Wisconsin senator persuaded the Senate in 1922 to authorize the Public Lands Committee to investigate. With presidential ambitions for the 1924 election, La Follette persuaded Tom Walsh in 1923 to chair the committee.

During his first decade in the Senate, Walsh was a true voice for the western Democrats, possessing much of their skepticism for the proposals of eastern environmentalists. He was even sponsor of the Walsh–Pittman Bill, with Senator Key Pittman of Nevada, providing for the leasing of oil on government lands, which La Follette had filibustered to death in March 1919. But chairing the Public Lands Committee brought a *volte-face* for Walsh.

In the first year of Warren Harding's administration, Washington wags were busy circulating rumors of corrupt deals, especially between the executive branch and oil men. President Harding signed an executive order in 1921 transferring control of two naval oil reserves, Teapot Dome in Wyoming and Elk Hills in California, from the Navy Department to the Interior Department, which then leased them to private oil companies.

Shortly after Harding's sudden, mysterious death in August 1923, Walsh's "Teapot Dome" Committee, after more than a year's preparation, opened hearings on October 25. At first, Walsh made little headway. Secretary of the Interior Albert Fall explained that the lavish additions to his New Mexico ranch were financed by a $100,000 loan from *Washington Post* publisher E.B. McLean, and Walsh could prove no connection to Teapot Dome. The *New York Times* claimed Walsh was up against a "stone wall," and Walter Lippmann called the investigation a "legalized atrocity ... in which Congressmen, starved of their legitimate food for thought, go on a wild and feverish manhunt, and do not stop at cannibalism."

But Walsh did not give up against a predominantly hostile press. He took a train to Florida to interview McLean, who admitted writing checks to Fall in 1921 but claimed they were returned uncashed. Suddenly, the case broke wide open in the press.[34]

The quiet but methodical Walsh called witnesses to prove that Secretary of the Interior Fall, a former Republican senator from New Mexico, had accepted bribes for the naval reserve leases from Edward Doheny and Harry Sinclair. Both Fall and Secretary of the Navy Edwin Denby resigned, with Fall imprisoned and fined. Although the entire story will never be known, Walsh asserted that Harding was nominated "pursuant to a deal" in the Blackstone Hotel, which promised Andrew Mellon, Albert B. Fall, and Harry Daugherty cabinet appointments.[35]

With his sharp prosecutorial skills, Walsh thoroughly pursued the scandal, though Doheny was a friend and a top California Democrat, who was also a confidant and business partner of a leading Democratic contender for the presidency, Senator William G. McAdoo of California. Walsh had supported the presidential nomination of McAdoo in 1920 and was nominally committed to him in 1924, though he wrote him: "You are no longer available as a candidate."[36]

Meanwhile, Montana's junior senator, Burton K. Wheeler, elected with Walsh's support in 1922, was launching an aggressive investigation of the Justice Department under Harding's attorney general, Harry Daugherty. The feisty Wheeler was threatened, had his files rifled, and was falsely charged with bribery, until President Coolidge fired Daugherty and replaced the head of the Federal Bureau of Investigation with his assistant, J. Edgar Hoover of A. Mitchell Palmer days.

Skillful handling of the Teapot Dome investigation made Tom Walsh the ideal man to chair the 1924 Democratic National Convention in New York, the most contentious presidential nominating convention in history. He also had the prerequisite compromise qualifications in a party divided down the middle: urban versus rural, Catholic versus Protestant, wet versus dry, North versus South, and East versus West. Who could be better qualified than a dry, Catholic, westerner like Tom Walsh?

Walsh walked a political tightrope in chairing the two-week convention in the steamy Old Madison Square Garden. The "two-thirds rule," which the Democrats were to abandon in 1936, provided that a candidate had to win the votes of two-thirds of the delegates to be nominated. This virtually assured a deadlock between Governor Al Smith of New York and Senator McAdoo of California, with Senator Oscar Underwood of Alabama also in contention.

But all the racial virulence in the party broke into the open when George Brennan, the Illinois boss, had the Smith campaign back an official condemnation of the Ku Klux Klan, which McAdoo did not support. The California senator was to be made to appear the candidate of the Klan. But the majority on the Platform Committee, including Walsh, wanted to condemn intolerance and racism but not the Klan by name. By one vote, a minority plank specifically condemning the Ku Klux Klan failed to win approval: 541$\frac{3}{20}$ to 542$\frac{3}{20}$.

Walsh as chairman had striven for harmony at all costs, though he clearly suffered from myopia on racial questions like most white politicians, including the progressives. But it should be noted that about 37 percent of McAdoo's supporters voted for condemnation of the Klan and that Walsh was joined by Bernard Baruch in supporting the western son-in-law of Woodrow Wilson. Although the fight over condemnation of the Klan undoubtedly hurt McAdoo, it also killed Smith's chances in 1924.

The convention voting dragged on from June 30 to July 8 for 100 ballots until McAdoo and Smith withdrew. And on the 102d ballot some 123 delegates even voted for the convention chairman, Tom Walsh. But on the 103d, John W. Davis of West Virginia, a distinguished Wall Street lawyer, was nominated by acclamation.

Immediately after Davis was nominated, a motion to adjourn was interrupted by "constant, persistant and innumerable cries, approaching unanimity and acclamation of 'Walsh,' 'Walsh,' 'Walsh.' " But when an Illinois delegate rose to place Tom Walsh in nomination for vice president, Chairman Walsh ruled him out of order. Later, Walsh rejected the nomination in a letter to the convention, and the delegates ratified Davis's choice of Governor Charles Bryan of Nebraska, brother of William Jennings.[37]

While the Democrats were meeting in New York, the Conference for Progressive Political Action was meeting in Cleveland, where it nominated Robert La Follette for president on the Progressive ticket. Ironically, La Follette selected as his running mate the other member of the duo, nicknamed "the Montana scandalmongers" by the *New York Tribune,* Burton Wheeler, who announced that he could not support Davis because of his close ties to Wall Street.[38]

But the country was in no mood for change. With both parties tacitly endorsing racism, in an era of pervasive classism, the nation elected to "keep cool with Coolidge" or bathtub gin and the other distractions of the Jazz Age.

William Allen White entitled his biography of Calvin Coolidge *Puritan in Babylon*. But the title also aptly described Tom Walsh, a most un-Irish second-generation politician who could never tell a good story but was known for his political integrity and private morality. The soft-spoken Walsh also exhibited a Puritan moral courage so missing in "Silent Cal."

In 1926, the issues of the Klan, corruption, and Democratic Party loyalty coalesced in a disputed Senate election in Iowa, where a progressive Republican, Smith Brookhart, in a close vote, "officially" defeated a conservative Democrat, Daniel Steck. Brookhart had alienated many Republicans by calling for an investigation of Attorney General Daugherty. In a 45 to 41 vote, the Senate seated the Democrat Steck, with the support of the Klan and conservative Republicans and Democrats, while Tom Walsh voted for the Republican Brookhart.[39]

In 1927, Walsh proposed a Senate investigation of the financing of gas and electrical services in the country. But conservative senators won support for Federal Trade Commission hearings and killed his proposal.

Encouraged by many prominent Democrats such as the historian and keynote speaker of their 1928 convention, Claude Bowers, Walsh was bitten by the presidential bug and briefly campaigned, until running a poor third in the California primary. But he had no organized following and came from a small state, in comparison with the Tammany-backed four-term governor of New York, Al Smith.

Walsh was the only realistic alternative to the flamboyant Smith. In a presidential contest that highlighted all the ugliness of the 1924 Democratic National Convention, one of the leading prohibitionists, Methodist Episcopal Bishop James Cannon Jr., called Walsh "the ablest, best qualified dry man in the Democratic Party." Bishop Cannon told reporters that he would "gladly support Senator Walsh for President" because he was "thoroughly incorruptible and a sincere dry" and also "an outspoken but not fanatical or priest-ridden Roman Catholic."

Cannon was upset at the encyclical of Pope Pius XI, "Fostering True Religious Union," intended to answer the 1927 Lausanne Conference for Christian Unity. The Pope announced that "this Apostolic See has never allowed its subjects to take part in the assemblies of non-Catholics." Bishop Cannon believed "that notwithstanding the bigotry and intolerance of the Roman Catholic Church, which had just been so amazingly emphasized by the papal encyclical, it would be part of the Smith Campaign to accuse his

opponents of bigotry and intolerance. The Walsh candidacy would eliminate that factor." But with Al Smith as the nominee, Bishop Cannon, a
Democrat, helped to swing five southern states to Herbert Hoover.[40]

Walsh's brief flurry in presidential politics left him with "no keen disap-
pointment or any great regret." He was reelected to the Senate for a fourth
term in 1930 and was particularly active in supporting relief measures during the depression and teaming up with George Norris on prolabor and
constitutional reforms.[41]

In 1932, Tom Walsh was elected permanent chair of the Democratic
National Convention in Chicago and supported Governor Franklin Roosevelt
of New York for the presidency. Upon winning the election, President-elect
Roosevelt, after much cajoling, persuaded Walsh, "no trusted friend of the
Money-changers," to accept the position of attorney general in the cabinet.[42]

But Providence had other plans. Tom Walsh had suffered a nervous
breakdown in 1917 when his wife Elinor died suddenly. Now, at seventy-
three, Tom Walsh, a lonely bachelor since his wife's death, decided to
marry a prominent Washington socialite and widow of a Cuban banker,
Señora Nieves de Truffin. The wedding was held on February 25, 1933, in
Havana, but on March 2, as the couple took a train north from Florida to
Washington for FDR's inauguration and Walsh's swearing-in as attorney
general, Tom Walsh suffered a fatal heart attack on board.

A leading Protestant journal editorialized upon his death: "The *Christian
Century* never has been fully reconciled to the fact that, after the Teapot
Dome exposures his party failed to seriously consider Senator Walsh as its
candidate for the presidency. He was the logical choice at the moment. Had
he been nominated, instead of the colorless John W. Davis, there would
have ensued a campaign in which the moral significance of the bribery of
government by big business would have been pressed home on the understanding of the nation at large. That might have done much toward heading
off the moral and financial catastrophe of 1929."[43]

Walsh and Lodge were both masters of pragmatic politics, but here the
comparison ends. Walsh was a moralistic progressive with a balanced skepticism that made him flexible. Lodge, however, placed party victory above
national concerns. Like Timothy Pickering, he knew how to appeal to the
American people's worst instincts, as he did in 1920 with what H.L. Mencken called "the Lodge sneer." But men like Senator Borah, who understood this, knew how easily the senator from Massachusetts could be
manipulated.

Thomas Marshall, Woodrow Wilson's Hoosier vice president for two
terms, in his 1925 memoirs heaped praise on Borah but wrote condescend-

ingly of Tom Walsh, whom he described as an "able lawyer, splendid debator, clean in manners and in morals," who "nevertheless was, and is, a politician." Such Americans with their uninformed contempt for politicians also profess a similar disregard for history.[44]

Walsh himself espoused a keener sense of history than the professionally trained historian Henry Cabot Lodge. In praising an article "In Defense of the Senate" by O.G. Villard, Walsh in a 1925 letter to the *Nation* warned of the "struggle to control the government by the malefactors of great wealth and others richer than any man ought to be." He mourned the effort to "reduce the American Congress to the humiliating position of the Roman Senate in the days of the decline of the Empire." But Walsh's Senate was still relatively powerful. Under a corrupting imperial presidency, the Senate would later sink to levels of decadence that Walsh never imagined.[45]

7

"Senator-at-Large of the Whole American People"

William E. Borah vs. George W. Norris (1920–1940)

The early life and career of George William Norris and that of William Edgar Borah followed a pattern similar to Tom Walsh's. Norris was born in 1861 in Sandusky, Ohio. In 1864—after the deaths of his father, Chauncey, of pneumonia and his only brother, John Henry, of battle wounds fighting with General William T. Sherman in Georgia—George, or "Willie," at the age of three, was the only surviving male in his family of six sisters and mother, the former Mary Magdalene Mook, a Pennsylvania Dutch girl. After growing up on the family farm, Norris attended Baldwin University for a year and then attained a bachelor's degree and an LL.B. from the Northern Indiana Normal School at Valparaiso. At first clerking and teaching school for two years, he then moved to Nebraska to practice law. That his integrity and independence inspired loyalty was evident in the way he never lost touch with his nine friends and supporters in a bitter contest for the presidency of the Crescent Literary Society at Northern Indiana. Though he lost the contest, they organized the LUN, the Loyal United Nine—or as their opponents called them "Lunatics under Norris"—who held an annual August reunion for fifty-nine years until 1941.

The seventh of ten children of a Civil War veteran, Borah was born near Fairfield, southern Illinois, in 1865. At sixteen he ran off with a traveling Shakespearean troupe to play Mark Antony, only to be brought home by his angry father. But William's histrionic gifts would later become his most notable characteristic. After moving to his married sister Susan's home in Kansas, he spent a year at the university in Lawrence, until dropping out to recuperate from tuberculosis. With Kansas in the depths of an agricultural depression in 1890, Borah took a train westward to settle in Seattle. But running out of money, he took the advice of an Idaho gambler and left the train at Boise, where he began to practice criminal law.

Both Norris and Borah were religious, though Norris never joined a church and Borah studied the Bible but was only nominally Presbyterian. Norris's creed evolved into a secular perfectionism, with one political scientist describing him as "a doggedly righteous man who never stopped battling for the Lord and the common people in a world of sinful men." Norris in his autobiography recalled asking his mother why she had planted a seedling of a fruit tree when she would never see it bear fruit. "I may never see this tree in bearing," Mary Norris replied, "but somebody will." Virtue required planting not only for the present but also for the future.

Both men had long marriages, but Borah was a notorious womanizer, known as the "Stallion of Idaho." As a young man, he reportedly spent "every night in a cathouse" with the proclaimed philosophy, "Better to pay for it before than afterwards." His marriage in 1895 to Mary O'Connell, daughter of Idaho Governor William J. O'Connell, appeared to have been of the shotgun variety after an abortion that left his wife sterile. They were married for almost forty-five years, until his death, and Mary, or "Mamie," was well known in Washington as "Little Borah," dying in 1976 at the age of 106.

Borah had affairs with two of Washington's most prominent women, who were rivals for his affection: Alice Roosevelt Longworth and Eleanor "Cissy" Patterson. Though married to Speaker of the House Nicholas Longworth, "Princess Alice," daughter of Teddy Roosevelt, soon became known as "Aurora Borah Alice," especially after Senator Borah reputedly fathered her only child, Paulina. "Cissy" Patterson, the divorced "Countess [Josef] Gizycka," novelist and gossip columnist, became the publisher of the *Washington Times-Herald*.

Norris's married life was more conventional, if not pragmatic. His first wife, Pluma Lashley, died shortly after the birth of their third daughter in 1901. After being elected to the House in 1902, before leaving for Washington, he married a McCook, Nebraska, teacher, Ella Leonard, who became mother to his three children. She was independent-minded and happily married to Norris, though they were childless, for more than forty years.[1]

Borah was a loner who rarely revealed himself, a party of one whose own self-confidence was his faith—strengthened into a political independence that always made him unpredictable. His favorite essay was Emerson's

"Self-Reliance," and he loved to dramatize his independent nature with such remarks as, "If the Savior of mankind would revisit the earth and declare for a League of Nations, I would be opposed to it." William Allen White recalled Borah as a fellow student at the University of Kansas. With an "obvious indifference to the opinion of others," Borah had "no side" but, as an older student among the freshmen, resembled "a big Newfoundland dog among smaller and more agile pups." For thirty-three years, Borah played such a role among very nimble senators, such as Henry Cabot Lodge. Borah's was a physical and oratorical presence *par excellence*.

A smaller, wiry man, Norris served in the U.S. Congress for forty years, the first ten in the House. He started out as a conservative lawyer, which he had been for the Burlington and Missouri (later Chicago, Burlington, and Quincy) Railroad. But in his second term, he returned his free railroad pass when he voted for greater federal control of the railroads. By 1910, he successfully led a coalition of insurgent Republicans and Democrats in curbing the inordinate power of Speaker of the House Joe Cannon. This most significant procedural revolution in House history provided for an elected Rules Committee without the Speaker as a member.

Borah, meanwhile, had become famous as a trial lawyer, especially as the prosecutor of "Big Bill" Haywood, secretary of the Western Federation of Miners, who was indicted for conspiracy in the murder of former Idaho Governor Frank Steunenberg. Borah lost the case to defense attorney Clarence Darrow but was praised for his eloquence and fairness to Haywood and the miners.

In 1907, Borah was elected by the Idaho legislature to the U.S. Senate. Since he had been a lawyer for timber and mining interests and had prosecuted labor unions, Nelson Aldrich appointed him chair of the Committee on Education and Labor. But Borah proceeded to disappoint the "boss" when he championed reforms. He sponsored bills to create the Labor Department and the Children's Bureau, to establish an eight-hour day on federal government contracts, and to investigate working conditions in the steel industry.

During his first term, Borah was also the chief sponsor of the income-tax amendment, which was ratified as the Sixteenth Amendment in 1913. He argued that the French Revolution was not caused by Robespierre but by the fact that the peasantry paid 85 percent of France's taxes. Borah also led the fight for the direct election of senators. It cut across party lines, pitting progressives like himself against conservatives like Cabot Lodge. Eventually, the joint resolution for direct election was ratified as the Seventeenth Amendment to the Constitution in May 1913.[2]

The Idahoan joined the "range senators" of the Northwest in bargaining on the Payne–Aldrich Tariff and finally supporting it. At the Republican National Convention in 1912, Borah was a leading supporter of Teddy Roosevelt but switched to William Howard Taft after he won the Republican nomination. Borah refused to bolt to the progressive Bull Moose Party, which nominated T.R. and Senator Hiram Johnson of California. Entering his second term in 1913, Borah became less progressive and more of an independent Ichabod.

In 1912, Norris was elected as a Republican senator in a Democratic landslide in Nebraska. He had supported the presidential candidacy of Teddy Roosevelt. But in office, Norris found himself generally supporting President Woodrow Wilson's "New Freedom" programs, especially the Federal Reserve Act and the Federal Trade Commission. Norris's "progressivism" anticipated his New Deal activism twenty years later.

Skeptical of the role of big government, Borah became more of a classical liberal critic of Wilson's New Freedom, opposing the establishment of the Federal Reserve Board: "What is the benefit going to be to the large business interests of the country, to the farming and agricultural interests[,] . . . of putting more money in the hands of banks to enable them to speculate it at an exorbitant rate of interest? Must we put it out to banks at three percent and see the people pay eight or nine percent? Who are we legislating for— the money lender or the money user?"[3]

Borah also opposed Wilson's Federal Trade Commission, under which monopolies, in his view, would regulate their regulators. Would not the monopolies come to control members of the FTC? While T.R. wanted to regulate "good" monopolies and Wilson and his friend Louis Brandeis wanted to eliminate all private monopolies, Borah called for the elimination of all monopolies—public and private. He also opposed Tom Walsh's amendment to the Clayton Antitrust Act exempting labor unions from the Sherman Act. But he was joined by Norris in opposing the entire Clayton Act, which Norris called "a fraud and a sham" and "the greatest victory of a legislative nature that had been won by the trusts and combinations within the lifetime of any man here."[4]

On the issues of American neutrality and entry into World War I, George Norris became nationally famous. Borah strongly supported appropriations for naval preparedness in 1916 and was as loyal as any Democrat in voting for a declaration of war in April 1917.

But Norris and Senator Robert La Follette led the opposition to American entry into the war. At first, they organized a semifilibuster against the Armed-Ship Bill in March 1917. It provided for the arming of American merchant ships in the Atlantic. In the final hours of the Sixty-fourth Congress, Norris was the last to speak against the bill, taking the floor on Sunday morning, March 4.

A wave of patriotic sentiment had swept the country a few days earlier, on February 28, when the Wilson administration released the text of the Zimmermann note. It was a message from an official in the German foreign office to its minister to Mexico, proposing a German alliance with Mexico "to reconquer the lost territory in New Mexico, Texas, and Arizona." President Wilson had already severed diplomatic relations with Germany after it resumed unrestricted submarine warfare on February 1.

America was in a state of armed neutrality; and on March 1, a day after the release of the Zimmermann telegram, the House overwhelmingly approved the Armed-Ship Bill. Its approval by the Senate would effectively push the United States into war, Norris feared, because of its broad grant of authority to the president to protect American rights on the high seas, especially since the lame-duck Congress would not be in session after noontime, March 4, when Wilson would be sworn in for a second term. The newly elected Sixty-fifth Congress was not scheduled to convene until December 1917.

In his speech to the Senate, Norris criticized the vague wording: "Under this bill the President can do anything; his power is absolutely limitless. The Constitution says the Congress has sole power to declare war. This [bill] in effect is an amendment of the Constitution, an illegal amendment. We are abdicating, we are surrendering our authority."

Norris next had to calm Robert La Follette, who, as the noon deadline approached, was prevented from speaking by the Democratic leadership, who wanted to embarrass him since they knew that a special session of Congress was now necessary. Norris sat beside La Follette remarking: "For God's sake don't do anything now. We've won the fight."

But the fight raged on. Mr. Wilson, waiting in the President's Room outside the Senate and furious at having to call a special session of Congress, denounced the "little group of willful men, representing no opinion but their own," who "rendered the great Government of the United States helpless and contemptible." Norris was compared in the press to Benedict Arnold and Aaron Burr; and Teddy Roosevelt called the opposition of Norris and others "treason."[5]

During the next few weeks, Norris offered to submit to a special recall election, but the Democratic governor of Nebraska refused. On March 26, at a rented hall in Lincoln, with no prominent politician to introduce him, Norris spoke to an audience of more than three thousand: "I have come to Nebraska to tell you the truth. You have not been able to get the truth from the newspapers." After speaking for more than an hour, he was forced to continue by the cheering crowd. He denounced the Wall Street brokers who "sat behind mahogany desks, coldly calculating the time until war could be declared and every drop of blood spilled in the trench, every tear shed by the mothers at home, could be converted into gold for [their] filthy pockets." In tones reminiscent of William Jennings Bryan, he scolded the stockbrokers: "You shall not coin into gold the life blood of our brothers."

Norris returned to Washington and was appointed to the committee to escort President Wilson into the House chamber on the evening of April 2. The president then delivered his famous speech calling for American participation in the war to make the world safe for democracy. But Norris was unmoved and, on April 4, denounced "the great combination of wealth" that controlled the American press and had "a direct financial interest" in American involvement in the war. He also stressed that "if, notwithstanding my opposition, we do enter it, all of my energy and all of my power will be behind our flag carrying it to victory."[6]

Borah had supported the Armed-Ship Bill, though deploring the president's steamroller tactics, and voted for a declaration of war because it was "in the defense and for the protection of the rights of the American people." But on other controversial matters during the war, Borah joined the progressives—including Norris, Hiram Johnson, and La Follette, who was temporarily weakened by efforts to expel him from the Senate for "treasonous" remarks in a Wisconsin speech.

Borah's independence was strengthened by his quiet announcement on April 28, 1917, that he would quit public life at the end of his term on March 5, 1919. In a confidential letter to a friend, he expressed concern that many of the wartime measures were at odds with his fundamental convictions: "I am unwilling to Prussianize this country in order to de-Prussianize Germany."[7]

In the area of civil liberties and war profiteering, Borah and Norris were united. They supported a flat excess-profit tax of 73 percent on all earnings above average profits for the years 1911 to 1913 but only won approval of a graduated tax to a maximum of 60 percent.

Norris and Borah were two of the six senators to oppose the Espionage Act of 1917. Borah warned his colleagues that wartime measures do not suspend other provisions of the Constitution, such as the First Amendment. And Norris denounced the further curtailment of civil liberties under the Sedition Act of 1918, which gave the postmaster general carte blanche to censor the mails in secret. Even if the postmaster general never used the arbitrary power in the act, its very existence was "the great evil," noted Norris. And he wondered how the nation could trust a man like the incumbent, A.S. Burleson, who had made political appointments to postmasterships in violation of civil service regulations.[8]

Both men had to fight a tidal wave of patriotic hysteria that swept teachers from their jobs, discriminated against German-Americans, and muzzled politicians. Norris was shocked to discover two liberal senators, Republican William Kenyon of Iowa and Democrat Henry Hollis of New Hampshire, favored the expulsion of Robert La Follette from the Senate for a wartime speech. Addressing the Nonpartisan League's convention in St. Paul, Minnesota, on September 20, 1917, La Follette referred to the causes of the American entry into the war: "I don't mean to say that we hadn't suffered grievances; we had—at the hands of Germany." He then said the grievance was our right to ship munitions to Britain without being torpedoed by German submarines. The Associated Press reported that La Follette said the United States had *no* grievances against Germany.

The next day, flag-draped vigilantism against La Follette swept America. President Nicholas Murray Butler of Columbia University, who led the firing of progressive historian Charles Beard as a professor, told an audience of the American Bankers Association that "you might just as well put poison in the food of every American boy that goes to his transport as to permit La Follette to talk as he does." A judge in Houston called for La Follette's execution by firing squad. The Wisconsin senator defended America's right to free speech but in a subdued way, until the war ended and the Senate dismissed the charges against him.[9]

But domestic repression under Wilson would go much further than suppression of free speech. In his campaign to suppress bolshevism, Wilson's attorney general, A. Mitchell Palmer, in 1919 and 1920 rounded up and deported radicals and suppressed their meetings, frequently without warrants. The "Red scare" was a domestic reaction to America's sending thousands of soldiers after the armistice to aid the enemies of the governing Communist Party in civil-war-torn Russia. In February 1919, Senator Hiram Johnson's resolution demanding withdrawal of American troops from Russia failed by one vote in the Senate. Borah and Norris strongly supported the measure, and Norris even suggested that President Wilson be impeached for sending American troops there.[10]

Borah changed his mind about running in 1918 and was easily reelected to the Senate, as was Norris, despite his opposition to the war. And they played an important role in postwar politics. Contradictions in Wilson's Fourteen Points—regarding Bolshevik Russia for Borah and Japan and China for Norris—led both men to become "irreconcilables," in opposition to the Treaty of Versailles.

Borah argued in the Senate that the only justification for American intervention in Russia was the German military threat. Since it had ended,

American troops should remain in Russia "only as long as it will take to get them out." According to Borah, President Wilson had "modified" his policy of noninterference in Russian affairs—number six of his Fourteen Points, which called for the evacuation of foreign troops and the determination by the Russians of their own destiny. The new goal, in Borah's view, was to destroy the Bolshevik government rather than to help the Russian people. He wondered why so many politicians were upset at the "despotism" in Soviet Russia, while so few had been concerned about tsarist despotism. "I take the position," the Idahoan concluded, "that the Russian people have the same right to establish a socialistic state as we have to establish a Republic."[11]

Similarly, Norris criticized President Wilson's abandonment at Versailles of the cardinal doctrine of his Fourteen Points: "open covenants of peace, openly arrived at." Norris especially opposed Section 156 of the Treaty of Versailles, which provided for all rights, privileges, and possessions of Germany in China to be awarded to Japan: "It must be remembered that Germany had no right in China that any honest man was bound to respect. What rights she obtained there she obtained at the cannon's mouth because China was unable to defend herself." The Shandong Peninsula, the ancient burial ground of Confucius and home for 30 million Chinese, was to be controlled by "the last nation on earth that China would have selected to control her had she been given a voice in the decision of her own destiny."

As an irreconcilable, Norris was popular with numerous anti-imperialist ethnic groups. He joined the American Commission on Conditions in Ireland and spoke to the Friends of Freedom for India in New York. He examined conditions in Korea, Egypt, Ireland, and India and concluded that "the most enlightened nations of the world are now almost barbarous." Great Britain and Japan "were determined to rule the world, and have the erroneous idea that they can get the confidence of honest people by shooting down, murdering and flogging folks, and terrorize them into submission." In denouncing the Treaty of Versailles, he asserted that no reservation would do. Only one amendment was needed, "and that amendment is to strike the whole thing out."[12]

But the chief irreconcilable was Borah, who dominated the Senate from 1920 into the thirties. During the crucial bipartisan conference on the treaty in January 1920, Borah got word that Lodge was about to work out a compromise on Article X and the League of Nations. On January 23, Borah organized a group of Republican "bitter-enders," who had learned of the secret conference, and sent for Majority Leader Lodge. Meeting them, Lodge protested his attempt at compromise: "Can't I discuss this matter with my friends?" As he leaned against the wall, Lodge then remarked: "Well, I suppose I'll have to resign as majority leader." "No, by God!"

exploded Borah. "You won't have a chance to resign! On Monday, I'll move for the election of a new majority leader and give the reasons for my action."

After a prolonged meeting, Lodge agreed to make no further concessions. And in a few days, the bipartisan conference broke down, and the irreconcilables doomed the treaty. Undoubtedly, Borah's account of his killing the treaty improved with each telling, especially by 1937, when he recounted it to Professor Thomas Bailey. But the story illustrates Borah's leadership role in the Senate.[13]

Both Norris and Borah were appalled at the corrupting role of money in American elections; and in 1922, they opposed the seating of Truman H. Newberry as a Republican senator from Michigan. He was accused of outbidding Henry Ford in purchasing the Republican nomination. Norris remarked: "They had a public sale up in Michigan . . . on . . . a seat in the United States Senate. The sale was public, the bidding was in the open, and the property was knocked down to the highest bidder." With the fall of Rome in mind, Borah mused: "We have traveled further over the road of money in politics in 100 years than Rome traveled in 500 years."[14]

Borah succeeded Lodge as chair of the Foreign Relations Committee in 1924 and became the second most prominent Republican in the country. He was wholly untarnished by the corruption of the Warren G. Harding administration. After pushing the Republican Party into opposition to the Treaty of Versailles, he only nominally supported Harding's campaign. Shortly before the Republican National Convention in 1924, President Calvin Coolidge desperately had the Secret Service search Washington for Senator Borah. When they finally found the Idahoan horseback riding in Rock Creek Park, they escorted him to the White House. There, President Coolidge greeted him: "We want you on the ticket." And Borah supposedly replied: "Which place, Mr. President?" to be sure he was not nominated for vice president.

Through the twenties, though Congress might recess, Borah was "always in session," complained Coolidge. The senator held a daily press conference. "Shortly after three o'clock each afternoon, all press trails lead to the office of Senator Borah," the *Christian Science Monitor* reported. In 1928, Borah was seriously promoted by friends for the presidency, but instead, he played the "Warwick role" in nominating the progressive secretary of commerce, Herbert Hoover, with whom he especially saw eye to eye on foreign affairs. The powerful senator was a rumored candidate for secretary of state.[15]

Borah was the charismatic leader, Norris his chief sidekick, of the handful of western progressives of both parties whom Senator George Moses of New Hampshire called "sons of the Wild Jackass." As one reporter put it, they had been "riding the Senate bareback for a decade." Borah, backed by Norris, had strongly supported diplomatic recognition of the Soviet Union, and both condemned Coolidge's landing of the marines in Nicaragua to protect American property.[16]

Norris, however, saw the constitutional implications more clearly when he supported an amendment by Senator John J. Blaine of Wisconsin to cut off funds for the 5,000 marines in Nicaragua. If Congress silently approved, said Norris, "the power of declaring war . . . will be entirely taken away by the executive." Borah opposed the Blaine amendment, and it was defeated. Despite an occasional imperial transgression by the presidency, during the twenties and early thirties the Senate was steering foreign policy.[17]

Borah became a major world figure with his efforts to outlaw war. After pressure from wealthy Chicago lawyer Salmon Levinson and the American Committee for the Outlawry of War, the reluctant Borah introduced his first resolution in 1923. It resolved that war between nations "should be outlawed . . . by making it a public crime under the law of nations, and that every nation should be encouraged by solemn agreement or treaty to bind itself to indict and punish its own international war breeders or instigators and war profiteers." Borah refused to support any peace plan to be implemented by force, and he won the support of such practical men as John Dewey.

In 1927, the French foreign minister, Aristide Briand, proposed a joint Franco-American treaty outlawing war between the two countries or at least assuring benevolent neutrality. When Secretary of State Frank Kellogg testified on the matter before the Senate Foreign Relations Committee, Chairman Borah interjected: "But, Mr. Secretary, the American counterproposal should be a pact to outlaw war between all nations of the world. We should point out that this is too important to confine only to this country and France." And then Senator George Moses grumbled: "That's the best way to get rid of the damned thing. Put the baby on their [France's] doorstep. Extend it to all nations. France would never consent to outlaw war with Germany."

In an article, Borah suggested that France could honor her Continental alliances and also sign a multipower antiwar pact. If, for example, Germany violated the pact, France would be released from the treaty and could proceed to aid, say, Belgium as part of a Franco-Belgian pact.

On August 27, 1928, in the Hall of Mirrors at Versailles, the Kellogg–Briand Pact was signed by fourteen countries. It eventually had sixty-two signatories and was to be implemented by moral force. Senator James Reed cast history's verdict on the pact when he called it an "international kiss." According to critics like Walter Lippmann, Borah failed to follow up on the treaty by providing the international judicial machinery needed.

Borah assisted in the establishment of the Borah Foundation for the Outlawry of War in Moscow, Idaho, in 1931, at whose dedication he denounced the Japanese invasion of Manchuria as a violation of the pact. But the only action he proposed was the withdrawal of Americans from China to prevent any provocation of Japan—an early form of appeasement.

The proud Idahoan increasingly revealed his capricious, unpliable side. He was what the father of outlawry, Salmon Levinson, called "a law unto himself." And although he commanded a dominant, and sometimes crucial, role in the Senate throughout the thirties, the era of the depression and rising militarism was not suited to his role as the "Great Opposer." His states' rights progressivism appeared reactionary to champions of the New Deal, though he supported most of the early New Deal legislation. Borah's career spanned the decline of the Senate oligarchy, as the depression but especially international crises contributed to the rise of the imperial presidency.[18]

George Norris, on the other hand, had always been more flexible, independent, and progressive than Borah. He supported T.R.'s Bull Moose candidacy in 1912 and bolted the Republican Party in 1928 to support Democrat Al Smith. The thirties, his fourth decade in Congress, were suited for Norris's persistently creative talents. He was a link between the old western progressives and the eastern New Deal liberals. And Franklin Roosevelt called him "the very perfect, gentle knight of American progressive ideals." As a virtual independent by 1932, Norris, the nominal Republican, became one of the strongest supporters of FDR's policies.[19]

Both Norris and Borah were outspoken in their attacks on monopolies. But Norris became more hated on Wall Street than even FDR after he delivered his "Spider Web of Wall Street" speech to the Senate in the final days of the Hoover administration. Pointing to an eight-foot-square chart, Norris said that it did not come close to showing all the corporations under Wall Street's control. "Instead of 120 major corporations shown here, there would be thousands." Each of the eight legs of the huge black spider represented a major banking firm, and a web of lines connected the eight with 120 major corporations, through interlocking directorates. Each line signified that the corporation and the bank had at least one director in common. These great bankers could control "practically any corporation of any size in the United States." But the banking houses, especially the House of Morgan, held "a position of absolute dominance in the power business."[20]

On the issue of public power, George Norris became famous. Almost single-handedly, he got Congress to support government ownership in the Muscle Shoals controversy. With the completion of the Wilson Dam in 1925 at the Muscle Shoals Rapids on the Tennessee River, the War Department had about 160,000 horsepower continually available for sale. With additional construction, Norris claimed that more than 300,000 horsepower could be available for the people of the South. He wanted to develop the Tennessee River and its tributaries as a unit, with power and storage dams for electricity and flood control. A new dam at Cove Creek, 250 miles from Muscle Shoals, was also needed. In the Senate debate of 1928, Norris acted as floor leader for his bill: "The Government owns Muscle Shoals now, it operates it now and the question is, Shall we turn it over to private monopoly or shall we keep it for all the people?" But President Coolidge pocket vetoed the bill.

Through Herbert Hoover's adminisration, Norris continued to hold off the leasing of Muscle Shoals electricity to private power interests. When Congress approved essentially the same bill in 1931, President Hoover issued a "blistering" veto message: "This is not liberalism, it is degeneration." Norris realized the issue could only be solved if the Democrats nominated the right man for president in 1932. He wrote in August 1932 that "if Roosevelt is elected it will undoubtedly be passed as soon as he is inaugurated and will no doubt be signed by him."[21]

On May 18, 1933, seventy-five days after his inauguration, President Franklin Roosevelt signed the Norris–Hill Bill into law. George Norris successfully fought off crippling amendments, especially in the House, and the Tennessee Valley Authority (TVA) was established, eleven years' after Norris introduced the first Muscle Shoals Bill in 1922. On August 1, 1933, the TVA Board of Directors announced that the projected Cove Creek Dam would be named the "Norris Dam."

During the thirties, the contrasts between Norris and Borah became more evident. When Norris celebrated his seventieth birthday in 1931, Borah was sixty-six. Norris bore "the simple, homely air of 'plain folk.' " Borah was always on stage and, like Daniel Webster, deserved the description "Godlike"—his "leonine head with a majestic mane." The Godlike William was also a great orator with an unsurpassed ability to arouse public opinion. But he did not have the temperament for routine committee work, and he often failed to follow through on his projects. Though he never resorted to personal attacks, his unpredictability gave him the appearance of shooting from the hip. Norris once joked: "Borah always shoots until he sees the whites of their eyes."[22]

Norris not only emerged as the leader of congressional liberals after the death of Robert La Follette in 1925 but, unlike Borah, he worked hard at the "nitty-gritty" of legislation. He introduced in 1924 the Norris–Sinclair Bill, the predecessor of the McNary–Haugen plan for the federal government purchase and sale of farm surpluses. He also joined another "son of the Wild Jackass," Tom Walsh, in braving the wrath of the utility companies. With the support of Walsh and Robert Wagner of New York, Norris was the author of the Norris–La Guardia Anti-injunction Act of 1932, which supported the right of labor to organize and bargain collectively, forbade the enforcement of "yellow-dog" contracts, and limited the use of injunctions in labor disputes.

The Nebraskan was almost solely responsible for the Twentieth Amendment to the Constitution, the "lame-duck" amendment. He had taken advantage of the constitutional anomaly in filibustering an end to the Armed-Ship Bill in 1917. The amendment shifted the date of presidential inaugurations from March 4 to January 20 and abolished the "lame-duck" session of the outgoing Congress, formerly held between the November election and the presidential inauguration.[23]

Norris supported FDR's 1932 and 1936 campaigns, whereas Borah nominally remained a Republican and even campaigned for the party's nomination in 1936. Though overwhelmed by Governor Alf Landon of Kansas, Borah succeeded in pushing the Republican platform to the left in an anti-monopoly stance. Like Norris, he supported most of the New Deal legislation—including the Securities and Exchange Commission, Social Security, the Wagner Labor Relations Act, and the Wealth Tax Act—and even broke with his party in supporting increased relief spending in 1938.

But Borah became the leading senatorial critic of the National Recovery Act (NRA). No other legislator exposed FDR's failure to control big business as effectively as Borah. He maintained that the NRA protected any kind of monopoly, destroyed the independents in industry, and provided the president with the information to propose laws, which only Congress had the power to make. The permissive business codes, under the umbrella of increased presidential power, he argued, could be used in price-fixing conspiracies against the consumer. The NRA, also, was an example of the way the New Deal enhanced the power of the executive at the expense of the legislature. Borah's fears were justified: the imperial presidency, with an accompanying corporatism, was beginning to take shape.

Borah was also more outspoken than Norris on the Agricultural Adjustment Administration (AAA) and Secretary of Agriculture Henry Wallace's policies. Norris made few complaints because Nebraska's farmers generally benefited from the AAA. But Borah warned that, though the AAA might have some virtues, it offered no permanent solution for the farmers. And he found the policy of crop destruction appalling while millions were starving.[24]

The two senators especially disagreed on FDR's so-called Supreme

Court packing bill of 1937. Senator Borah was the first to challenge the president, when on May 31, 1935, Roosevelt told a press conference that the Supreme Court's decision holding the NRA unconstitutional took the country back to "horse and buggy" days. When FDR soon threatened to "pack" the Court, Borah told a radio audience that the president had enough power under the Constitution without infringing upon the powers of the courts. But the issue came to a head after FDR's electoral landslide of 1936 when the Supreme Court ruled as unconstitutional the AAA, the Guffey Coal Act, and the New York Minimum Wage Law. On February 5, 1937, President Roosevelt submitted a bill to reorganize the federal judiciary. It gave the president the authority to appoint one judge to the Supreme Court and inferior courts for every justice over the age of seventy who refused to resign or retire within six months. Under the bill, membership of the current Supreme Court would be increased from nine to fifteen justices.

Norris had long desired to curb the power of the Supreme Court. In 1935, he suggested to FDR an amendment preventing a bare majority on the Supreme Court from ruling a law passed by Congress unconstitutional. Norris wanted a four-fifths majority of the Court. In 1936, after the high court ruled the AAA's processing tax unconstitutional by a 6 to 3 vote, Norris commented: "The People Can Change the Congress, but Only God Can Change the Supreme Court." He concluded that the Court, "for all practical purposes, is a continuous constitutional convention." The senator reluctantly endorsed the president's proposal as constitutional but thought it only a temporary measure. He worried that under FDR's plan, for example, there could still be decisions by an 8 to 7 vote. Norris favored two constitutional amendments: one calling for a set term of office for judges and another permitting Congress to override a "veto" of the Supreme Court.

Roosevelt's packing plan went nowhere because Congress objected to this imperial power play by the president. Progressive Republican Senator Hiram Johnson, who had supported FDR's reelection in 1936, expressed concern about his landslide victory: "There will be nobody to stop him, and but few to protest. All sorts of experiments we may see, some of which will give us the cold shivers." Johnson also worried that Norris was "so infatuated with his TVA . . . that he regards Roosevelt as a god."

But overconfident political gods can on occasion be defeated by determined political mortals. A progressive liaison of Borah, for the Republicans, and Senator Burton Wheeler, Tom Walsh's associate, for the Democrats, organized FDR's first major legislative defeat. A sudden change in the Supreme Court's outlook also helped, as it upheld as constitutional the Railway Labor Act, the Frazier–Lemke Farm Mortgage Moratorium Act, the Wagner–Connery Labor Relations Act, and the Social

Security Act. But the president's strategy paid off when the elderly Justice Willis Van Devanter retired in August 1937 and FDR nominated in his place Senator Hugo Black of Alabama, "a worthy representative of the people," in Norris's words, despite Black's earlier, brief membership in the Ku Klux Klan.[25]

Toward the issue of civil rights for African Americans, both Borah and Norris turned a morally blind eye. They joined most of white America in benign neglect, if not active discrimination against "Negroes." And Borah's opposition to the Wagner–Costigan Antilynching Bill succeeded in preventing cloture of a southern filibuster in 1935.

With the depression, the rise in southern white lynchings of blacks increased to more than one per month in the early thirties. Some were even held in a gruesome, carnival-like atmosphere with the victim brutally mutilated and burned. Yet FDR told Walter White, head of the NAACP, in May 1935, when he came to the White House at Eleanor Roosevelt's invitation: "If I come out for the antilynching bill now, they [southern Democratic committee chairmen] will block every bill I ask Congress to pass to keep America from collapsing."[26]

Borah and Norris were not bigots. Borah's apologists pointed out that, as a young lawyer in 1903, he had prevented the lynching of two blacks in Nampa, Idaho. And Norris appointed one black out of the three Senate staff appointments he made in 1928. But both men had little understanding of the plight of African Americans when even the black Americans' perhaps greatest white friend, Eleanor Roosevelt, reverted to the imprinted childhood prejudices of her great-aunt from Georgia who reared her, when the adult Eleanor used the terms *darky* and *pickaninny* in her autobiography.[27]

Norris and FDR worried about the constitutionality of the antilynching bill. After all, the states were supposed to guarantee the most fundamental human right, life itself. And Borah, in opposing southern cloture, said he would support any constitutional measure to end lynching but added: "If the states cannot enforce law, who can?"

Borah claimed to believe in social reform and states' rights. So he favored woman suffrage if granted by a state but voted against the Nineteenth Amendment granting woman suffrage.[28] He was against lynching but opposed to the antilynching bill. The only exception was his support of Prohibition and the Eighteenth Amendment because he said that interstate commerce made local-option prohibition impossible to enforce.[29]

As late as 1938, Norris opposed Senator Robert Wagner's antilynching bill as "unconstitutional." The not-so-virtuous Nebraskan claimed that winning enough votes for cloture against a southern Democratic filibuster was impossible. But this time a private letter, chastising the father of the TVA, came from Walter White of the NAACP: "But what, my dear Senator Norris, is the worth to a man of an electrically lighted home if he can be taken from that home as easily as from a cabin lighted by candles, and burned to death by a howling mob?" White and Norris continued corresponding and generally saw eye to eye, such as on confirming Senator Hugo Black for the Supreme Court.[30]

But American entry into World War II began to unravel segregation in American society. Despite the increased militancy of the NAACP, the Senate remained a bastion of racism and segregation. George Norris, however, ended his career as a "fighting liberal." He launched a battle in 1942 that placed him in the forefront of civil rights leaders. How could the United States fight against Hitler and fascism abroad and not move toward broader equality at home, he wondered. Norris organized a campaign to abolish the poll tax in federal elections, despite the opposition of many southern admirers. Senator Tom Connally of Texas said he did not think "in his closing days the Senator should stab in the back those who have been voting with him on liberal legislation."

At first, Norris was the only member of a Judiciary Subcommittee to vote for an anti-poll-tax bill. Since the House had voted for the Geyer–Pepper Bill overwhelmingly and the Senate had unanimously favored the abolition of the poll tax for men in the military service, Norris thought the bill would have a good chance if it got to the floor of the Senate. He drafted an elaborate report, aided by the bill's cosponsor, Senator Claude Pepper of Florida. And the Judiciary Committee accepted his report by a 13 to 5 majority vote.

The fighting liberal quoted Senator Carter Glass's remarks in 1902 as a member of the Virginia Constitutional Convention. Glass, who drafted the Virginia poll-tax bill that year, said its purpose was to disfranchise "146,000 ignorant Negro voters." When Norris's anti-poll-tax bill reached the Senate floor, one reporter wrote that it threatened "to extend democracy to 10,000,000 voteless Southern Citizens."

Norris's views on democracy and equality had been evolving. In August 1929, at the unveiling of a statue of Abe Lincoln in Freeport, Illinois, he equated economic and racial slavery: "What doth it profit if we strike the chains of slavery from the black man and permit monopoly to forge the same chains upon millions of our own race?" In 1942, at the end of his career, he challenged wartime America to live up to the ideals for which white and black Americans were fighting. But he could not win the necessary two-thirds vote for cloture against the southern filibuster. Only after the war and the emergence of Martin Luther King and the civil rights movement did Congress approve in 1962 the anti-poll-tax amendment in federal elections, which was ratified in 1964 as the Twenty-fourth Amendment to the Constitution.[31]

History proved to be much kinder to the energetic Norris than to the grandiloquent Borah, largely because of the horrendous cataclysm of World War II, which William Borah did not live to see. Norris was probably the only prominent American to be "right" on both world wars. He opposed American entry into World War I, and he understood Hitler's threat to the world in the 1930s.

Like so many of the western progressives, Borah suffered from isolationist myopia. He was not anti-Semitic: when he advised President Hoover to appoint Benjamin Cardozo to the Supreme Court and was told that the president was advised that there should not be two Jews (Brandeis was the other) on the Court, Borah replied: "Anyone who raises the question of race is unfit to advise you concerning so important a matter." Though he deplored the Nazi persecution of the Jews, he opposed any change in immigration laws to give Jewish refugees asylum in the United States because of the "hundreds of thousands" of hungry and unemployed American citizens. He also opposed the various extensions of the Neutrality Act of 1935, especially the cash-and-carry provision. Another isolationist, Senator Arthur Vandenberg, called this policy the "doctrine of transferred risk," because it made the United States the ally of the nation with the largest navy, the United Kingdom.

Even FDR's administration did little to protest Hitler's aggression in rearming Germany, reoccupying the Rhineland, and persecuting the Jews. Finally, on October 5, 1937, President Roosevelt publicly urged a "quarantining" of aggressors to ensure peace; but Senators Borah, Wheeler, and Gerald Nye denounced him as a "warmonger."[32]

Simultaneously, George Norris drastically modified his views. He strongly supported an increase in the size of the American navy, and it was Japanese aggression that led to his change of mind. The undeclared Sino-Japanese war, beginning in July 1937, and Japan's "barbarous" conduct in China, together with the sinking of the USS *Panay* by Japanese planes, demonstrated to Norris "that Japan is an outlaw nation, with no regard for justice or her duty to humanity." He also denounced the alliance among Japan, Italy, and Germany as an agreement to "help one another in their efforts to destoy the civilization of the world."[33]

By the spring of 1938, Borah singled out as "sensible" the views of Joseph P. Kennedy, ambassador to the Court of St. James. Kennedy wrote Borah from London: "The more I see of things here, the more convinced I am that we must exert all of our intelligence and effort toward keeping clear of any involvement." Borah blamed Britain for the dismemberment of Czechoslovakia. It would not have been such a cold-blooded betrayal if the United Kingdom had been frank with the small republic, he thought. But England selfishly hoped to protect herself by encouraging Hitler's drive eastward: "The Munich Pact makes the violation of treaties a cardinal tenet of modern diplomacy[,] . . . makes the mere name of treaty a byword and a kissing."

In late 1938, Borah was planning to visit Herr Adolph Hitler at his invitation. The senator also opposed President Roosevelt's request to repeal the arms embargo, in the debate on the Neutrality Act in early 1939. But when the president declared at a press conference, "Our frontier is on the Rhine," Borah knew his trip had to be canceled. Even after Nazi troops entered Prague in March 1939, Borah declared: "If Hitler is as wise as I believe him to be, he has no designs whatsoever on France." *Mirabile dictu!* Yet Borah did realize that Hitler by 1939 was more powerful than Napoleon in 1812 and worried that the *führer* would be corrupted by power.[34]

Unfortunately for the memory of William Borah, he coined his most famous phrase in a press conference after the German invasion of Poland, September 1, 1939, when Britain and France declared war. He accused the United Kingdom and France of "pulling their punches" on the western front because, "having discharged their duty to Poland," they could still negotiate terms with Germany. "There is something phony about this war," he said. One would think Britain and France "would do what they are going to do while Germany and Russia are still busy in the East, instead of waiting until they have cleaned up . . . there." With his "phony war" theme, Borah even believed that "the chances are increased for peace."[35]

In the last few months of his life, Borah hoped to keep America out of the European "slaughter pen" and opposed any effort to lift the arms embargo. During the seven months of the "phony war" between the fall of Poland and the invasion of Belgium and Holland, Borah died, on January 19, 1940. The sincere idealist was spared democracy's commitment to the ruthless realism of Winston Churchill, in order to combat the greatest barbarism humanity had yet witnessed. "Saint Borah," as Harold Ickes called him, remained consistent until the end. Borah remarked in 1922: "I do claim that I shall leave this post of service without ever having compromised upon a single fundamental political belief which I entertain." But was his hubris compromising a higher moral principle in this "good war"?[36]

Norris, perhaps a gentler idealist, was also more of a pragmatist. He attributed Neville Chamberlain's "disgraceful surrender" at Munich to the *Luftwaffe*'s control of the air. So Norris supported continued revision of the neutrality law. When FDR called a special session of Congress during the fateful month of September 1939, Norris became the chief spokesman for the president's proposed revision of the neutrality law, which would lift the arms embargo for the "Allies" on a cash-and-carry basis. The *Portland Oregonian,* in an editorial, remarked that "if the neutrality law is changed by this Congress to omit the arms embargo, it would not be surprising if future historians should credit the victory more to Senator Norris of Nebraska than to Mr. Roosevelt himself." Norris argued that "absolute neutrality is an impossibility," given the present world situation, and that failure to repeal the embargo would be helping the Axis powers. With Senators Borah, Nye, and Vandenberg opposing, the Senate revised the Neutrality Act by a 63 to 30 vote.[37]

Although increasingly concerned with an imminent world war, Norris, champion of free speech during World War I, continued to be a watchdog for civil liberties. In 1940, he was particularly outspoken about J. Edgar Hoover's "disgraceful and indefensible" use of the FBI to arrest and harass veterans of the Abraham Lincoln Brigade, who had fought for the loyalists in the Spanish Civil War. These "premature anti-Fascists," J. Edgar Hoover thought, were the same as communists. With the memory of Hoover's conduct during the Red scare of 1919, Norris denounced Attorney General Robert Jackson's "whitewashing" investigation of the matter, even though the soon-to-be Mr. Justice Jackson of the Supreme Court, who would later be chief prosecutor at the Nuremburg trials, was one of Norris's closest friends.

Norris, who had served for eight years as a Nebraska judge, at various times during the New Deal was mentioned for the Supreme Court, to which he once advocated the appointment of a "philosopher, instead of a lawyer." He had the mind of a great judge as he worried in a speech to the Senate on the eve of the nation's entry into World War II that "wrong" methods used by the FBI could "mean the destruction of human liberty in the United States." The war and its aftermath would challenge American civil liberties as seldom before.

Norris finally went down to defeat in November 1942, running as an independent in a three-way race and losing to Republican Kenneth Wherry. The Republican establishment finally got its revenge on the man who had become one of the strongest advocates of the New Deal. Even in 1957, years after his death, Republicans prevented the turncoat from being honored as one of the five "outstanding" senators, whose portraits would hang in the Senate reception room. Though Norris led in the votes of a panel of scholars, receiving 87 votes to 86 for runner-up Henry Clay, *Life* magazine claimed Norris's nomination was blocked by, among others, Nebraska's Senator Roman Hruska, who had nominated Kenneth Wherry as an "outstanding" senator. By an ironic twist of fate, Hruska in 1970 helped to kill President Richard M. Nixon's nomination of G.H. Carswell to the Supreme Court by publicly admitting that although Carswell was a mediocrity, the millions of mediocre Americans deserve a representative on the high court.[38]

George Norris died at McCook, Nebraska, on September 2, 1944, as the American army was fighting its way into Germany. During the almost two years after he left the Senate, he was, in the words of another progressive Republican, Mayor Fiorello La Guardia of New York, "the Senator at large of the whole American people." Norris was a frequent university lecturer, usually discussing topics concerning the postwar world, such as "Peace without Hate." Eleanor Roosevelt grieved at the time of his defeat because his reputation for "integrity and courage" gave "youth a belief in its own idealism." Though he served in Congress for forty years and was a man of limited means, he refused to take a congressional pension.

During his final years, Norris did not lose his sense of outrage. When William Witherow, president of the National Association of Manufacturers, asserted that the United States was not fighting the war to give milk to Hottentot babies or to build a TVA on the Danube, Norris was quick to reply at a testimonial dinner. Norris called Witherow's remarks "shallow minded" and reminded his audience that if World War II was only being fought "that the selfish idea of wealth will prevail," then "we shall have fought this war in vain."[39]

Without the massive Websterlike appearance and cocksure philosophy of Borah, George W. Norris acted upon a strong democratic faith generally with humility, though some of his critics would agree with Republican Senator Peter Norbeck that Norris was "just the material that martyrs are made of. He would dearly love to be a martyr, but he would want a very good stage setting, or it would not be worth while." When asked on Lincoln's birthday in 1936 whether Abe Lincoln would support the New Deal if he were alive, Norris replied: "Lincoln would be just like me. He wouldn't know what the hell to do." But George Norris almost always did know.[40]

IV

The Imperial Presidency
and the Supine Senate (1940–1990)

As the Watergate crisis was escalating, Arthur M. Schlesinger Jr. in 1973 coined the phrase "imperial presidency," which was popularly used to describe the constitutional depredations of the Richard M. Nixon presidency. But his book appeared to have been inspired not only by the "ominous" latter days of Nixon but also the trauma of Vietnam, or the "presidency rampant." In a 1989 epilogue, Schlesinger quoted Alexis de Tocqueville from a century and one-half earlier: "It is chiefly in its foreign relations that the executive power of a nation finds occasion to exert its skill and its strength. If the existence of the American Union were perpetually threatened, if its chief interests were in daily connection with those of other powerful nations, the executive would assume an increased importance." The quotation was especially relevant to the Civil War, World War II, and Cold War eras.[1]

The power of the Senate had increased not only under its oligarchy from Nelson Aldrich to Henry Cabot Lodge but even under populists such as William E. Borah, as times demanded during the twenties and thirties. Franklin Roosevelt trod very carefully in international waters during his first two terms, though the depression enhanced his personal power. But the outbreak of World War II dramatically changed everything, as Tocqueville predicted. Washington became the "capital of the free world" as its "very look" was transformed, though the transition to an imperial presidency and a supine Senate was almost imperceptible.[2]

The major battle in the Senate during the forties was waged among Republicans as the Democrats generally followed their presidents, and the chief combatants were two former isolationists from neighboring states,

Bob Taft of Ohio and Arthur Vandenberg of Michigan. As most of his isolationist allies were snuffed out politically during or shortly after the war, Vandenberg's conversion to internationalism in 1945 arguably came from self-interest.

Vandenberg would call for a nonpartisan, which became a bipartisan, foreign policy in dealing with postwar Europe and the Middle East. With a Republican victory in the Senate elections of 1946, he became chair of the Senate Foreign Relations Committee and president pro tempore when the office of vice president was vacant. In effect, he also served as a kind of second secretary of state from 1945 to 1949, anticipating virtually every move of the Harry S. Truman administration in foreign policy.

The Vandenberg Resolution in 1948 became a "sense of the Senate" basis for American participation in mutual defense pacts under the auspices of the United Nations General Assembly, where the Soviet Union could not cast a veto. The resolution was also the foundation document of the North Atlantic Treaty Organization (NATO), which Vandenberg fathered and for which he won Senate approval in 1949. He carried a majority of Republicans with him, but not Taft.

Taft had a free hand in shaping Republican domestic policy in opposition to what he considered to be the excesses of the New Deal continued by President Truman. And Vandenberg supported him in this. But the two men split on American commitment to arms for NATO, as Taft worried whether massive American armaments in Europe were the best way to stop the advance of communism. What about the cost and the effect on the American economy? What about the deterrent effect of nuclear weapons? But Taft's presidential campaigns weakened his position in the Senate, and he lost to candidates of the eastern internationalist establishment, Thomas E. Dewey and Dwight D. Eisenhower, who were committed to Vandenberg's foreign policy views.

By the outbreak of the Korean War in 1950, Vandenberg's fear of a "chain reaction" of communist revolutions from the Dardanelles to the China Sea had been realized. With the loss of China, the Soviet detonation of a nuclear bomb, and sensational revelations about Soviet spies, anticommunist paranoia swept the country and was intensified by McCarthyism. Vandenberg's concept of mutual defense and collective security was stretched to include virtually the entire planet, and even Taft was caught up in the tidal wave of patriotism. Vandenberg's policies paved the way for the presidency of General Eisenhower, who defeated Taft in 1952.

The "imperial presidency" grew in strength from the 1950s through the 1980s, though not without some setbacks, such as the Vietnam War and

Watergate. But the domestic scene also demanded a strong presidency when a bus boycott by poor blacks in Montgomery, Alabama, almost led to a second civil war. The civil rights acts were pushed through the Senate by the passive resistance tactics of southern blacks, led by Dr. Martin Luther King Jr.; but their passage was also aided by the power of an "imperial president" in the aftermath of the assassination of his predecessor. Lyndon B. Johnson used the foreign menace of communism to unite the country at home. But his abuse of power in Vietnam destroyed his presidency and undermined his Great Society reforms.

Two figures stand out in the era of the supine Senate, Hubert Humphrey and Strom Thurmond. Humphrey inspired many of the programs of the New Frontier and Great Society, from the Peace Corps to fair housing, and was one of the strongest white advocates of civil rights. But his desire to be president was overweening, as he became a political insider in 1961 after his defeat by John F. Kennedy. Always anxious to please, Humphrey was manipulated by Lyndon Johnson as his vice president and politically ruined by him. The pathetic fate of Humphrey was that of most Kennedy–Johnson liberal Democrats, who supported the military buildup in Vietnam under Johnson's guise of a Great Society for Southeast Asia that would even include a "TVA" (Tennessee Valley Authority) on the Mekong River. Not even the gimmicky interregnum of Jimmy Carter could save the Great Society.

The year 1968 was a turning point in modern American history. Humphrey was nominated by a splintered Democratic Party, but Nixon was elected by a white backlash to integration and to programs of the Great Society. The architect of Nixon's electoral strategy was Senator Strom Thurmond of South Carolina. Although it was successful in 1968, it was even more so in 1972 with Governor George Wallace out of the race. Thurmond laid out his law-and-order, patriotic, anti–big government beliefs in his 1964 address to South Carolinians that announced his conversion from Democrat to Republican and his endorsement of Senator Barry Goldwater for president. This speech, in effect, became the foundation document for Republican presidential victories not only in 1968 and 1972 but also in 1980, 1984, and 1988. Thurmond helped to bring the old and new South into the Republican Party just as population and electoral votes were moving from a Northeast power base to a South–Southwest Republican stronghold. Thurmond's values united white southerners with white suburbanites. As he gradually accepted integration and became the first southern senator to hire a black for his staff, he increasingly talked about law and order and pushed the missile and military buildup, which greatly aided the southern and southwestern economy. His laissez-faire views also led him to support

Reaganomics and to encourage a rise in mergers. Thurmond understood the power structure of an imperial presidency.

Such an imperialistic age, with its emphasis on secrecy and national security, inevitably produced an age of hubris, accompanied by a "culture of narcissism," a generation of yuppies, and a supine Senate. Examples of hubris abound, from the Kennedys' manipulation of the media in publishing *Profiles in Courage* to the conduct of Senators Fulbright and Mike Mansfield on Vietnam. But there were still examples of courage or virtuous fortitude, such as Wayne Morse's opposition to the Gulf of Tonkin resolution and Sam Ervin's conduct during the Watergate crisis.

In the words of a student of virtue among the Founding Fathers, Ralph Ketcham, we are still, like Jefferson, trying "to accommodate the relatively new principle of government by consent to the ancient principle of respecting only governments that cultivated virtue, or, what is the same thing, resisted partial, self-interested views." But Jefferson also knew that a democracy cannot expect to have a virtuous Senate represent a nation that does not encourage the habits of virtue. A study of democracy and liberty, written a century ago, might well have been observing the United States over the past greedy decade. "It is an evil omen for the future of a nation," W.E.H. Lecky wrote, when men of "colossal fortunes" but questionable character become objects of admiration.[3]

8

Shaping Pax Americana

Robert A. Taft vs. Arthur H. Vandenberg (1940–1950)

The nation's attention focused on San Francisco airport for the arrival of the *Bataan,* the plane carrying General Douglas MacArthur home from Korea on April 18, 1951, while across the country in his hometown of Grand Rapids, Michigan, Arthur Hendrick Vandenberg lay dying of cancer. The following day, while the obituary pages paid tribute to the Michigan senator, that "old soldier" did not fade away but mesmerized the country in a nationally televised address to a joint meeting of Congress. The death of Senator Vandenberg coincided with President Harry Truman's firing of MacArthur as commander of U.N. forces and the firestorm of criticism that followed. With three out of four Americans opposing the president's action, the Republican senator's death appeared to symbolize the end of the bipartisan foreign policy he had championed. Both parties had begun to compete with each other in the rush to the patriotic Right.[1]

Yet a deep division remained within the Republican Party. Vandenberg, who had supported MacArthur for the presidency in 1944, became a staunch internationalist after the war and supported the eastern wing of the party. His principal rival was "Mr. Republican" of the Senate, Robert A. Taft of Ohio (son of former President William Howard Taft), who was skeptical of wealthy easterners and their Europe-first attitude. Ironically, while losing the Republican presidential nomination to the candidate of the eastern establishment in 1952, Dwight D. Eisenhower, Taft unwittingly won the verbal battle on foreign policy issues, as they were both swept along in the tidal wave of McCarthyism.

As early as 1942, Taft predicted a "real battle on the character of the peace to be sought" and "a direct fight for control of the [Republican] party machinery": "I believe it would be fatal to the future of the Party if [Wendell] Willkie and [Henry] Luce[,] . . . together with the wealthy crowd in the East, succeed in their aim." As a good nationalist with a dash of isolationism, he attacked the idealism of Willkie and Franklin D. Roosevelt (FDR). Taft opposed the establishment of an "international WPA [Works Progress Administration]" and "a policing of the entire world by the Anglo-Saxon race." But in the flush of the great Allied victory in 1945, Taftite isolationism was made to seem unpatriotic by the Democrats.[2]

Born in Grand Rapids in 1884, Vandenberg was five years older than Taft. After attending the University of Michigan but not graduating, Vandenberg edited the *Grand Rapids Herald* for more than twenty years. On June 30, 1913, he delivered an impressive speech upon the presentation of the statue of Senator Zachariah Chandler from the state of Michigan to the "National Hall of Fame" in the U.S. Capitol. When congratulated for his eloquence by Vice President Thomas R. Marshall, Vandenberg expressed the hope to make such a speech in the Senate, representing Michigan. His desire was fulfilled when he was at first appointed and then elected to the Senate in 1928, where he became one of the leading isolationists during most of FDR's presidency, though he preferred the word *insulationist*.

A member of the Senate Foreign Relations Committee for twenty-three years, Vandenberg remained in the isolationist camp for the first fifteen. He cosponsored with Gerald P. Nye of North Dakota in 1934 the resolution establishing the committee to investigate the munitions industry. Unlike western progressives, Vandenberg opposed most New Deal measures. But he was especially active in foreign policy, supporting the Neutrality Acts but opposing the repeal of the arms embargo to aid the United Kingdom in 1939. When the Senate approved the Lend-Lease Bill in 1941, he "had the feeling" that he "was witnessing the suicide of the Republic." During World War II, however, without the encouragement of President Roosevelt until 1945, Vandenberg sought common ground in planning postwar policy and so became a principal architect of a bipartisan foreign policy.[3]

A "very bright" student with "too practical a mind," as one philosophy professor described him, Robert Taft graduated from Yale excelling, according to his biographer, in "rote learning" and an unquestioning

faith in "the essential justice" and "propriety of the American social system." First in his class, he was also first at Harvard Law School, with his
father, the president, noting: "Bob has taken the highest marks that have
been taken in Harvard for fifteen years." Refusing offers from prestigious
Wall Street law firms because they were "so aggressive," young Bob Taft
returned to Cincinnati to practice law and enter politics. Turned down for
the army during World War I because of poor eyesight, he volunteered to
assist in Herbert Hoover's relief program. He first worked in the Food
Administration in Washington but then moved to Paris, as Hoover's legal
adviser, in the American Relief Administration. There he came to share his
boss's disillusionment with the selfishness of the Allies after the "war to
end wars." He moaned: "The whole structure of international politics seems
to have reappeared in very much its old form." In Paris, he also hobnobbed
with the bright young men of the peace delegation, including John Foster
Dulles and his brother Allen, nephews of Secretary of State Robert Lansing.

Returning to Cincinnati in 1920, Taft, still in his father's shadow until
the chief justice's death in 1930, at first rose slowly in politics. He served
for six years in the Ohio state House of Representatives and, after four years
off, eight years in the state senate. And in 1938, entering his fiftieth year,
Robert Alphonso Taft was elected U.S. senator from Ohio.

Unlike Vandenberg, Taft was not handsome and presidential-looking but
more professorial, as his large eyes peered through rimless spectacles.
Though neither man was given to small talk, Vandenberg was more loquacious, if not a bit pompous. Taft was dignified, but naturally reticent, and
seemed, especially for a politician, too sober and serious. And as Taft
entered the Senate, Vandenberg was already "presidential," as a dark-horse
candidate in 1936, who had declined the vice presidential nomination.

Both men married sweethearts of their youth. Elizabeth Watson, Vandenberg's first wife and mother of his three children, tragically died of a brain
tumor while they were still young. Shortly afterward, he wed Hazel Whittaker, who, he joked, was the only thing he got out of his short stay at the
University of Michigan, where they met. Martha Bowers was as talkative as
her husband, Bob Taft, was reserved. She was the daughter of his father's
solicitor general and had attended the Sorbonne. The witty Martha proved a
better campaigner than her husband.

The two senators were both *"papabile"* in 1940, but Taft was a serious
candidate for the presidency at the Philadelphia convention that nominated
Wendell Willkie. Again, at the 1948 Philadelphia convention, Taft was a
serious challenger to the eventual nominee, Governor Thomas E. Dewey of
New York, as Vandenberg assumed a new "senior statesman" role. But the

starring roles the two men would play in foreign affairs in the late forties would not only elect General Eisenhower president in 1952 but shape the international "Pax Americana" for the next four decades.[4]

As far as the American press and public were concerned, Arthur Vandenberg made a complete about-face when he rose in the Senate on January 10, 1945, to deliver the most famous speech of his life—literally "a speech heard round the world." Actually in 1944, he had been saying many of the same things, for he realized: "The whole world changed—the factors of time and space changed—with World War II, and I changed with them." He was also anxious "to clarify and strongly assert the position of America from the standpoint of those of us who had been so-called 'isolationists' prior to Pearl Harbor." And he must have had on his mind the fate of his friend and fellow member of the munitions committee Gerald P. Nye of North Dakota.

On December 7, 1941, Nye suffered the misfortune of addressing the last public rally of the America First Committee in Pittsburgh, as the news broke of the Japanese attack on Pearl Harbor, with its approximately two thousand American victims. Nye's noninterventionism appeared traitorous to many, even though he would vote for war against Japan and Germany. Before Pearl Harbor, he had been tagged "the *führer* from North Dakota" and, together with fellow America Firsters Charles Lindbergh and Burton Wheeler, denounced as "arch traitors who would have sold out their country." Interventionists labeled Nye and others "Fascists" in the same way liberal internationalists after World War II would be called "Communist fellow travelers." The term *isolationist* turned derogatory and helped defeat Nye for reelection to the Senate in 1944.[5]

Political expediency, then, would suggest a dramatic change for Vandenberg in his perceived position on foreign policy. In preparing his statement, Vandenberg privately thought the Republican Right needed to be "far more realistic about the 'social revolution' which has swept the entire world." His views involved the future of capitalism as well as the future of democracy: "I am very certain that the capitalistic system will *not* survive (nor will the Republican Party) unless we meet 'social liberalism' with forward-looking 'capitalistic liberalism.' " He was paving the way for a bipartisan foreign policy supporting a multinational corporate liberalism.[6]

Vandenberg's celebrated speech warned against America's becoming a "silent partner" in the "grand alliance" against the Axis, while the outspoken Winston Churchill and Joseph Stalin asserted their "unilateral" aims. Otherwise, America would fall victim to "the unity which Jonah enjoyed when he was swallowed by the whale." The "real question always becomes": "Where does real self-interest lie?" And he then singled out the Soviet Union: "Russia's unilateral plan appears to contemplate the engulfment, directly or indirectly, of a surrounding circle of buffer states, contrary to our conception of what we thought we were fighting for in respect to the rights of small nations and a just peace. Russia's announced reason is her insistent purpose never again to be at the mercy of another German tyranny. That is a perfectly understandable reason. The alternative is collective security."

James Reston of the *New York Times,* noting how enthusiastically the American people responded to the speech, observed: "What he did was merely to express and symbolize their change." Vandenberg's speech also came on the eve of the Yalta Conference in February 1945. During the previous year, he had been lobbied by his sizable Polish constituency in Michigan to press for a tougher stance toward the Soviet Union; and he was only too willing to become their chief legislative spokesman.[7]

FDR's administration seized the opportunity offered by Vandenberg when, as the president was returning from the Yalta Conference, the State Department announced that the Michigan senator had been appointed a delegate to the United Nations Conference on International Organization, opening in San Francisco, April 25. Although Vandenberg accepted, he wrote to his confidant John Foster Dulles that he would not go as "a stooge." The senator was especially upset at the "indefensible" accession of Polish territory by the Soviet Union at Yalta. He also opposed the apparently "unconscionably immoral" recognition of the Soviet-backed Lublin government, which had branded as "traitors" General Wladyslaw Anders and the Polish soldiers "who bore the brunt of the ghastly Cassino battles." In a letter by the president, Vandenberg reiterated his "profound conviction that we *must* organize the postwar world on the basis of effective, collective security."[8]

Vandenberg's leadership position in foreign policy was strengthened by his participation at the founding of the United Nations, but especially, after FDR's death, by his influence on President Truman. With a willingness to label as "appeaser" anyone "too persistently urging the Soviet view point," Vandenberg was horrified when Secretary of State Jimmy Byrnes proposed to the Senate Foreign Relations Committee, just before he left for Moscow in December 1945, "an exchange of atomic scientists and scientific information with Russia." Vandenberg recorded that everyone on the committee was opposed to such an exchange until the Soviet Union ended the practice of "hermetically sealing herself up behind 'iron curtains.'" The senators were also unanimous in their opposition to shortening the period of American nuclear superiority. Vandenberg considered such a policy "sheer appeasement," and Truman backed him on the question.

Byrnes's days as secretary of state were numbered when he returned from Moscow on December 29, 1945. The president would send him a memo in January with the accompanying remark: "I am tired [of] babying the Soviets." Under pressure from Vandenberg, who called for an end to the "miserable fiction" that confronting American-Soviet differences would endanger world peace, Byrnes addressed the Overseas Press Club on February 28, 1946. His speech was full of Truman's toughness: "We cannot [Truman's emphasis] *allow aggression* to be accomplished by *coercion* or *pressure* or *subterfuges* such as *political infiltration.*" The press dubbed the speech "the Second Vandenberg Concerto," as the secretary of state abandoned his policy of conciliation and announced his personal declaration of the Cold War.

Byrnes would hang on as lame-duck secretary of state until January 1947. Though, in Vandenberg's words, Byrnes "loitered around Munich," the Irishman from South Carolina left office as *Time*'s 1946 "Man of the Year." But Vandenberg could declare in May 1946: "The appeasement days are over." And Henry Wallace, shortly before being fired by Truman as secretary of commerce, in September 1946, would tell the president that "Jimmy Byrnes in effect was under the control of Vandenberg. At any rate, Vandenberg had the veto power over him."[9]

Vandenberg was up for reelection to the Senate in November 1946, and he was in the unique position of being attacked by both the *Chicago Tribune* and the *Daily Worker*. Colonel Robert McCormick's newspaper called Vandenberg's efforts toward a bipartisan foreign policy a "partnership in iniquity" because he was "abandoning the principles of Americanism." The *Tribune*'s cartoons even portrayed him as Benedict Arnold, while the Communist *Daily Worker* featured frequent attacks on Vandenberg, which he put to good use. "I am flattered to find myself at the top of the Communist 'purge' list all around the world," he wrote, and as for the political fallout, he knew the Michigan electorate understood that "they are 'dropping a letter to Stalin in the mailbox' when they drop their votes into the ballot box."

Vandenberg was reelected in a landslide. But more important, the Republicans won control of both the Senate and the House for the first time since 1930. And Vandenberg's position was further strengthened when he became chairman of the Senate Foreign Relations Committee and president pro tempore of the Senate. Democratic Senator J. William Fulbright even suggested that President Truman appoint Vandenberg, Taft, or some other prominent Republican, secretary of state, and, with the vice presidency vacant, resign the presidency in his favor. The president responded to the proposal by referring to the Arkansan as "half-bright." Vandenberg was probably more powerful remaining where he was, and he strengthened his position by nurturing a "cordial" relationship with Taft and by shrewdly deferring to him on domestic issues.[10]

In fact, 1947 was Bob Taft's "year." One reporter claimed that he had more influence on the Republican Party than any senator since Charles Sumner, and the *New Republic* lamented: "Congress now consists of the House, the Senate, and Bob Taft." While Wallace White of Maine was nominal majority leader, he took directions from Taft. And Taft assumed his first committee chairmanship, of the newly designated Labor and Public Welfare Committee, where he formulated and rewrote a much harsher House bill that became the Taft–Hartley Bill. It curtailed the Wagner Labor Act of 1935, which union leaders regarded as their "Magna Carta." Taft's bill banned the closed shop, forbidding the hiring of nonunion workers. It also outlawed secondary boycotts and was tagged a "slave-labor bill" by the unions. Looking forward to union support in the presidential election of 1948, President Truman vetoed the bill, but the Eightieth Congress overrode his veto.[11]

The year 1948 will always belong to Harry Truman, highlighted by his dramatic come-from-behind victory over "the little man on the wedding cake," Governor Thomas E. Dewey of New York. At least, Truman triumphed personally. But on foreign policy questions, Vandenberg dominated the scene, winning support for the Marshall Plan and the North Atlantic Treaty Organization (NATO). Vandenberg was, in fact, a co–secretary of state in 1947 and 1948 with General George Marshall.

Vandenberg had become the key person in the Congress and in the country for any dramatic change in foreign policy. On February 27, 1947, President Truman and Secretary Marshall called Vandenberg and other congressional leaders to the White House for a briefing on the threat of a Communist victory in the civil war in Greece. Britain, under economic pressure at home, was forced to end military assistance there. Vandenberg agreed to support Truman's request for $250 million for Greece and $150 million for Turkey, but he warned the president that, to win public support, he would have to "scare hell out of the American people." In a letter to a skeptical constituent, Vandenberg justified his support in terms of a "chain reaction," or what would be called later in Southeast Asia the "domino theory": "Greece must be helped or Greece sinks permanently into the communist order. Turkey inevitably follows. Then comes the chain reaction which might sweep from the Dardanelles to the China sea.... I do not know whether our new American policy can succeed in arresting these subversive trends (which ultimately represent a direct threat to us). I can only say that I think the adventure is worth trying as an alternative to another 'Munich' and perhaps to another war (against the occurrence of which every human effort must be made)."

At 1:00 P.M. on March 12, 1947, President Truman addressed a joint session of Congress, with Vandenberg and Speaker Joe Martin presiding. The president called for immediate aid for Greece and Turkey. But in the speech, he announced what became known as the "Truman Doctrine" and, in a single sentence, shaped American foreign policy for the next four decades: "I believe that it must be the policy of the United States to support free peoples who are resisting attempted subjugation by armed minorities or by outside pressures."

Though George Kennan, the head of the State Department's Policy Planning Staff and author of the concept of "containment," protested that the "Truman Doctrine" was "more grandiose" than anything he had ever conceived, Truman went ahead with his depiction of a worldwide struggle between freedom and slavery. He had to sell his plan as Vandenberg advised. Ironically, the comprehensive plan could be interpreted as a kind of reactionary "Holy Alliance" against leftist revolutions, since all anti-Communist nations were to be equated with "free" ones, even if they were right-wing dictatorships.[12]

Taft at first dragged his heels with a month of embarrassing questions for Vandenberg, such as "What was the evidence to suggest, as Truman seemed to claim, that a communist takeover of Greece would spread throughout the Middle East?" The Ohioan then grudgingly announced his support. "I don't like the Greek-Turkish proposition," he commented in a letter, "but I do recognize that perhaps we should maintain the *status quo* until we reach some peace accommodation with Russia. I don't like to appear to be backing down." But he qualified his position: "I do not regard this as a commitment to any similar policy in any other section of the world." Taft also advocated American withdrawal "as soon as normal economic conditions are restored." Clearly, Vandenberg would now have to worry about Taft's support when the price tag of the Truman Doctrine became evident in the "Marshall Plan."[13]

At the Harvard commencement on June 5, 1947, in the presence of fellow honorary degree recipients General Omar N. Bradley and T.S. Eliot, Secretary of State George C. Marshall announced the most sweeping plan of American foreign aid in history. With a large red shield inscribed "Veritas" centered above the Ionic columns behind him, the secretary presented his plan to save Western civilization. After being compared to George Washington by President James Conant, Marshall appealed to the humanitarian instincts of the 8,000 assembled participants: "The truth of the matter is that Europe's requirements for the next three or four years of foreign food and other essential products—principally from America—are so much greater than her present ability to pay that she must have substantial additional help or face economic, social, and political deterioration of a very grave character." He also called it "logical" for the United States to "assist in the return of normal economic health in the world, without which there can be no stability or assured peace."

The genius of the Marshall Plan was that it contained something for everyone. For humanitarians, it offered aid to rebuild war-torn Europe. For farmers and exporters, it meant a strong export trade. For staunch anti-Communists, it proposed to prevent Communist subversion and, by rebuilding the Wehrmacht, to counter the Red Army threat.[14]

Taft grew steadily more critical of the European Recovery Program, or Marshall Plan, through 1947, especially after he announced his candidacy for the presidency on October 24. He began more forcefully to resist the idea of a bipartisan foreign policy. His foreign and domestic policies were cut from the same cloth. Excessive government lending abroad would artificially stimulate demand and create inflation at home. At times, he even sounded like the New Left of the post-Vietnam era: "If we throw our dollars around and try to run the show, we are going to give the Communists further arguments against us for trying to be imperialistic."

Taft's philosophy was unsuited for the generation of the G.I. Bill but was a more articulate and intelligent version of the politically successful Reaganomics. His wife, Martha Bowers, a more colorful campaigner, summed up their attitude toward government: "We've got a 'highboy' government in Washington—one bureau on top of another, and the New Dealers are like termites in the drawers." Taft himself, while scrupulously honest, was often tactless when handling reporters. After complaining that excess demand led to higher food prices, he told one press conference: "Eat less meat and eat less extravagantly." The message was quickly distorted into "eat less," as he was compared to Marie Antoinette.

The Ohioan, however, found it difficult to reconcile his anticommunism with opposition to foreign aid. He was increasingly vulnerable to the charge of "isolationism," as Clark Clifford bragged in 1947 that the Truman administration had "adroitly stolen" the anti-Communist issue from the GOP. Making foreign policy an issue in the 1948 election hurt Taft in his race for the Republican nomination, when the majority of Republicans in the Senate and the country supported Vandenberg's bipartisan approach.[15]

Michigan's senior senator strengthened his position as leader of a bipartisan foreign policy on New Year's Day 1948 by quashing a "Vandenberg-for-president" movement. With the words, "I am confident that I can best serve my country by completing my present term in the Senate," like senators stretching back to Thomas Hart Benton, Vandenberg's perfect timing reinforced his personal standing among colleagues and his commitment to the Marshall Plan. With virtually all segments of American society, from isolationists to socialists, testifying in its behalf before the Senate Foreign Relations Committee, which he chaired, Vandenberg was said to have "killed the opposition to the Marshall Plan with kindness."

The administration bill carried a price tag of the then stupendous amount of $17 billion for the plan over its entire four-and-one-fourth-year life span. With about twenty Republican senators, including Taft, demanding revisions, Vandenberg began negotiations with the State Department and eventually worked out an agreement for an initial authorization of $5.3 billion for the first twelve months. But House right-wing Republicans balked. They approved $5 billion for fifteen months and stalled until the eve of the Republican National Convention in mid-June. Taft then stepped in and announced that the Senate would stay in session until its "moral commitment" to the administration had been met; and the House backed down, as Congress adjourned for the Philadelphia convention.[16]

Taft's statesmanship, however, did not win him the Republican nomination. The convention turned to Governor Thomas Dewey, and the party's eastern establishment won again. Dewey and his advisers John Foster Dulles and McGeorge Bundy refused to make foreign policy a campaign issue, as Taft would have, and gave Vandenberg a free hand.

Support for the Marshall Plan, and even more, was strengthened among the American public by events in Europe. The Soviet Union was busy fortifying its position in Eastern Europe, as it purged all anti-Communist opposition in rigged elections in Hungary in 1947. But world attention especially focused on the Communist coup in Czechoslovakia in February 1948, with the second "defenestration of Prague" in the suicide of national hero Foreign Minister Jan Masaryk. The coup dramatized the limitations of American foreign policy while Congress debated the funding of the Marshall Plan. And who could forget the fate of Czechoslovakia at the hands of another dictator at Munich a decade earlier?

Again, Vandenberg stepped in. After consulting Secretary Marshall, John Foster Dulles, and top congressional and military leaders, but principally Undersecretary of State Robert Lovett, Vandenberg drafted what Dulles would compare to the Monroe Doctrine as a milestone in American diplomatic history. The "Vandenberg Resolution" was a "sense of the Senate" statement advising the president to seek mutual defense arrangements for a secure "free world" under the U.N. Charter, but outside the Security Council, where the Soviet Union could exercise a veto. On June 11, 1948, after just eight hours of debate, the Senate approved the Vandenberg Resolution by a vote of 64 to 6, after rejecting an amendment by Senator Claude Pepper of Florida to strike all references to possible American military aid.

The Vandenberg Resolution called for "progressive development of regional and other collective arrangements for individual and collective self-defense" under the U.N. Charter.[17]

The seedling of the North Atlantic Treaty Organization had been planted, but no one could foresee the way it would grow to maturity in two years. Vandenberg's resolution was the first planting. The North Atlantic Treaty, in April 1949, was the second growth, followed by the third in October 1949, a commitment to military aid in the Mutual Defense Assistance Program. It finally blossomed into the commitment of American troops under the leadership of General Eisenhower in June 1950. Fertilizing the growth was the expanding Communist "aggression," ranging from the Berlin blockade to the explosion of the first Soviet atomic bomb in August–September 1949, and then to the Communist victory in China the following December.[18]

"Give 'em hell!" Harry's upset election as president in his own right in November 1948 accompanied, and was perhaps the result of, the Democrats' carrying both houses of Congress. Bipartisanship appeared to be dead when civil war broke out among Senate Republicans, the more isolationist and conservative group supporting Taft as chairman of the Senate Republican Policy Committee and the more internationalist, preconvention Dewey supporters voting for Henry Cabot Lodge Jr. Though Vandenberg was closer to the Lodge "rebels," he greatly respected Taft's handling of domestic affairs and voted for him. But the split exacerbated differences among Republicans, especially over the upcoming ratification of the North Atlantic Treaty.

Though Vandenberg was rumored to be Marshall's successor as secretary of state, he indirectly informed the president through Leslie Biffle, secretary to the Senate Democratic majority, that such an appointment would kill bipartisanship. Truman then appointed Dean Acheson, whom Taft and others considered supercilious, if not arrogant. Though not temperamentally close to Acheson, as he had been with Marshall and Lovett, Vandenberg still proposed to continue his bipartisanship. Acheson was very condescending in his memoirs about "a large mass of cumulonimbus cloud, often called Arthur Vandenberg, producing heavy word fall" and expressed jealousy of the senator's "penchant for stealing the limelight." Secret testimony, however, published in 1976 after Acheson's memoirs, revealed that Vandenberg saved Acheson's nomination as secretary of state when public opinion was running strongly against it because of Alger Hiss's indictment for perjury a month earlier and Acheson's public statement that Hiss and he "remain friends." In the executive session of the Senate Foreign Relations Committee, chaired by Vandenberg, the senator guided the stiff secretary designate in his testimony, pointing out to him that "whether we like it or not we confront a problem of public relations here." Vandenberg then got a commitment from Acheson as he asked: "I am sure that you would not think, for instance, of appointing Mr. Hiss this afternoon to a position in the State Department if you were there." "That is quite right," Acheson replied, and quashed the opposition.[19]

But Vandenberg's differences with the Taft Republicans could not be so easily papered over. The split over the Senate ratification of the North Atlantic Treaty during the summer of 1949 marked not only the denouement of Vandenberg's influence and the beginning of its decline along with his health, but also the growing rift between Taft and the important Republican internationalists looking ahead to the 1952 presidential campaign. And the arguments presented by Taft and Vandenberg would reverberate through foreign policy debates over the next forty years. The formation of NATO with nine Western European countries, Iceland, and Canada emphasized America's resolve to contain Soviet expansion. But its key clause, proclaiming that an attack against one would be considered an attack against all, committed the nation, for the first time since the 1778 Franco-American alliance, to war in support of other nations outside the Western Hemisphere.

The language of the debate was increasingly hyped. Senator Frank Porter Graham of North Carolina called the Vandenberg Resolution the "Magna Carta of new hope for freedom in a Communist-assaulted world." And Vandenberg himself would use rhetoric, perhaps appropriate for his time, that would distort American foreign policy in the 1960s. He wrote a constituent: "When Mr. Hitler was contemplating World War Two, I believe he would have never launched it if he had any serious reasons to believe that it might bring him into armed collision with the United States. I think he was sure it would not do so because of our then existing neutrality laws. If an appropriate North Atlantic Pact is written, I think it will exactly reverse this psychology so far as Mr. Stalin is concerned if, as and when he contemplates World War Three. Under such circumstances, I very much doubt whether World War Three happens."

Taft was most opposed to the military aid part of the pact and argued that the Soviet Union did not want war and was already checked by America's possession of the atomic bomb: "A few more obsolete arms in Europe will not concern them in the least." Again, he sounded like some of the anti-Vietnam activists of the sixties: "Today we have quietly adopted a tendency to interfere in the affairs of other nations, to assume that we are a kind of demigod and Santa Claus to solve the problems of the world. It is easy to slip into an attitude of imperialism where war becomes an instrument of public policy rather than its last resort."

In July, the Senate ratified the North Atlantic Treaty, despite Taft's opposition, by a vote of 82 to 13. He then led a futile attempt to cut the military part as Vandenberg, soon to be operated on for cancer, delivered his last "full-dress" Senate speech on September 20. In urging and winning military implementation of the Treaty, he called the bill "the finest possible example of constructive responsibility in collaboration with a responsive State Department. A widely divided Joint Committee sought and found substantial common ground. . . . I think the bill is in honorable keeping with our Treaty obligation. I think it is definitely and specifically in the interests of our own intelligent self-interest. I think it is discouragement to war. I think it is prime and vital peace insurance for us and for the free world."[20]

At the moment of his greatest and final triumph, Vandenberg, in the same way William Pitt Fessenden had worried about the country's "madness" in 1866, observed the pall of fear enveloping the nation in 1949. "The whole country is in a state of nerves," he wrote: "Everybody is under tension. Nothing is right. The whole tenor of Senatorial correspondence has changed. Everybody is mad about *something*—and they seem to love to 'take it out' on their members of Congress. . . . Oh well—we survived the Civil War and I guess we can survive this. *This too shall pass.*"

As Vandenberg slowly passed from this world over the next eighteen months, the "shocks of 1949," according to historian Eric Goldman, "loosed within American life a vast impatience, a turbulent bitterness, a rankor akin to revolt." President Truman compared the era to that which produced the Alien and Sedition Acts of 1798, but a more apt comparison might be the "Red scare" under his Democratic predecessor in 1919. In March, a Justice Department employee, Judith Coplon, was arrested as a Soviet spy, and Congressman Richard Nixon called for a congressional investigation: "This case shows why the department may be unfit and unqualified to carry out the responsibility of protecting the national security against Communist infiltration." Nixon made a national reputation for himself investigating Alger Hiss, whose perjury indictment worked its way through the courts in 1949.

Hiss, the sophisticated, first-in-his-class graduate of Harvard Law School and law clerk to Supreme Court Justice Oliver Wendell Holmes Jr., had risen rapidly in the State Department as an adviser to President Roosevelt at the Yalta Conference and as a member of the American delegation at the United Nations Charter Conference. Hiss was the epitome of the eastern liberal elite, and when Whittaker Chambers, an ex-Communist senior editor of *Time,* charged Hiss with being a Communist at least since 1934, Nixon pressed the House Un-American Activities Committee (HUAC) to continue its investigation of Hiss.

Though not staking his political career, the way Richard Nixon did, on the anti-Communist paranoia sweeping the land, young, lackadaisical Congressman John F. Kennedy demonstrated that even the eastern elite were not immune to the hysteria of the moment. He did not accept the State Department's view that China was on the verge of collapse because of Chiang Kai-shek's corrupt and incompetent administration. And the former Harvard government major even attacked one of Harvard's dons, China expert Professor John King Fairbank: "So concerned were our diplomats and their advisors, the Lattimores and the Fairbanks, with the imperfection of the democratic system in China after 20 years of war and the tales of corruption in high places that they lost sight of our tremendous stake in a non-Communist China. . . . This House must now assume the responsibility of preventing the onrushing tide of communism from engulfing all of Asia."

Spy stories fed the paranoia, as they reportedly occupied 32 percent of the combined front pages of the New York daily newspapers during one week in June. The HUAC published a booklet entitled *Spotlight on Spies*. Then, on September 22, the very day the Senate approved arms for NATO, the Truman administration shocked the country with the announcement of the Soviet Union's first atomic explosion. And as Chiang's Nationalist government fled to its island fortress of Formosa in December, abandoning mainland China to Mao's Communists, the China lobby, with support from right-wing Republicans, talked of the American "betrayal" of China. The charge of being "soft on Communism," which at first worked to the Democrats' advantage in winning support for the Truman Doctrine and NATO, would now backfire on them in Asia.[21]

The month after the fall of China, the conviction of Alger Hiss on perjury charges on January 21, 1950, ignited a firestorm of Republican criticism of the Truman administration. And on February 3, when the news broke that Dr. Klaus Fuchs, a British physicist who had worked on the Manhattan Project, had been arrested as a Soviet spy, a *Chicago Tribune* headline shrieked: "REDS GET OUR BOMB PLANS!" But it was a Lincoln Day speech to the Republican Women's Club of Wheeling, West Virginia, that stole most of the headlines and smudged American politics with sham patriotism for the next four years.

"McCarthyism" was born when a little-known, ineffectual, but opportunistic senator from Wisconsin delivered that Wheeling speech. Parts of Senator Joseph R. McCarthy's speech were lifted from one given by Richard Nixon in the House, warming up for his senatorial campaign in California. Parts came from newspaper clippings about Communist infiltration of the State Department. But according to newsmen present, McCarthy waved a collection of papers and wailed: "I have here in my hand a list of 205—a list of names that were made known to the Secretary of State as being members of the Communist Party and who nevertheless are still working and shaping policy in the State Department."[22]

At first, McCarthy's buffoonery was not evident to most senators, as with Major Esterhazy in the Dreyfus Affair. Rationality was a rare commodity in American politics at that time, and Taft, the dominant Republican leader with the declining health of Vandenberg, found himself drifting further away from bipartisanship, pulled there by the Republican Right and the China lobby. Foreign policy and internal security had become partisan issues.

When the Russian-trained North Korean Army crossed the 38th parallel on June 25, 1950, bipartisanship was restored briefly as the Congress and the country united behind President Truman. The U.N. Security Council, with the Soviets still absent protesting the exclusion of Communist China, unanimously endorsed a joint U.N. "police action" to stop the aggression; and President Truman appointed General Douglas MacArthur supreme commander of U.N. forces.

But the Korean War quickly became "Mr. Truman's War," as far as most Republicans were concerned. Had not the president encouraged North Korean aggression by withdrawing American troops in 1949? Was not the error compounded by Secretary of State Acheson's public statement on January 12, 1950, that Korea should not be included within America's "defensive perimeter"? Was it not reasonable to think, in Congressman John F. Kennedy's words, that "McCarthy may have something" in his charges about Communist infiltration of the State Department?

With the death of Vandenberg, the bipartisan Republicans were almost overwhelmed by McCarthyism. The only hope for these Europe-first internationalists was the new commander of NATO forces, General Eisenhower. But Taft was swept along in the anti-Communist tide because, as a close friend recalled, he was "rabid on the subject of communism." And if Andy Jackson, Zachary Taylor, and Ulysses S. Grant were formidable as war heroes, how much more so "Ike," the consummate politician who could accommodate egos the likes of Churchill and General Bernard Law Montgomery.

Taft became more of a prisoner of the China lobby and McCarthy than he would have liked, as the bubble of his popularity expanded during the controversy over the firing of General MacArthur. Though that bubble burst in the Republican primaries of 1952 and Taft lost the nomination to Eisenhower, he converted Ike through Dulles to a more rhetorically aggressive foreign policy. "Containment" of communism under the Democrats was insufficient, as the word *liberation* was used more frequently to describe the Eisenhower–Dulles policy. And as Taft preferred, Ike would step up the production of atomic weapons as a better deterrent than ground forces.

Ike was the typical organization man in the best, high-minded sense of the description. He successfully directed the Allied war effort as a sort of chairman of the board and was ideally suited to lead the country and the "free world" during the 1950s. He stood for a corporate liberalism at home and abroad that appealed to the eastern establishment and to the American business community. Critics like Republican Senator William Jenner of Indiana despaired over the way Ike's brain was like a pillow in retaining the impression of the last person who sat upon it. But part of Ike's political strength was his inability to articulate his views. Incoherence served as a public asset, until the cocksure rhetoric of his successor overcame the lethargy of the 1950s but created new pitfalls.

The relationship between Taft and Vandenberg set the tone for American policies for about forty years. But they should not be blamed for the excesses to which some of their policies led. Their *pas de deux* for five years, with all its turns, reveals more about the next four decades than detailed analyses of the Truman and Eisenhower administrations.

According to Taft's biographer, many senators found Vandenberg "loquacious" and "fond of flattery." On one occasion, Taft asked his wife "to butter Van up." But the witty Martha wrote: "I tried manfully, but he buttered himself so thoroughly that I really couldn't find a single ungreased spot." But Vandenberg was the master at greasing everyone else. With an ego not unlike Benton's, Vandenberg controlled his ambition and strengthened his standing in the Senate and the country. His greatness lay in his growth over the years and the honorable way he used the power entrusted to him. Vandenberg, with greater simplicity than Taft, also exhibited greater self-awareness. In writing about a radio broadcast of Sigmund Romberg's music, "the most thrilling musical program I ever heard," Vandenberg observed: "The announcer said that musical 'highbrows' consider Romberg 'low-brow' and that 'low-brows' consider him 'high-brow' and therefore he considers himself 'middle-brow.' I guess that's where I land when it comes to music." And that's where he lands when it comes to understanding American politics of his era. Being "middle-brow" was his major strength and weakness.

Taft lacked not only an appreciation of music but also a sense of aesthetics. He was totally unsuited for an age seeking charisma in its political leaders. Yet he kept running for president and weakening his position in the Senate. Taft was the kind of conservative contrarian whose views were easily misinterpreted, such as his opposition to the Nuremberg war crimes trials. He preferred that the Nazi leaders be executed by court-martial, or imprisoned like Napoleon, rather than convicted under the pretense of justice. His prickly conservatism also revealed a contempt for aggressive money making, as he worried about President Eisenhower's appointing too many "big businessmen" to his cabinet. Taft possessed a sense of irony so rare in American politics. Never one to fool himself, he once wrote: "What gives one pause in politics is the number of nuts who write you with approval."[23]

As Vandenberg's concept of collective security grew to include each continent and then the entire planet and, in effect, the universe, the imperial presidency was strengthened by the constant crises of the Cold War. Real or fabricated external threats to the United States enhanced the power of the president and weakened that of the Senate. Through distraction and neglect, patriotism, mingled with paranoia, weakened domestic reform efforts, such as Senator Hubert Humphrey's, and played into the hands of conservative opponents, such as Senator Strom Thurmond. The cult of secrecy on "national security" grounds would lead to the abuse of presidential power at home as well as abroad, from the Vietnam War through Watergate to the Iran–Contra scandal. Ironically, it was the conservative Robert Taft who warned the Senate in 1951: "The result of a general practice of secrecy . . . has been to deprive the Senate and Congress of the substance of the powers conferred on them by the Constitution." The Cold War created not only an imperial presidency but also a supine Senate.[24]

9

The "Politics of Joy" and "Uncle Strom's Cabin"

Hubert H. Humphrey vs. Strom Thurmond (1950–1990)

During the week of July 12, 1948, when the Democratic National Convention met in Philadelphia, two new figures entered the national political arena, where one of them still contests in 1996: Mayor Hubert Horatio Humphrey of Minneapolis and Governor James Strom Thurmond of South Carolina. The convention dutifully nominated Harry Truman for president, but the major battle centered on the civil rights plank in the platform, with Humphrey and Thurmond playing major roles.

The regular Democrats wanted to continue to placate southerners with the pious platitudes of the 1944 platform, but a minority plank was presented to the convention by Mayor Humphrey. It urged the adoption of the 1946 President's Commission on Civil Rights, which called on the federal government to outlaw lynching, to form a commission to curb discrimination in employment, to guarantee African American voting rights in the South, and to open the military to all races.

In the most stirring speech he ever gave, Humphrey told the convention and the nation at the time of the Berlin airlift: "We cannot use a double standard. Our demands for democratic practice in other lands will be no more effective than the guarantee of those practices in our own country." Referring to the executive order ending segregation in the armed forces issued by the president, the mayor told the cheering delegates: "Harry Truman has had the courage to give the people of America the new emancipation proclamation." And in his most incisive and memorable sentence,

Humphrey summed up the challenge to the party: "The time has arrived for the Democratic party to get out of the shadow of states' rights and walk forthrightly into the bright sunshine of human rights."

Walking forthrightly out of the convention after it surprisingly approved the minority plank were delegates from Alabama and Mississippi. Governor Thurmond stayed to defend his position on civil rights at the last session. But the dissidents from sixteen states hastily arranged a gathering in Birmingham on July 17, which quickly became another convention. To the strains of "Dixie" the States' Rights Democrats nominated Governor Thurmond for president and Governor Fielding Wright of Mississippi for vice president.

Thurmond's so-called Dixiecrats placed another strain on Truman's campaign since the president already had to worry about Henry A. Wallace's Progressive Party on the left. Despite the polls, Truman won by more than 2 million popular votes, though the switch of 21,000 votes in Ohio and Illinois to Governor Thomas E. Dewey, or the defection of the Democratic electors of North Carolina and Texas to Thurmond, would have thrown the election into the House of Representatives. Thurmond's Dixiecrats laid the foundation for the Goldwater-Republican "southern strategy," which would elect Richard M. Nixon in 1968, Ronald Reagan in 1980, and George Bush in 1988.[1]

Born on May 27, 1911, in Wallace, South Dakota, Hubert Horatio Humphrey grew up in the small town of Doland, South Dakota, population 600, where his father, H.H. Sr., was a druggist. "Pinky," as he was known, was the second of four children of H.H. and Christine Sannes. His father was an outgoing free-thinker, who nevertheless joined the Methodist church with his children and wife because there was no Lutheran church in town for her. Christine was a strict churchgoer, who took the children to Sunday school every week, while Hubert Senior stayed at home reading Tom Paine and the anti-Christian Robert Ingersoll. The big-hearted father was known for his generosity, even hiring an embezzler just released from prison, and—much to his wife's horror—was pleased with Pinky's popularity among the black roadbuilders to whom he sold newspapers. Pinky's Aunt Olga noted how older people liked the young boy: "He would do things for them, little errands, always willing no matter what they'd ask—sure, he'd go." The young Hubert was also influenced by his Methodist minister, the Reverend Albert Hartt, whose son Julian, later a Yale professor, became a close friend. The Reverend Hartt introduced the young man to such radio evangelists as Harry Emerson Fosdick and Father Charles Coughlin—an interest Humphrey never lost as he requested the Reverend Robert Schuller of the Crystal Cathedral to preach at his funeral.

Hubert experienced much of the pain of the depression. His parents lost their home and moved to the larger town of Huron. After one year at the University of Minnesota, he dropped out and, from the age of twenty to twenty-six, worked in his father's drugstore. But after he married Muriel Buck, she saved $675 by 1937 so that Hubert could finish his degree at Minnesota. Graduating Phi Beta Kappa in political science, he won a teaching fellowship at Louisiana State University, where he wrote a master's thesis on the political philosophy of the New Deal.

Returning to Minneapolis in 1940, Humphrey eked out a living teaching adult education courses through the Works Progress Administration (WPA) as he became the father of a daughter and son. He ran unsuccessfully for mayor in 1943, at first seeking support from Dr. Walter Judd, who had been a medical missionary in China and had defeated an isolationist incumbent in the Republican primary for a seat in the House of Representatives in 1942. Humphrey told Judd: "My father was a total Populist—he wanted to break up everything. But I've been studying political science over at the University and down at Louisiana State, and I know you can't do that sort of thing." Despite his middle-of-the-road pragmatism, Humphrey lost his first campaign.

But in 1945, with united labor support and considerable business backing, Humphrey was elected mayor of Minneapolis. Immediately, however, he made enemies with his more left-wing labor backers by nominating the only J. Edgar Hoover–FBI-trained member of the police force as its chief. Reelected overwhelmingly in 1947 as mayor, Humphrey then set his sights on the U.S. Senate race in 1948. His strong anticommunism set the tone of his campaign against the "totalitarians of the Left." In attacking that element in the Democratic-Farmer-Labor (DFL) Party who were supporting Henry Wallace's Progressive Party, Humphrey won the support of the majority of the DFL. In championing the Truman Doctrine, he told his Americans for Democratic Action supporters: "We're not going to let the political philosophy of the DFL be dictated from the Kremlin. You can be a liberal without being a Communist, and you can be a progressive without being a Communist sympathizer, and we're a liberal progressive party out here. We're not going to let this left-wing Communist ideology be the prevailing force because the people of this state won't accept it, and what's more, it's wrong." In this way, the anti-Communist, liberal Humphrey was elected senator by a middle-class farmer–labor coalition.[2]

While becoming the "No. 1 prospect for liberalism in this country," according to *Time,* with "the cyclonic attack of an ad salesman," Humphrey revealed a character flaw in his efforts to subdue McCarthyism in the country. He fought the Communists in the Electrical Workers union in Minnesota and confronted them in Senate hearings in 1952. But in the summer of 1954 he outdid all of the Red baiters. Republican Senator John Marshall Butler of Maryland had submitted a bill that empowered the attorney general to haul any "Communist-infiltrated" organization before the Subversive Activities Control Board, which might then deny a labor union, for example, the right to engage in collective bargaining. The unions were horrified, and Senator Humphrey rushed to their defense, proclaiming: "I am tired of having people play the Communist issue." He then introduced an extreme substitute amendment that banned the Communist Party. Membership should be a crime because, he said, "the Communist party isn't really a political party, it's an international conspiracy." Confessing that he was "tired of hearing this talk of twenty years of treason," under Democratic presidents from 1933 to 1953, Humphrey's efforts may have helped the Democrats recapture the Senate and the House in November 1954. Approved 85 to 0, the Communist Control Act of 1954 in its final version contained the Butler Bill without its antiunion provisions and the Humphrey amendment with all penalties for party membership removed. Liberals could joyfully proclaim their anti-communism before the November elections, echoing Humphrey's sentiments: "These rats will not get out of the trap."

Out in South Dakota, young Professor George McGovern bristled at the prediction of an old University of South Dakota historian. Angry at Humphrey's disregard for the First Amendment and basic constitutional rights, Professor Herbert Schell saw "a flaw in Humphrey's political character that will keep him from becoming president of the United States." The professor's observation turned into a remarkable prophecy of the role of anti-Communist ideology in shaping Humphrey's conduct as vice president and presidential candidate from 1965 to 1968. Liberal Democrats would be held hostage by Conservative Republicans for being "soft on Communism" from the period of McCarthy paranoia into the Reagan era.[3]

The marriage of Strom Thurmond's parents united two of the oldest families of Edgefield, South Carolina. Eleanor Gertrude Strom was the daughter of a prominent physician; and John William Thurmond, a state legislator and U.S. attorney, was, according to a state chief justice, "the ablest all-round lawyer who ever appeared before the Supreme Court of South Carolina." The family into which James Strom Thurmond (he later dropped the "James") was born on December 5, 1902, as the second of six children, regularly attended Edgefield's Baptist church and was known for its strict moral code. Like John C. Calhoun's, Thurmond's life was strongly rooted in a South Carolina county and relatively well to do.

Graduating from Clemson College in agricultural science and English at the age of twenty, Thurmond taught agriculture for five years before being elected Edgefield County superintendent of education in 1928. He then studied law as an apprentice to his father and tied a graduate of Harvard Law School for first place in the South Carolina bar exam of 1930. Serving in the state senate from 1933 to 1938, he was then elected a circuit court judge by the General Assembly. Though exempt from military service, he volunteered for the army the day Congress declared war on Germany.

If Calhoun was the army candidate for president in 1824, Thurmond's service in World War II made him one of the principal supporters of the Pentagon in the Senate. Crash-landing in a glider in Normandy on D-Day, Thurmond fought in five battles of the First Army in Europe before being transferred to the Pacific theater. He was awarded the Legion of Merit, the *croix de guerre,* and the Purple Heart, among other citations. Discharged as a lieutenant colonel, he eventually rose to the rank of major general in the army reserves.

Returning to his job as circuit judge in January 1946, Thurmond soon announced his intention to run for governor of South Carolina and won an eleven-man race for the Democratic nomination in August, which assured his election in the one-party state. In his first year in office, the forty-four-year-old governor married Jean Crouch, a twenty-one-year-old college graduate. As an omen of a long and active life and career, *Life* magazine carried a picture of the engaged couple, with Strom in tennis shorts standing on his head and the caption: "VIRILE GOVERNOR demonstrates his prowess in the mansion yard day before wedding."[4]

Prune juice, teetotalism, and religious fundamentalism became mainstays of Thurmond's life. In the peak of health at sixty-six, he remarked: "I lay [*sic*] on the floor every morning, and I throw my feet over my head twenty or thirty times to keep the blood flowing to my head. Your brain has to be fed by fresh blood, and if you don't exercise, your brain won't be supplied." When his beloved wife, Jean, died of brain cancer in 1960, he stayed in physical and mental shape and, a few years later, fell in love with an even younger woman than Jean had been when they first met—Nancy Moore, Miss South Carolina of 1966. The couple waited until after Nixon was safely elected in December 1968 to get married: he was sixty-six and she, twenty-two. She presented the childless Thurmond with four children, but as the youngest reached adulthood, the couple announced their separation in 1991.[5]

Despite his national prominence as States' Rights presidential candidate, Governor Thurmond ran a close race for the U.S. Senate against incumbent Olin Johnston in 1950 but lost. When, however, Burnet Rhett Maybank, the senior senator, died suddenly of a heart attack on September 1, 1954, an amazing situation developed. Maybank had been renominated for another six-year term by the state Democratic Party convention, which was tanta-mount to reelection since he had no Republican opposition. On the night of Maybank's funeral, the state Democratic executive committee nominated, without a primary, state Senator Edgar A. Brown of Barnwell County, the most powerful man in the legislature. This would guarantee Brown a six-year term without a popular election. Strom Thurmond quickly organized a write-in campaign and, with the support of fourteen of sixteen of South Carolina daily newspapers, won the general election in a landslide. Thurmond became the first person in history to be elected by write-in votes to either the Senate or the House.[6]

The man who would play a modern Calhoun entered the Senate the year following the U.S. Supreme Court decision, *Brown* v. *Board of Education of Topeka,* which ruled that "separate but equal" public schools for blacks violated the Fourteenth Amendment. It marked the beginning of the end of segregation in American society, and Senator Thurmond led the opposition the way that other South Carolinian had fought abolition a century earlier. Thurmond inspired and helped to draft a "Declaration of Constitutional Principle," or "Southern Manifesto," published on March 12, 1956, and signed by nineteen senators and eighty-one congressmen, pledging to resist the desegregation ruling by all legal means.

But another movement had already begun in the South. On December 1, 1955, in Montgomery, Alabama, a courageous black seamstress' by the name of Rosa Lee McCauley Parks refused to give up her seat to a white male and move to the back of a bus reserved for Negroes. Her subsequent arrest inspired the Montgomery Improvement Association (MIA), led by Dr. Martin Luther King Jr. On March 22, 1956, Dr. King, president of the MIA, was convicted of violating the Alabama antiboycott statute. Within ten days of the "Southern Manifesto," King's trial had begun to mobilize national support for the Montgomery bus boycott, which would inspire a populist movement that, through passive nonviolence, would integrate the nation. Congress and white America would ultimately have no choice but to implement the principles of the Declaration of Independence, held by Thurmond and others to be in conflict with the Constitution.

Back in the Senate, which was about to vote on the Civil Rights Bill of 1957, Thurmond delivered the longest filibuster in history, lasting twenty-four hours and eighteen minutes. The rather innocuous bill set up a Civil Rights Commission to enforce voting rights by prosecuting any offense in refusing to register black voters that could be defined as civil contempt. Humphrey supported the watered-down compromise, to be enforced with small fines and no jury trial. King knew that the bill, to be administered by a languid Dwight D. Eisenhower administration, was only symbolic. The bill passed by a 60 to 15 vote but made Thurmond in his losing cause a hero to white southerners.

Thurmond became a respectable countersymbol to Dr. King during the "Camelot" days of President John F. Kennedy (JFK). But when the senator crossed the aisle to become a Republican in 1964 and support Barry Goldwater for president, he signaled a different strategy that would shape American politics from 1968 onward.[7]

Hubert Humphrey was at his prairie-populist best in the late 1950s, but he was usually reined in by the Senate majority leader, Lyndon Baines Johnson (LBJ). During the Eisenhower years, Humphrey saw little in the way of legislative achievement but used the Senate to mobilize public opinion in support of the many bills he introduced involving civil rights, Medicare, and nuclear disarmament. He proposed the idea of a Peace Corps in 1957 and saw it become the symbolic beginning of the New Frontier program of President John F. Kennedy. Humphrey also anticipated the Job Corps in his Youth Conservation Corps and the "Food for Peace" program in his proposal for using farm surpluses for foreign aid. He also originated the food stamp program but shrewdly got the support of conservative Republican Representative Robert Dole of Kansas as sponsor when it was enacted in 1964. A bill of Humphrey's eventually became the Occupational Safety and Health Act of 1970 under President Nixon.[8]

From 1955 to 1960, Humphrey generally deferred to Majority Leader Johnson on the crucial matter of civil rights. Unlike Thurmond, Humphrey was willing to compromise his convictions, as he at first persuaded liberals not to fight to change the two-thirds cloture rule that permitted southerners to filibuster civil rights bills to death. Walter White, an aging leader of the National Association for the Advancement of Colored People (NAACP), called this action "[a]bject surrender." And when Humphrey and others introduced individual civil rights bills with no possibility of passage, Senator Allen Ellender of Louisiana contemptuously accused them of doing so "as political sops to pressure groups and for no other reason." Even Johnson's conversion to supporting part of Humphrey's civil rights bill in 1957 came only after the majority leader, in the words of Senator Paul Douglas of Illinois, "gutted the bill." The Civil Rights Act of 1957 was emasculated by such amendments as one supported by organized labor providing for the right of a jury trial to state officials accused of not complying with court orders on voting rights. No southern jury at the time would have voted for conviction. The jury trial amendment, according to Vice President Nixon, was "a vote against the right to vote." The act was the first legislation of its kind since Reconstruction, but it would take the peaceful pressure of southern blacks, not congressional or presidential leadership, to enact the civil rights legislation of the 1960s.[9]

As early as 1956, Humphrey's presidential ambition would begin his undoing. After Adlai Stevenson had locked up the Democratic nomination in primaries against Senator Estes Kefauver, Humphrey thought he had a commitment from the former Illinois governor to become his vice presidential running mate and decided to announce his candidacy. But Stevenson thought otherwise and threw the nomination open on the convention floor. Despite LBJ's help, on the first ballot Humphrey ran eighth in a field of nine. As states began to shift their votes, two candidates emerged: Kefauver and Senator John F. Kennedy. And to add to Humphrey's consternation, Kefauver had won the Minnesota primary against a Humphrey-backed slate. A tearful Kefauver pleaded with a tearful Humphrey to break the deadlock. When Humphrey announced his support for Kefauver, the Minnesota delegates switched from their favorite son to Kefauver and helped him defeat Kennedy, who had the support of most of the South, including Texas. Humphrey had been humiliated, and Kennedy's graceful concession speech gave the handsome young senator good national exposure. In perspective, after the Eisenhower–Nixon landslide, Humphrey had done Kennedy a favor, as JFK told the Gridiron Dinner two years later: "I might have won that race with Senator Kefauver—and my political career would now be over."[10]

Humphrey rebounded quickly from the embarrassment, but Kennedy would snatch victory from the jaws of defeat. Aided by his wealthy "Founding Father," Joseph P. Kennedy, who brought Hollywood into American politics in the new media age, John Kennedy, in effect, began his 1960 presidential quest with his concession to Estes Kefauver. JFK was tailor-made for television, and his Merlin–father created Camelot. He would finagle the awarding of the Pulitzer Prize for biography in 1957 for his son's book *Profiles in Courage,* when it was not even one of the nominated finalists. Everywhere Humphrey looked between 1958 and 1960, Kennedy and his wife Jackie appeared on magazine covers and were featured in television interviews. Humphrey was running not only against an individual but against a wealthy family corporation, a parvenu dynasty conjuring an aura of royalty, possessing innumerable connections in the media and politics.

Humphrey could only compete on the issues, and there was no competition. Kennedy's record was a poor shadow of Humphrey's. But Humphrey was again a patsy, as in 1956. Despite Kennedy's well-managed and well-financed campaign, he appeared the underdog against Humphrey in the crucial state of West Virginia. Kennedy had defeated Humphrey in the Wisconsin primary in Humphrey's own backyard, but analysts had noted the great number of Catholic crossover voters for Kennedy and likewise Lutheran voters for Humphrey. (Nixon would carry Wisconsin in the general election.) And the overwhelmingly Protestant and rural West Virginia, where Humphrey was the early favorite, was to be the major test for the Catholic Kennedy, as far as the national media were concerned. The myth of Al Smith's defeat by anti-Catholic bigots in 1928 was perpetuated. But the Harvard-educated war hero was no Al Smith. And just to be certain, Kennedy forces imported Franklin D. Roosevelt Jr., son of the president who had been so popular in poverty-stricken Appalachia, to accuse Humphrey of being a draft dodger in World War II. The poorly financed Humphrey campaign was also no match for Joe Kennedy's millions. Thousands of Protestants were to prove they were not bigots by voting for the underdog, created by the media, against a Protestant with a far superior legislative record.[11]

Oscar Wilde wrote: "In this world there are only two tragedies. One is not getting what one wants, and the other is getting it." Such was the case with Hubert Humphrey's selection by LBJ as his running mate in 1964. Humphrey had become a power in the Senate, being elected whip to Majority Leader Mike Mansfield of Montana, who succeeded LBJ after he was elected vice president. Humphrey became a major architect of New Frontier and Great Society policies. But presidential ambition, reinforced by what Doris Kearns [Goodwin] has called a "psychological dependency" on Johnson, proved Humphrey's undoing when he was chosen vice president, perhaps the epitome of political dependency.

Almost from the moment of their landslide victory over Barry Goldwater and William E. Miller in November 1964, President Johnson began to emasculate his vice president–elect. When Humphrey gave the impression that he would become the administration spokesman on education, Johnson called in White House reporters and told them: "Boys, I've just reminded Hubert that I've got his balls in my pocket." But the president's machismo would color his attitude not only on the vice president but also on the war in Vietnam.

In February 1965, after the Viet Cong attacked the American base at Pleiku, Johnson ordered retaliatory bombing of North Vietnam. When, three days later, the Viet Cong killed twenty-three Americans at Quinhon, Humphrey at a National Security Council meeting called for a delay in retaliation, especially since Soviet Premier Aleksey Kosygin was visiting Hanoi. The others in attendance recommended immediate bombing. A week later, Humphrey sent the president a memo, advising him to "cut losses" while the administration was still politically strong, and warning him that escalation and bombing would lead to mounting opposition at home. Why adopt Goldwater's tactics when, in the election, "we stressed not enlarging the war" and won a landslide victory? But Humphrey soon told Thomas Hughes, the chief of State Department intelligence who drafted the memo, that it "infuriated" Johnson. The president immediately shut the vice president out of Security Council meetings. And the country was singing, in the words of satirist Tom Lehrer, "Whatever became of Hubert?"

Vietnam would prove the undoing not only of Humphrey but also of the liberal Democrats, who, under Senator William Fulbright's leadership, had given Johnson carte blanche to do as he saw fit under the Tonkin Gulf Resolution. After the passage of the Voting Rights Act of 1965 and the president's proclamation to a Howard University commencement, "We Shall Overcome," as Dr. King moved north to march for fair housing in Chicago, Johnson in September 1965 abolished the civil rights council headed by the vice president. And Humphrey acquiesced. Johnson's abandonment of civil rights virtually coincided with his escalation of the war in Vietnam. Humphrey was shocked in July 1965 when marine corps commandant General Wallace Greene told him: "Mr. Vice President, you must understand that it will take no less than five hundred thousand troops on the ground to do what we must do to carry out our mission and bring an end in Vietnam." Humphrey, anxious to get out of Johnson's "doghouse," was soon outdoing the president by warning the country to "be prepared for a long, ugly, costly war." Humphrey was convinced that the overwhelming majority of academics and college students supported the draft and the policy of escalation, as he called his hecklers communists.[12]

After Johnson announced his intention to send ground troops to Vietnam on July 28, 1965, his policy was supported with growing public enthusiasm for the next year. The chairman of his Council of Economic Advisers, Gardner Ackley, in a letter to Johnson two days later, observed: "We are certainly not saying that a Vietnam crisis is just what the doctor ordered for the American economy in the next 12 months. But on a coldly objective analysis, the over-all effects are most likely to be favorable to our prosperity." Predicting a rapid growth in productive capacity, Ackley forecast "more butter, and if needed, more guns." Charles De Gaulle's assessment of Winston Churchill and the English might well apply to Johnson and the Americans: they both possess a merchant mentality with their short-range aims. Humphrey had jumped back on the Johnson bandwagon.

Humphrey was to become in 1966 the chief evangelist for LBJ's policies, against those of the newly elected senator from New York, Robert F. Kennedy (RFK), who was suggesting that the Viet Cong be included in the South Vietnamese government. On February 7, Humphrey began a two-and-one-half-week, highly visible trip to Saigon and other Asian capitals. Naive especially on military matters, he was easily brainwashed by General

William Westmoreland and others. He sketched for his staff a draft report for the president in Vandenbergesque language: "The big picture must be shown, the big picture that Mansfield, Fulbright, [Wayne] Morse all missed. The Vietnam situation is a dramatized, concentrated example of what the Communists intend to do elsewhere. . . . The danger of China is a plague—an epidemic, and we must stop that epidemic. . . . This is not a fight about Saigon. If this is only a fight about Vietnam, then you are not going to get my kid." Regarding RFK's suggestion, Humphrey told the press: "Putting the Viet Cong in the Vietnamese government would be like putting a fox in the chicken coop." And Arthur Vandenberg's "chain reaction" theory became the "domino theory." Shortly after his return to Washington, Humphrey told the American Federation of Labor and Congress of Industrial Organizations (AFL-CIO): "Vietnam today is as close to the United States as London was in 1940."[13]

Humphrey, elevated from the Senate to the vice presidency, was no longer his own man, and his presidential benefactor was to become a political albatross. A reaction among the "silent majority" of Middle America was developing against the big-government programs of the Great Society. And the old New Deal coalition had begun to break down in the South after the passage of the Civil Rights Acts. The Tet Offensive of January 31, 1968, put the lie to Johnson's Vietnam policy and forced his withdrawal from the presidential race that year. But Humphrey, in announcing his candidacy for the presidency, revealed how increasingly insensitive he had become.

In the aftermath of Martin Luther King's assassination, as thousands of flag-draped coffins were being returned from Vietnam, Vice President Humphrey announced his candidacy for the Democratic presidential nomination. He typically bubbled over and extemporized, unwittingly calling his platform "the politics of joy." His inappropriate remark, headlined the next day, made him look silly at the beginning of his presidential quest.

But the nation's attention was focused in May 1968 on the two Senate liberals competing in the primaries, Bobby Kennedy and Eugene McCarthy. After Kennedy won Indiana and Nebraska handily, "Clean Gene" won Oregon by 6 percent. California was to be crucial, but politics was forgotten temporarily that early morning of June 5, when Bobby Kennedy was shot and killed. As Muriel Humphrey said, "The bullet that killed Bobby Kennedy also wounded Hubert." But it also wounded the election process and, in the words of the vice president, would "sour the whole public, and particularly the Democratic party, on the election and on the democratic process."[14]

Humphrey had the nomination locked up after the other Minnesotan, Gene McCarthy, suffering a nervous breakdown, failed to rally the antiwar forces, despite his narrow loss to Kennedy in California. But was the nomination worth anything, especially after the riotous Democratic National Convention in Chicago? Humphrey came close to defeating Nixon in the general election, winning 42.7 percent of the popular vote to Nixon's 43.4 percent. But in the electoral college, the vote was not so close: Nixon 301, Humphrey 191, and George Wallace 46. The Democratic answers in 1964 had been so simple, so right; the complex questions of 1968, confronting the Democratic liberals, had no easy answers for ghetto blacks, antiwar students, and confused suburbanites. The nation would turn to the "new Nixon" with a "secret plan" to end the war in Vietnam.[15]

Just as in England after an era of Gladstonian Liberal reform, the public would turn to Disraeli's Conservatives for a patriotic breathing spell, so in 1968, the American voters would choose a more conservative, apparently patriotic course. Hubert Humphrey might be compared to Herbert H. Asquith, the last Liberal prime minister of the United Kingdom, in 1916. Just as those World War I Liberals were pulled apart by often conflicting constituencies—suffragettes, Irish nationalists, labor unions—so, too, were the Democrats of the Vietnam era by theirs: antiwar students, prowar "hard hats," ghetto blacks, and traditionally Democratic southern whites. Just as "playing the Orange card" of Ulster unionism became a successful tactic to unite British Conservatives, so would a "southern strategy" of racist hue be devised by Republicans to appeal to a white Middle America, both in the North but especially in the new, potentially Republican South, frightened by the growing political strength of African Americans. And the architect of that conservative, southern strategy was a senator who was not intoxicated by presidential ambitions, Strom Thurmond.

In 1964, Thurmond at long last decided on political consistency and became a Republican, supporting the losing cause of Barry Goldwater. The South Carolinian supported the Republican-southern coalition 90 percent of the time during the 1963–1964 sessions, the second highest of all southerners, with only Senator Sam Ervin of North Carolina ahead of him at 91 percent. And on Soviet–American relations, Thurmond, a major general in the army reserve, saw eye to eye with Senator Goldwater of Arizona, a major general in the air force reserve.

Thurmond had been at odds with the Kennedy administration from the start. When presidential adviser Arthur M. Schlesinger Jr. asserted that creation of a welfare state was a good defense against communism, Thurmond shot back: "Welfare statism is like Communism in its mistrust of individual liberty and its reliance on state control." In 1961 and 1962, he attacked the nation's "no win" foreign policy and pushed the Senate Armed

Services Committee into investigating the muzzling of high-ranking officers by Pentagon civilians under Secretary of Defense Robert McNamara. Thurmond's staff examined the 1,500 censored speeches the secretary had submitted to the committee, and the senator singled out for criticism such deleted phrases as: "Communist conspiracy directed toward absolute domination of the world," "Communism encompassing Marxism, Fabian Socialism, Socialism," "Soviets have not relented in the slightest in their determination to dominate the world and to destroy our way of life." On January 15, 1962, Senator Thurmond became the first member of Congress to call the nation's attention to the construction of Soviet missile sites in Cuba. On August 31, he announced that the Russians had deployed "at least four intermediate range ballistic missiles" in Cuba. Thurmond's intelligence gathering had scooped the president, and the nation's confrontation with the USSR in October 1962 led to the removal of the missiles and their Soviet technicians.[16]

The nation knew Thurmond chiefly for his opposition to the Civil Rights Act of 1964 and the Voting Rights Act of 1965. He clothed his implicit racism in the rhetoric of strict constitutional construction. In supporting the *Dred Scott* decision, he argued that "the War between the States was brought on because the social revolutionaries refused to stop at the constitutional barrier cited by the Supreme Court." After the Civil War, in his view, the Fourteenth Amendment was "legislated and imposed by force of arms . . . to preserve the outward appearance of legality." The *Brown* decision of the Supreme Court in 1954 revealed that "the intent of the Framers of the Constitution and previous judicial decisions could be ignored."

Thurmond for a moment in 1964 turned into a playful Preston S. Brooks, the congressman from his home county of Edgefield who had beaten Senator Charles Sumner with his cane. The physically fit Thurmond merely wrestled Senator Ralph Yarborough of Texas to the floor outside the door to the Commerce Committee room, in a futile effort to prevent a quorum in a vote on the confirmation of former Governor LeRoy Collins, a racial moderate, to head the new federal Community Relations Service, created by the Civil Rights Act.[17]

As a not-so-playful muscular Christian, Thurmond, benefiting from J. Edgar Hoover's wiretaps of Martin Luther King's phones, had employed some of Joe McCarthy's tactics in August 1963. He rose in the Senate to denounce the organizer of the March on Washington, Bayard Rustin, for "sexual perversion" and inserted a police booking slip into the *Congressional Record*. For weeks before the march, Thurmond also presented to the Senate numerous newspaper reports charging communist connections with civil rights workers. Thurmond obviously hoped to smear the Southern Christian Leadership Conference and the civil rights movement.[18]

In his address to the people of South Carolina on September 16, 1964, Thurmond explained why he was joining the Republican Party and supporting Goldwater for president:

> The Democratic Party has abandoned the people. It has turned its back on the spiritual values and political principles which have brought us the blessings of freedom under God and a bountiful prosperity. It has breached the trust reposed in it by the people. It has repudiated the Constitution of the United States. It is leading the evolution of our nation to a socialistic dictatorship.
>
> The Democratic Party has forsaken the people to become the party of minority groups, power-hungry union leaders, political bosses, and big businessmen looking for government contracts and favors.
>
> The Democratic Party has encouraged lawlessness, civil unrest, and mob actions.
>
> The Democratic Party . . . has sent our youth into combat in Viet Nam, refusing to call it war. . . .
>
> The Democratic Party now worships at the throne of power and materialism.

Many of his themes would echo down through the Nixon, Reagan, and Bush campaigns.[19]

But Thurmond and his aide Harry Dent most significantly became the chief architects of Goldwater's southern strategy. Though it failed in LBJ's 1964 landslide, it would become a winning strategy for Nixon in 1968 and 1972, Reagan in 1980 and 1984, and Bush in 1988. Due largely to Thurmond's efforts, Goldwater carried, in addition to his home state of Arizona, the five southern states of South Carolina, Georgia, Alabama, Mississippi, and Louisiana. The addition of these southern states plus North Carolina would have elected Nixon in 1960, without Illinois and California. Strom Thurmond's strategy for the 1968 presidential campaign had become clear.

Thurmond was to play a senatorial Warwick in 1968. He was not one of those many post-Eisenhower senators using the upper chamber as a trampoline to reach the presidency or vice presidency. He worked daily at his political push-ups in his Senate fiefdoms of the Armed Services and Judiciary Committees. Just after extracting from Richard Nixon a pledge to support the ABM (antiballistic missile) system, Thurmond endorsed the former vice president at the Republican Nominating Convention in Miami. Also in return for lining up southern delegates for Nixon, Thurmond was given veto power over Nixon's running mate, which the Senator used against Senator Mark Hatfield of Oregon and ex-Governor William Scranton of Pennsylvania. When the list was narrowed to two, Governor John A. Volpe of Massachusetts and Governor Spiro T. Agnew of Maryland, the choice was an obvious one. Wooing Strom Thurmond and the south required Agnew.

Wags in Washington during Nixon's first year in office referred to the White House as "Uncle Strom's Cabin." The southern strategy of Thurmond and his former assistant Harry Dent, now on Nixon's staff, was partially successful in winning the election, though George Wallace carried four of the five southern states Goldwater had carried in 1964 and came close to throwing the election into the House of Representatives. But South Carolina went for Nixon. The election symbolized a sea change in American politics because most of the voters for Wallace's American Independent Party were using it as a "way station" in deserting the Democratic Party for the Republican, the way Thurmond had in his temporary independence. In effect, Thurmond's influence in the Republican Party was strengthened by the strategy for an "emerging Republican majority" during the 1970s and 1980s. His rhetoric anticipated the polarizing speeches of Vice President Agnew. During his successful campaign to prevent the confirmation of Abe Fortas as chief justice, Thurmond asked the nominee to comment on the 1957 Supreme Court decision, *Mallory* v. *United States:* "Does not that decision, Mallory—I want that word to ring in your ears, Mallory— . . . shackle law enforcement? Mallory, a man who raped a woman, admitted his guilt, and the Supreme Court turned him loose on a technicality. . . . Is not that type of decision calculated to encourage more people to commit rapes and serious crimes?" Thurmond's words would echo down to the election of 1988, when his protégé, Lee Atwater, made the name of another convicted rapist, Willie Horton, ring in the ears of the American public.[20]

Hubert Humphrey took his narrow defeat by Nixon gracefully, and he was reelected to the Senate from Minnesota in 1970. But his focus was still on the White House, and he made one last try in 1972. As far as many antiwar Democrats were concerned, however, he was a tainted candidate. Though he won more votes in the primaries than Senator George McGovern, the Democrats nominated the South Dakotan, who lost forty-nine states and the election to President Nixon. Humphrey, who detested fund-raising, was also humiliated during Watergate by having his 1972 campaign manager, Jack Chesnut, convicted of accepting illegal campaign contributions.

In 1976, Humphrey was tempted to run in the New Jersey primary on June 6, as a last-ditch effort to stop Jimmy Carter. But he fortunately decided against it, as he was diagnosed with cancer in September and had his bladder and prostate removed. In addition to being reelected to the Senate in November, he did have the joy of seeing his protégé, Senator Walter F. Mondale, elected vice president.

In 1977, Humphrey's cancer was diagnosed as terminal, and the whole political establishment knew. He was honored in many ways: a new Health,

Education, and Welfare building was named after him, and he was invited to address the Senate and the House. He fought cancer as vigorously as he campaigned: once, in 100-degree heat at a Minnesota high school, as the entire band lay prostrate on the ground, Hubert rolled on in his hour-long address.

At Humphrey's funeral in the Capitol rotunda in January 1978, Vice President Mondale eulogized his friend and mentor: "He taught us how to hope and how to love, how to win and how to lose. He taught us how to live, and, finally, he taught us how to die." He was probably the most accessible of all the politicians of his era, and the most lovable. But did this reflect an inordinate desire to be liked—a fatal flaw in politicians?

Gene McCarthy testily remarked of "Fritz" Mondale during his campaign for the presidency in 1984 that he had the soul of a vice president. Perhaps Humphrey did, too. He confessed in the aftermath of his 1968 presidential campaign: "I ought not to have let a man who was going to be a former President dictate my future." Shortly before he died, a *Washington Post* poll of a thousand insiders on Capitol Hill voted Humphrey the "top senator" of the past seventy-five years. Hubert Humphrey definitely had the soul of a great legislator, and an unbroken senatorial career of almost thirty years might have placed him almost on the level of Senator George Norris were it not for Humphrey's overweening desire to be president. If LBJ had passed over Humphrey in 1964, would Senator Humphrey, not Gene McCarthy or Bobby Kennedy, have led the antiwar movement in 1968? Probably not, given Humphrey's vulnerability to charges of being "soft on Communism."[21]

The White House may have been "Uncle Strom's Cabin" during the Nixon presidency, but it took a "Sunbelt strategy"—an updating of the "southern strategy"—and Reagan's political coattails in 1980 to elect a Republican Senate for the first time in twenty-six years and to turn the influential Judiciary Committee into Uncle Strom's Committee. As chair, he began immediately to influence policy by abolishing the Antitrust Subcommittee. The full Judiciary Committee assumed control, and the chair and the majority were thus able to limit investigations of antitrust matters. This was an important symbolic move ushering in the decade of mergermania.

Through the eighties, Thurmond remained an important link to the South and to Christian fundamentalists for the Reagan administration. The senator applauded Reagan's Justice Department decision in 1982 to grant federal tax exemption to such racially discriminatory schools as Bob Jones University, where Thurmond was a trustee. It expelled students for interracial dating and marriage, but Thurmond called Justice's policy an end to "trampling on religious and private civil rights." When the Supreme Court later ruled such exemptions illegal by a vote of 8 to 1, the undaunted Thurmond pressed for a more conservative Court. By 1991, Thurmond was still extreme in his anticrime philosophy when he led the Bush administration's efforts to legalize the "exclusionary rule." The Senate defeated his amendment, which would have allowed police to admit into evidence in court "items seized during warrantless searches," as Majority Leader George J. Mitchell of Maine, a former judge, condemned Thurmond's proposal for its "totalitarianism": "That's Communism. . . . That's China. That's not America." Thurmond and his supporters maintained that such evidence should be considered, as long as the search was conducted under the "good-faith" belief that a crime had been committed.[22]

Thurmond remained an important symbol of the new electoral strategy for the presidential elections of 1984 and 1988. His protégé Lee Atwater, a young political scientist from South Carolina, had served as Reagan's southern regional coordinator in 1980 and would eventually move up to become George Bush's campaign manager in 1988. Atwater claimed that the Sunbelt, with its 266 electoral votes—four fewer than a majority and still growing in numbers, according to the rising population in large southern and western states—was the key to Republican victories for at least the rest of the century.

Atwater even turned the tables on his old mentor Strom in 1988 when the senator endorsed Robert Dole before the South Carolina primary. It was to be held on the Saturday before the Super Tuesday primaries. Recognizing that the greatest strength of Bush was his attachment to Reagan and that Thurmond's popularity could not be transferred to Dole, Atwater enticed Dole to challenge Bush in South Carolina, even though the state Republican organization under Governor Carroll Campbell was supporting the vice president. Bush won South Carolina with 48 percent of the vote and all of the delegates, to 21 percent for Dole and 19 percent for Pat Robertson. Bush was then boosted to his landslide victory the following Tuesday, winning sixteen states to none for Bob Dole. South Carolina had played a role in nominating a president that was beyond the wildest dreams of John C. Calhoun.[23]

Today's Calhoun, Senator Strom Thurmond of South Carolina, ironically found himself a states' rights champion of an imperial presidency. It had all taken place as the Senate became a mere "launching pad" for the presidency. Nineteen out of the thirty-two nominees for president and vice president of the Democratic and Republican National Conventions from 1960 to 1988 were current or former senators. With the rise of the imperial presidency after the four terms of FDR, but especially as a result of the nation's becoming an imperial world power, the executive dominated the legislative branch. The seat of power was 1600 Pennsylvania Avenue, not Capitol Hill.

A story about JFK illustrates the power shift. When an acquaintance visited young Congressman John F. Kennedy, Representative Kennedy remarked: "I have to get to the Senate, because that's where the action is." When the same person visited Senator Kennedy in the 1950s, the Senator said: "I have to get to the White House—that's where the action is." Kennedy's comments reflected the attitudes of most post–World War II liberal Democratic senators, especially Hubert Humphrey.[24]

Thurmond, a major general as well as a senator, understood the "military-industrial complex" and, despite his states' rights philosophy, took advantage of the imperial federal structure. Because of his staunch anticommunism, he was content with usurpers of executive power such as J. Edgar Hoover and William Casey. The liberal Democrats, with their FDR–New Deal obsession, permitted the Senate to drift into becoming a mere appendage to the executive branch, where "the action" was.

Just as Woodrow Wilson wrote during the Spanish-American War that the presidency was always strengthened during wartime at the expense of the Congress, even more so was the huge, ever-expanding executive branch of the Cold War era. Not even the trauma of Vietnam, the excesses of Watergate, or the absurdities of the Iran–Contra affair weakened the power of the president. As Suetonius wrote about Emperor Tiberius Caesar, the imperial president had merely to appear to consult the Senate, as he kept them "guessing by his carefully evasive answers and hesitations." The club of 100 members—each his or her own political party—failed, often by default, to perform its proper constitutional role. And the "Keating Five" and other examples of corruption revealed a body that was hardly a forum for virtue or even wanted to be.[25]

Epilogue

Virtue Misapplied

Modern Heroes in an Age of Hubris

On June 1, 1950, the freshman senator from Maine and the first woman to become an influential member of the male-dominated club rose in the upper house to issue a "Declaration of Conscience." It focused on the paranoia sweeping the country since Senator Joseph R. McCarthy delivered his speech to the Republican Women's Club of Wheeling, West Virginia, in February waving a list of "205" members of the Communist Party working in the U.S. State Department. "I speak as a Republican. I speak as a woman. I speak as a United States senator. I speak as an American," she said. Recently, she maintained, the Senate "has too often been debased to the level of a forum of hate and character assassination, sheltered by the shield of congressional immunity." She reminded the nation of

> some of the basic principles of Americanism:
>
> > The right to criticize;
> > the right to hold unpopular beliefs;
> > the right to protest;
> > the right of independent thought.

Her manifesto called on the Republican Party not to ride to electoral victory on "the Four Horsemen of Calumny—Fear, Ignorance, Bigotry and Smear."

Senator Margaret Chase Smith was joined in her "Declaration" by six other Republicans while all the Democrats ran for shelter during those crazy times of the Korean War and the McCarthy era until the Senate finally summoned the courage to censure him in December 1954. The cause of

Margaret Chase Smith's courage, according to Senator John F. Kennedy's observation on personal courage a few years later, was "shadowed by a veil which cannot be torn away." Yet the absolute truth of that phrase camouflages the moral torment implicit in every act of real courage. Such acts were relatively rare in a supine Senate under an imperial presidency. What the ancient Greeks called hubris, or insolence growing out of excessive pride, came to dominate American politics and culture during the Pax Americana after World War II.

Yet virtue, misapplied, can turn to vice. It did for Senator Smith on June 1, 1970, when, from her same desk in the Senate, she delivered her "Declaration of Conscience, II." She had strongly supported the U.S. policy in Vietnam, including President Richard Nixon's "incursion" into Cambodia and Vice President Spiro Agnew's attack on the media. But her personal confrontation with students at Colby College, who shouted obscenities at her after the killings at Kent State University, scared her. She was well intentioned: she said she was trying to get the nation to "Cool it." Her focal point this time was "the anarchism of the extreme Leftists," and she warned that "repression is preferable to anarchy and nihilism to most Americans." Unlike 1950, this time she overlooked the abuse of power by those in authority. Though she was right to attack the "antidemocratic arrogance" of the "extreme left," Margaret Chase Smith failed to understand what it meant to be a conservative. And so did the conservative Freedom House in making her chair of its board for her statement on "repression." Senator Smith, with excessive pride, summed up her career in a book, *Declaration of Conscience,* published shortly before her retirement. Her memoir unwittingly dramatizes the way heroism and hubris, Januslike, test everyone for a lifetime. Courage in one crisis does not guarantee virtuous conduct in another, especially in the dangerous waters of historical analogy.[1]

A clear case of hubris and arrogant abuse of history was the awarding of the 1957 Pulitzer Prize in biography to John F. Kennedy's *Profiles in Courage.* It was a classic example of political manipulation by Ambassador Joseph P. Kennedy, with the caveat that "politics" often influence the awarding of Pulitzers, Nobels, and other prizes. The academic judges had recommended five biographies, among them Alpheus T. Mason's *Harlan Fiske Stone,* James MacGregor Burns's *Roosevelt,* and William N. Chambers's *Old Bullion Benton.* Yet the official Advisory Board ignored the recommendations and, out of the blue, selected *Profiles.* Apparently, it was not the hand of Providence at work but that of the "Founding Father."

America was ready to be seduced by a young Lancelot of the "G.I. generation." JFK had already made a graceful appearance on the national stage in his narrow defeat for the vice presidential nomination in 1956, and *Profiles* had appeared in serialized form in *Harper's, Collier's, Reader's Digest,* the *New York Times Magazine,* and the *Boston Globe.* NBC-TV's *Kraft Theatre* presented an hour's dramatization of Edmund Ross's "courage" in preventing the impeachment of Andrew Johnson. Not surprisingly, then, a member of the Pulitzer board, Joseph P. Pulitzer Jr., would later say: "It was not history as much as it was a journalistic achievement at that time—and a political achievement. I think that's the point." Of course, the quiet lobbying of the ambassador and family friend Arthur Krock, one-time editor of the *New York Times* and member of the faculty of Columbia University's School of Journalism, helped. The following month, June 1957, a new Gallup poll showed Jack Kennedy leading Senator Estes Kefauver 50 percent to 39 percent for the Democratic presidential nomination of 1960.

Media-packaged heroism is as old as American party politics. And America the Guinevere was tiring of its old Arthurian hero in the White House. Although the nation still "liked Ike," the romantically sappy fifties sought a new "Shane" or "Ben Hur." And why not the purple-heart hero of PT-109 and author of the Krock-crafted *Why England Slept* and now a Pulitzer Prize–winning historical study of heroic acts in American history? Never mind that JFK wrote, at most, a small part of the book. He was not about to share the prize with Ted Sorensen and the team of professors who did most of the research and writing. In accepting the Pulitzer Prize for himself, Senator Kennedy exhibited a hubris just below the level of Napoleon's during his coronation as emperor, when he seized the crown from Pope Pius VII and crowned himself. But the arrogance of power would appear in more virulent form in later imperial presidents.[2]

American involvement in Vietnam was one long history of hubris, especially regarding the Senate's role. And the Tonkin Gulf Resolution demonstrated what a docile body it had become between the Dwight D. Eisenhower and Lyndon B. Johnson administrations. At issue were the president's role as commander in chief of U.S. armed forces and the constitutional authority of Congress to declare war. When President Eisenhower requested congressional approval of his authority to send American forces to the Middle East, if necessary, in 1957, the Middle East Resolution was thoroughly debated, often behind closed doors, in the Senate. Senator J. William Fulbright complained that the resolution would give the president a "blank check," and Senator Richard Russell of Georgia prophetically remarked that the resolution would make Congress "an appendage of the executive branch of the Government" on the war powers question. Senator

Wayne Morse of Oregon called the resolution "a clear violation of the constitutional power of the President," and Hubert Humphrey worried about a "predated declaration of war." The Senate debated the resolution for twelve days and passed it in amended form by eliminating the reference to congressional authorization. When Eisenhower sent troops to Lebanon, he did so on his authority as commander in chief. Senatorial resistance was further worn down by the Cuba and Berlin resolutions of 1962. Wayne Morse was to be the only senator to have opposed both the Middle East Resolution of 1957 and the Tonkin Gulf Resolution in 1964.[3]

When on August 2, 1964, the U.S. destroyer *Maddox*—"its mission to play games with the North Vietnamese radar"—provoked an attack, the groundwork was laid for the first bombing of the North, and after the second, perhaps fabricated attack, the Tonkin Gulf Resolution. The Senate and the American people only knew that U.S. forces had been attacked, though eight months later, the president, musing to reporters about the difficulty of obtaining hard facts, quipped, "For all I know, our Navy was shooting at whales out there." Three days after the second attack, the Senate, on August 7, overwhelmingly approved a resolution granting the president authority to use such force against the North Vietnamese as necessary, even if it led to war. The only dissenters were old progressive Republicans-turned-Democrats, Wayne L. Morse of Oregon and Ernest Gruening of Alaska.

Dean of the University of Oregon Law School and member of the War Labor Board, Morse was elected to the Senate as a progressive Republican in 1945. But he switched to the Democrats in 1955 and served in the Senate until replaced by Robert Packwood in the traumatic election of 1968. Gruening came from a similar political background. Having graduated from Harvard Medical School, but entering journalism and serving as editor of the *Nation* during the 1920s, he supported reform Republican Fiorello La Guardia for mayor of New York. Appointed territorial governor of Alaska in 1939, Gruening became a champion of Alaskan statehood and represented Alaska in the U.S. Senate from 1959 until his defeat in the 1968 Democratic primary by real estate developer Mike Gravel. Senator-to-be Gravel ran an especially sleazy campaign, in which a TV film portrayed him as a liaison between the U.S. Army and the French underground during World War II, though Gravel only turned fifteen in 1945. Gruening remarked on his defeat: "I began to understand how Bob La Follette felt when he lost to Joe McCarthy."

Both of the dissident senators were throwbacks to a George Norris–Thomas J. Walsh progressivism. But Morse had a special interest in international law and a shrewd skepticism about the integrity of LBJ, which prepared him for the Tonkin debate. In 1955, when Morse had switched to the Democrats, he broke a tie in the Senate to aid them in forming the majority and to elect Johnson majority leader. And in 1957, the Oregonian perceived the shallowness of the Civil Rights Bill that most senators and observers viewed as a great victory for the Texan: "I disagree with my Majority Leader on the nature of the bill. I think this so-called Civil Rights Bill shows that civil rights for the time being for millions of colored people are dead, so far as effective protection of their right to vote is concerned." Morse was not about to be fooled by President Johnson's imperial feint in appearing to consult the Senate over the Tonkin Gulf incident, nor was Gruening. Two cantankerous old men opposed the unanimous endorsement of the imperial will of the president: the House voted 416 to 0.[4]

"I don't think that there was anybody any more independent or tougher-minded than Wayne was," Senator William Proxmire of Wisconsin remarked of Morse. In opposing the Tonkin Gulf Resolution, Morse's words would haunt the generation of the sixties: "I believe that history will record that we have made a great mistake in subverting and circumventing the Constitution of the United States ... by means of this resolution. ... [W]e are in effect giving the President ... warmaking powers in the absence of a declaration of war. I believe that to be a historic mistake." In the words of a historian of the war, the U.S. Senate "had seen fit to acquiesce without any serious challenge to the manipulations of the executive branch." As the war escalated, backed by the authority of the resolution, Gruening wondered whether the Tonkin Gulf incident was "another Reichstag Fire." The resolution was a good example of the way an imperial presidency should operate: personal power exercised privately. Morse's courage was a product of intelligence and integrity: he was his own man.[5]

In contrast to Morse's heroic act, as 85 percent of the nation approved of the raids that the Tonkin Gulf Resolution supinely endorsed, Senator J. William Fulbright, chair of the Foreign Relations Committee, was the president's vassal. In 1959, Majority Leader Johnson had made him chair of the prestigious committee, even referring to him as "my Secretary of State." And Fulbright exulted in his behind-the-scenes exercise of personal power. He had been a supporter of the Dwight Eisenhower–John Foster Dulles "Cold War" foreign policy and was manipulated by LBJ into conning such skeptics as Senators John Sherman Cooper of Kentucky and Gaylord Nelson of Wisconsin, who questioned the open-ended nature of the resolution. Fulbright would have to apologize publicly to Nelson after President Johnson continued to escalate the war with the backing of the resolution. Morse would later blame Fulbright more than Johnson for the Vietnam disaster. More Oxonian than Arkansan, Senator Fulbright, a Rhodes scholar like

Dean Rusk and Walt Whitman Rostow, had been tagged by President Harry S. Truman as "an overeducated Oxford SOB." Though the senator may have been corrupted by his own arrogance, he sought penance for his act of hubris, publishing *The Arrogance of Power* in 1966. In fact, his "sense of guilt" has been "a powerful goad" ever since.[6]

Another who especially knew better was the former professor of history and Asia expert who succeeded Johnson as majority leader in 1961, Senator Mike Mansfield of Montana. Born of Irish immigrant parents in Greenwich Village in 1903, Mike Mansfield lost his mother at the age of three and was sent by his father to live with an aunt and uncle in Great Falls, Montana. He dropped out of school before finishing eighth grade, and when the United States entered World War I in 1917, he joined the navy at the age of fourteen. He subsequently served in the army and the marines before meeting Maureen Hayes, a schoolteacher, who insisted that he finish school before she would marry him. He not only completed high school but eventually obtained an M.A. in history at Montana State University, where he joined the faculty to teach Latin American and Far Eastern history and political science. And in 1942, he was elected to the House, replacing Jeannette Rankin, the Republican pacifist who did not run for reelection after casting the lone vote in Congress against American entry into World War II. President Franklin D. Roosevelt sent Mansfield on a secret mission to China in 1944, and President Truman offered to appoint him assistant secretary of state in 1949. But he stayed in the House and was elected to the Senate in 1952. In 1956, LBJ appointed him Democratic whip; Mansfield succeeded Johnson as majority leader in 1961. The senator from Montana was "a decent, gentle, kind man, and keenly intelligent," wrote Bobby Baker, secretary to the majority; and he said working for Mansfield after working for Johnson was "like lolling on the beach as opposed to picking cotton."

Mansfield had been one of President Kennedy's closest friends in the Senate. As early as 1962, Mansfield had visited Saigon at Kennedy's request and returned with a private report that was so pessimistic that it angered the president. During the summer of 1965, when President Johnson made the crucial decision to send combat troops and escalate the war, Mansfield privately advised against it, warning of growing discontent in the United States and mindful of the disastrous French experience. He had supported the Tonkin Gulf Resolution and continued to support each increase in the number of troops. The senator felt that, as majority leader, he had to stand loyally behind the president of his own party.

Mansfield often referred to Tom Walsh as his hero. But Walsh was more self-actualized, as he grew in his office and even broke with the president of his own party. Mansfield apparently gave no thought to resigning his leadership post in protest of policies he opposed. He suffered from that special form of hubris which immobilizes intellectuals who know what is right but are incapable of acting.

But Mansfield was trapped like most Americans in July 1965, when LBJ announced the first big escalation of the war. The Vandenbergian rhetoric of twenty years was now to be applied to Vietnam, and the "chain reaction" theory became the "domino theory." In announcing an increase of 50,000 troops (he had secretly agreed upon 100,000), LBJ told a press conference: "Nor would surrender in Vietnam bring peace, because we learned from Hitler at Munich that success only feeds the appetite of aggression. The battle would be renewed in one country and then another country, bring[ing] with it perhaps even larger and crueler conflict, as we have learned from the lessons of history." Even those who knew the real "lessons of history" were swept along in supporting propagandistic history to justify the actions of an imperial presidency. In camouflaging his military buildup, President Johnson called for a kind of Great Society for Southeast Asia, proposing a dam on the "vast Mekong River" that would "dwarf even our own TVA [Tennessee Valley Authority]." Mike Mansfield's Senate gave almost rubber-stamp approval to President Johnson's power as commander in chief.[7]

The Senate became the setting for one of the most majestic and tragic dramas of American history in 1968, as two Irishmen tried to use a presidential election to change the course of history but failed. Each was motivated by both hubris and heroism. Senator Eugene J. McCarthy of Minnesota was the Benedictine-educated professor who considered himself the genuine liberal Catholic of the 1950s, in contrast to JFK. Senator Robert F. Kennedy (RFK) of New York was the charismatic heir of his assassinated brother.

There was special irony in the roles the two men played. McCarthy, the sometime poet, became the man of action, who acted decisively in late 1967 and announced his candidacy for the presidency. He would challenge the incumbent in the primaries of his own party. And on the night of March 12, 1968, he shocked the country by winning a moral victory in the New Hampshire primary against President Johnson (42 percent to LBJ's 49 percent and within 1 percent of the president's vote when Republican write-ins were counted). But it was a Pyrrhic victory for "Clean Gene," as the antiwar forces would be divided by another candidacy a few days later.

On the morning of March 16, in the same Senate Caucus Room where his brother had announced for the presidency eight years earlier, Bobby

Kennedy abandoned his Hamletlike stance and joined the political fray. The tough-minded Irish politician had turned idealist in what was probably a losing role. His hubris would not trust the political outcome to the quixotic McCarthy. And for one challenging the imperial presidency, Bobby Kennedy's campaign began on a confused note: "At stake is not simply the leadership of our party and even our country, it is our right to the moral leadership of this planet." Such "moral" leadership was LBJ's rationale for a Great Society for Southeast Asia. And as for Bobby's hubris in spoiling Gene's victory, Murray Kempton summed up the attitudes of thousands of McCarthy supporters in a telegram to Ted Kennedy: "Sorry I can't join you. Your brother's announcement makes it clear that St. Patrick did not drive all the snakes from Ireland."[8]

Eugene McCarthy was not devoid of political aspirations. He had coyly accepted LBJ's overtures as one of the finalists in the vice presidential sweepstakes of 1964, much to the consternation of his old mentor Hubert Humphrey. But it was McCarthy who was made to look a fool by the president. And this grudge may have been a motivating factor in his challenging Johnson. But Bobby's entry into the race stirred up McCarthy's old animosity toward the Kennedys. Who was the real liberal, the real Irishman, the real Catholic? It carried with it all the rivalry midwestern and western Irish Catholic reformers felt toward their eastern, more conservative counterparts, Archbishop John Ireland of St. Paul versus William Cardinal O'Connell of Boston, Senator Tom Walsh of Montana versus Governor Al Smith of New York, and Catholic-educated McCarthy versus Harvard-educated Kennedy. But blue-collar whites, who also liked George Wallace, preferred Bobby to Gene because, in RFK's words, "Gene comes across as Lace Curtain Irish to those people. They can tell I'm pure Shanty Irish." For Gene, Bobby's tactics in 1968 were "cheap and petty" and resembled those in his campaign against Senator Kenneth Keating of New York.[9]

When McCarthy confessed that he was a stalking-horse for Sir Thomas More, not Bobby Kennedy, he was alluding to the highly acclaimed movie and play *A Man for All Seasons,* about the historical figure. Just as More opposed the Machiavellian aggregation of power by Henry VIII, so, too, would McCarthy attempt to limit presidential power by running for the presidency. In a poem in the spring of 1967 called "The Lament of an Aging Politician," McCarthy wrote:

> I have left Act I, for involution
> And Act II. There mired in complexity
> I cannot write Act III.

The senator explained that "Act I states the problem. Act II deals with the complications. And Act III resolves them. I'm an Act II man. That's where I live—involution and complexity." McCarthy was a poet frustrated with the impotence of the Senate. He was caught up in his Act II role as presidential candidate for the next three months and could not foresee the tragedy of Act III.[10]

Bobby evoked the "divine right of Kennedys" in competing against "Clean Gene," but to loyal supporters of McCarthy, he was merely opportunistic. And in the May Oregon primary, with its higher percentage of white middle-class liberals and smaller number of African Americans than Indiana, McCarthy won a solid victory and tarnished the charisma of the heir apparent. The Minnesotan arrogantly but accurately proclaimed: "It's narrowed down to Bobby and me. So far he's run with the ghost of his brother. Now we're going to make him run against it. It's purely Greek: he either has to kill him or be killed by him. We'll make him run against Jack. . . . And I'm Jack." In style, perhaps, Gene was closer to Jack in his progressive but aloof Whiggishness, in contrast to Bobby's passionate man-of-the-people. The night before the California primary, TV news carried their contrasting styles: McCarthy exhorting his supporters as Shakespeare portrayed Henry V before the battle of Agincourt and RFK singing "Moon River" off-key with his friend the black football player Roosevelt Grier. In California, Bobby had freed himself from the ghost of his brother, but Act III continued the Greek tragedy: Bobby's ghost would haunt Gene and the entire Democratic Party. Heroism was dead, and hubris would become the major trait of American politics for the next two decades.[11]

A curious, almost lugubrious form of hubris affected liberal Democrats in their championing of the Kennedy name. Jack Newfield of the *Village Voice,* in a worshipful biography of Bobby in 1969, gave the impression that RFK was almost totally motivated by reading Albert Camus and that his campaign was the ultimate existential experience. Newfield's "memoir" contributed to the cult as it concluded: "The stone was at the bottom of the hill and we were alone." This solipsistic hubris flourished on the American Left for the next two decades. A campaign worker for Senator Gary Hart, who ran as a Kennedy look-alike in 1984, summed it up. Explaining her support for Hart, she identified with him as one of the sixties people who "grew up with a kind of hope that we really could right all of the wrongs in the world."[12]

On the other hand, given the nature of the supine Senate, was Eugene McCarthy's decision not to run for reelection in 1970 an example of his arrogant pride or independent courage? Certainly, most politicians could not understand giving up such power and status, especially Hubert Humphrey, who took advantage of the vacancy and was reelected to the Senate. Dr. Edgar Berman, Humphrey's friend and physician, wrote that Hubert and Bobby Kennedy liked each other but were both puzzled by McCarthy's conduct. Dr. Berman described McCarthy as having the "attention span" of "a wayward child." The physician accounted for McCarthy's "delinquent nature" with a quote from H.L. Mencken: "He took great pleasure in throwing a dead cat into the carriage of the rich and powerful as it passed him in the alley." Twentieth-century Americans do not have much time for such impractical, Swiftian characters as Eugene McCarthy, but the poet–politician obviously hopes that time may do him justice.[13]

The epitome of hubris in the seventies was the man elected president in 1968. Richard Nixon was the stereotypical "imperial president" who would do violence to the Constitution. And his chief adversary in the public eye was a most unlikely nemesis, Senator Sam Ervin of North Carolina. The old judge was often rated the most conservative senator, even ahead of Strom Thurmond. It was to be especially ironic, then, that Ervin became the chair of the Watergate investigating committee.

"Like Ulysses, all of us are a part of all we have met," Sam Ervin told the Senate in 1959, as he reflected on his lawyer–father Samuel J. Ervin Sr.: "He implanted in my youthful heart a love of law and a hate of tyranny. All the things I have met since the days of my youth have intensified this love and this hate." Though a graduate of the University of North Carolina at Chapel Hill and Harvard Law School, Samuel J. Ervin Jr. was cut from whole cloth in his early years and possessed that kind of virtue the Romans so admired. In fact, his life presents a consistent pattern and a special integrity.[14]

Ervin's arrival on the national scene occurred shortly after the momentous Supreme Court decision *Brown* v. *Board of Education of Topeka,* handed down on May 17, 1954. That decision, eliminating segregation in American public schools, would shape much of Ervin's political career for the next two decades. In June, Ervin was sworn in to succeed Senator Clyde R. Hoey of North Carolina, who had died suddenly of a heart attack. Safely elected in 1956, Ervin was fortuitously appointed to the Senate Judiciary Subcommittee on Constitutional Rights, where he fought every civil rights bill between 1957 and 1968.

Without any political organization, and with virtually no opposition, Sam Ervin won three six-year terms in the Senate in 1956, 1962, and 1968. His biographer described him as "the intellectual darling of the segregationists" and their "legal crutch" who gave their cause "a veneer of legal class." Ervin certainly was no hero as he took the obvious path on civil rights to be reelected in the South. His first two full terms in the Senate were wasted: one observer called him "a great man whose mind is in chains." But he was consistent in his opposition to the growing power of the central government: "The proponents of current civil rights legislation, many of them undoubted men of good will, would, in an attempt to meet a genuine problem concerning the inflamed nature between the races in this country, trounce upon an even more pressing need—the need to preserve limited, constitutional government in an age of mass bureaucracy and centralization."[15]

But Ervin's final term in the Senate would coincide with Nixon's years in the White House, and no man was better prepared for his moment of glory. Ervin was ideally equipped to challenge the depredations of the imperial presidency surrounding Watergate.

When, in 1960, Sam Ervin succeeded to the chair of the Senate Judiciary Committee's Constitutional Rights Subcommittee, civil libertarians were alarmed. But Ervin's strict constructionist views provided a consistency in his positions that often made them libertarian. He was a staunch advocate of freedom of the press and fought almost single-handedly against Nixon's preventive detention bill for the District of Columbia in 1970, when most of the liberals were afraid to speak out in the aftermath of the Cambodian "incursion" and Kent State. He argued that "the supreme value of civilization is the freedom of the individual to be free from governmental tyranny." But he was one of only eight senators to oppose the Equal Rights Amendment for women, viewing it as a "potential blunderbuss" that was unnecessary because of the equal protection clause and the Civil Rights Act. Senator Sam also, perhaps, harbored some guilt over being tongue-tied on Vietnam. Privately convinced that the war was unconstitutional, Ervin refused to confront Lyndon Johnson and so, according to one biographer, was "being untrue to himself."

Perhaps Ervin's greatest legislative triumph came when he tacked his "Indian Bill of Rights" to the Fair Housing Bill of 1968. When Majority Leader Mike Mansfield got a ruling from the chair that Ervin's bill was not germane to civil rights, the North Carolinian stood up and replied: "Mr. President, inasmuch as the ruling of the chair scalps the Indians, I appeal from the ruling of the chair and ask the Senate to reverse it." The Senate not only overturned the ruling 54–28 but approved his amendment 81–0, as reservation Indians were guaranteed the rights of other Americans.

The chair of the special Senate Watergate investigating committee had been accused of being a racist and a sexist because of his views on the Constitution. But in a 1967 letter of his placed in the *Congressional Record,* Ervin portrayed himself as a libertarian: "But we will not fool history as we fool ourselves when we steal freedom from one man to confer it on another.

When freedom for one citizen is diminished, it is in the end diminished for all. It is not the 'civil rights' of some but the civil liberty of all on which I take my stand." Ervin was the perfect person to combat the constitutional violations of CREEP (the Committee to Reelect the President).[16]

Sam Ervin considered the facts of the Watergate "crime" obvious: five burglars were caught—in his words—"red-handed" inside the headquarters of the opposition party "with money in their pockets belonging to President Nixon's reelection campaign." The senator reminded the chief witness at the hearings, John Dean, former White House counsel who charged President Nixon with a role in the cover-up, that Article II of the Constitution states that the president "shall take care that the laws be faithfully executed." Ervin then asked Dean: "Do you know anything that the President did or said at any time between June 17 [1972: the break-in] and the present moment to perform his duty to see that the laws are faithfully executed in respect to what is called the Watergate affair?"

Ervin constantly displayed a sense of history, especially British and American constitutional history, to educate the American public on their own Constitution. When John D. Ehrlichman claimed that the burglary of Daniel Ellsberg's psychiatric records would have been perfectly legal if the president had approved it on the grounds of "national security," Ervin mentioned two favorite examples of his in disagreement. He recalled the prophet who "described the mountain of the Lord as being a place where every man might dwell under his own vine and fig tree with none to make him afraid." The senator also quoted William Pitt the Elder on the issue before the American Revolution: "The poorest man may in his cottage bid defiance to all the forces of the crown. It may be frail, its roof may shake, the wind may blow through it, the storm may enter, but the King of England cannot enter. All his force dares not cross the threshold of the ruined tenement." Then, looking at Ehrlichman, Ervin responded: "And yet we are told here . . . that what the king of England can't do, the president of the United States can."

Senator Ervin tried to place the Watergate affair in historical perspective, perhaps with some hyperbole, as he called it "the greatest tragedy this country has ever suffered." He said that he used to think that the Civil War was the nation's worst tragedy, "but I do remember that there were some redeeming features in the Civil War in that there was some spirit of sacrifice and heroism displayed on both sides. I see no redeeming features in Watergate." But at least there was one unlikely hero, Sam Ervin, who exhibited the qualities of virtue that the Founding Fathers admired.[17]

But hubris became a more pervasive trait of the eighties. For some, the lesson learned from Nixon's disgraced fund-raiser and secretary of commerce, Maurice H. Stans, once named accountant of the year, was how to shred records and to cook the books. By the time of the Iran–Contra scandal, the country did not have the stomach for another Watergate, especially since the scandal touched upon the powers of the imperial presidency in foreign affairs. Hubris was disguised as heroism: a convenient hero was found in Lieutenant Colonel Oliver North, handsome, bedecked with medals, and cloaked in national security. No wonder a book characterized our nation as *The Cynical Society*. And who were its heroes? Manipulative media decided for the masses, while cynical elites, smug and comfortable, sneered from their balconies at slavish populace and virtuous citizens alike. Tocqueville warned us never to expect a wise government "to originate in the votes of a people of servants."[18]

Afterword

An inspiring paper was read at the first meeting of the American Historical Association in 1884 by its president, Andrew Dickson White, who worked in many fields of history and whose hero was William Pitt Fessenden. President White, of Cornell University, complained about "excessive specialization" in historical studies that fastened upon graduate students "the character of petty annalists." To balance such special work, he advocated "thoughtful study of great connected events."[1]

This book, hopefully, is such a study and will challenge our cynical age when excessive specialization or cultural fragmentation abounds in historical research. With skeptical deconstruction as a philosophy, can a scholar—teacher make sense out of anything, much less the complexities of the past? Without a sense of direction—that is, bias—history cannot be written, only chronicles by "petty annalists."

Christopher Lasch's *Culture of Narcissism* is especially relevant. He criticized an article by David Donald on a "sense of the irrelevance of history": "The 'lessons' taught by the American past are today not merely irrelevant but dangerous. . . . Perhaps my most useful function would be to disenthrall [students] from the spell of history, to help them see the irrelevance of the past, . . . [to] remind them to what a limited extent humans control their own destiny." Lasch denounced such despair and demoralization. He called the past "a political and psychological treasury from which we draw the reserves (not necessarily in the form of 'lessons') that we need to cope with the future." *Narcissism* argues that American culture's "indifference to the past . . . furnishes the most telling proof of that culture's bankruptcy."

Abraham Lincoln biographer Donald would undoubtedly reply with Lincoln's famous remark, "I claim not to have controlled events but confess plainly that events have controlled me." And there are hundreds of examples of deriving the wrong lesson from history, one of them being the constant comparison during the 1960s of appeasement at Munich with opposition to an American war in Vietnam. Although both Lasch and Donald are right—each in his own way—and each can easily be misinterpreted, the pendulum has clearly swung too far toward Donald's skepticism.

Each time we turn the kaleidoscope of history, Clio grants us another surprising view. For example, David Donald declared confidently about the Reconstruction: "But it does not greatly help us ... to learn that Benjamin F. Butler loved his wife and Charles Sumner hated his." My own chapter on Reconstruction refutes this. Sumner's relationship with his wife, among other factors, affected his relationship with Fessenden, which influenced the outcome of the Fourteenth Amendment and the course of the Reconstruction. And the same chapter portrays the way Lasch's view can be carried too far in the myths drawn by certain radical historians from their "political and psychological treasury" in the Reconstruction, which they use to "cope with the future." Though historians should strive to be "gods in spirit," we are all "moles in vision," digging "our little tunnels as straight as we can."[2]

Skepticism about the reliability of virtue and courage need not turn to cynicism. Humankind can still sink to the level of a Kurt Waldheim or surprisingly rise to the heights of a Raoul Wallenberg. Though thousands of mini–Donald Trumps are flourishing, there is still an occasional Ralph Nader. Searching for heroism does not necessarily lead to hagiography. The parallel lives of senators can give us a better understanding of the difficulty for every human to live a life of virtue.

Most obvious among the several kinds of heroes in this book are those who grew more courageous in office: from the swaggering Thomas Hart Benton to the judicious Thomas J. Walsh and to the consummate politician Arthur H. Vandenberg. The rude but sophisticated Benton grew more outspoken in his defense of liberty and the Union at a time of national schizophrenia. The timid Walsh, after a nervous breakdown in 1917 and a bout of cowardice over national security in 1918, developed into a spokesman for sanity and compromise in 1920 and an opponent of massive corruption in 1923. Vandenberg's statesmanship slowly evolved, and he became a master politician, who, when possessing great power, never abused it. All three men were populists who understood the need for virtue in leaders.

Three other heroes stand out for their consistent, lifelong virtue: the honest William Pitt Fessenden, the humane George Frisbie Hoar, and the master builder George W. Norris. A kind of Down East Lincoln, Fessenden possessed a deep sense of integrity and humanity. But his hatred of "humbug" brought out his Swiftian sarcasm, which created enemies. The shrewd multimillionaires of the Gilded Age Senate tolerated Hoar's virtue of a bygone age, which constantly reminded them of the principles of the Declaration of Independence. Norris remained a fighting liberal through his thirty years in the Senate.

Three other virtuous men were symbols of movements: John C. Calhoun, states' rights; Charles Sumner, abolitionism; and William E. Borah, isolationism. All three were men of integrity, never deviating from their principles. And the personal fortitude of each became a political force in its own right. But the armor of all three contained big chinks: Calhoun's, slavery; Sumner's, hubris; and Borah's, appeasement. For them, as Shakespeare put it, "Virtue itself turns vice, being misapplied."

No two senators had a better understanding of political power than Henry Cabot Lodge and Strom Thurmond. Both of them thought they belonged to the elect: Lodge to the Brahmins', and Thurmond to God's. Both were content to make the Senate their power base. The sneering Lodge stared contemptuously down on any form of idealism, and the evangelical Thurmond thought he was God's muscleman in the temple of justice.

The remaining five all hoped to use the Senate as a trampoline to the presidency: Rufus King, James Monroe, John Sherman, Robert A. Taft, and Hubert Humphrey. Monroe made it, but what did he really accomplish? Like most politicians, of course, all five reflect their own times, but would Sherman and Humphrey have been more significant figures had they not been so busy running for president? Humphrey did, of course, inspire some of the best programs of the Kennedy–Johnson administrations. But Taft, of the five, comes closest to greatness: every Senate needs one as a critic, though his anticommunism, like Humphrey's, became obsessive.

In a society that celebrates the nihilism of the lowest common denominator, we need a government that cultivates virtue; but this can only be accomplished with the consent of the governed. Only a people that exercise and breathe virtue can expect a virtuous government. A line from Tom Walsh's speech in Missoula, Montana, on the fourth of July 1910 is appropriate: "The very existence, therefore, of free institutions is dependent upon . . . the character as upon the capacity of the citizenry." Such a virtuous electorate can then hope to have an occasional Fessenden to write home to a son or daughter: "I can say with truth that I have never either sacrificed any political principle or even concealed an opinion, and I have never sought a nomination to office. I have not the shame of recollecting that I owe my success to unworthy means. . . . I trust that all my sons will ever be guided by the same rule, as they may be certain that no honor can ever repay them for the loss of their own esteem."[3]

A Note on Sources

After searching the careers of more than 1,800 senators, I selected two to compare and contrast for each era based on their tenure, force of personality within the Senate, and historical significance. Some of these were subjects of biographies of many thousands of pages. Of course, these figures also appeared in the biographies of contemporaries and more specialized studies of their respective eras. My notes and research covered at least 50,000 pages of reading.

In only one case did I find it advisable to quote from primary sources directly: the William Pitt Fessenden Papers at Bowdoin College, Maine. Even though all of my quotations from these papers have appeared in print before in several studies, I double-checked them because my interpretation of his role in the Civil War and Reconstruction varies so much from that of most Reconstruction historians.

Finally, all of my notes serve as one bibliography of hundreds of books, monographs, articles, and so forth. Special thanks are due to the Senate Historical Office and the manuscript collections at the Library of Congress and Bowdoin College Library.

Notes

Introduction

1. John F. Kennedy, *Profiles in Courage* (New York, 1956), 1, dust jacket, xv; Jefferson to Robert Skipwith, August 3, 1771, in *The Papers of Thomas Jefferson,* Julian P. Boyd, et al., ed. (Princeton, NJ, 1950–), 1:76–80; Arthur M. Schlesinger Jr., *The Imperial Presidency,* 2d ed. (Boston, 1989), 428; Paul K. Longmore, *The Invention of George Washington* (Berkeley, CA, 1988), 9; Jeffrey C. Goldfarb, *The Cynical Society: The Culture of Politics and the Politics of Culture in American Life* (Chicago, 1991); Garry Wills, *Inventing America: Jefferson's Declaration of Independence* (Garden City, NY, 1978). For an especially good discussion of virtue and leadership in the Federalist period, see Ralph Ketcham, *Presidents above Party: The First American Presidency, 1789–1829* (Chapel Hill, NC, 1984).

2. Benton and Tocqueville, quoted in Richard A. Baker, *The Senate of the United States: A Bicentennial History* (Malabar, FL, 1988), 167–70. See also Robert A. Wilson, ed., *Character above All: 10 Presidents from FDR to George Bush* (New York, 1995).

3. The other members of the committee were John F. Bricker of Ohio, H. Styles Bridges of New Hampshire, Richard Russell of Georgia, and Michael J. Mansfield of Montana. Norris and Bridges had been archenemies over the TVA. See Richard Lowitt, *George W. Norris: The Triumph of a Progressive, 1933–1944* (Urbana, IL, 1978), 470–71; Herbert S. Parmet, *Jack: The Struggles of John F. Kennedy* (New York, 1980), 394; "Report of the Special Committee on the Senate Reception Room," including appendix C, 1–125, Senate Report 85–279 (85th Cong., 1st sess.).

4. "Senate Reception Room," 18–19, 21–23, 29, 46, 54, 59, 68–69, 81, 96–98, 106, 112, 120.

5. W.E.H. Lecky, *Democracy and Liberty,* 2 vols. (New York, 1896), 1:397; Alexis de Tocqueville, *Democracy in America,* 2 vols. in 1, ed. J.P. Mayer, trans. George Lawrence (Garden City, NY, 1969), 694; *Congressional Record,* March 12, 1959, vol. 105, part 3 (86th Cong., 1st sess.), 3974–78.

Part I Introduction. The Patrician Age (1789–1820)

1. Alvin M. Josephy Jr., *On the Hill: A History of the American Congress* (New York, 1980), 38; Gordon S. Wood, *The Creation of the American Republic, 1776–1787* (Chapel Hill, NC, 1969), 553–64.

2. Jefferson and Madison, quoted in Noble E. Cunningham Jr., ed., *The Making of the American Party System, 1789 to 1809* (Englewood Cliffs, NJ, 1965), 10–18.

3. See H. Trevor Colbourn, *The Lamp of Experience: Whig History and the Intellectual Origins of the American Revolution* (Chapel Hill, NC, 1965), esp. 198.

Chapter 1. "Last of the Romans":
Rufus King vs. James Monroe (1789–1820)

1. Richard A. Baker, *The Senate of the United States: A Bicentennial History* (Malabar, FL, 1988), 22; Harry Ammon, *James Monroe: The Quest for National Identity* (New York, 1971), 54–59; Robert Ernst, *Rufus King: American Federalist* (Chapel Hill, NC, 1968), 53–63.

2. Ammon, *Monroe*, 7–49; Ernst, *King*, 36–37, 161–62, 230; Henry Wise, quoted in Arthur Styron, *The Last of the Cocked Hats: James Monroe and the Virginia Dynasty* (Norman, OK, 1945), viii.

3. Ernst, *King*, 92–117, 118–34; Ammon, *Monroe*, 72–73, 81–82.

4. Ernst, *King*, 135–49; Alvin M. Josephy Jr., *On the Hill: A History of the American Congress* (New York, 1980), 44–45; Baker, *Senate*, 6–7.

5. Edgar S. Maclay, ed., *Journal of William Maclay: United States Senator from Pennsylvania, 1789–1791* (New York, 1890), 315, 234; Ernst, *King*, 162–66; Ammon, *Monroe*, 83.

6. Ammon, *Monroe*, 83–84, 109–110; Ernst, *King*, 194–95; Josephy, *On the Hill*, 86, 92–94.

7. Ernst, *King*, 181–94; Ammon, *Monroe*, 104–7, 87–88.

8. Ammon, *Monroe*, 108–56; Ernst, *King*, 219–75, 410, 263–64.

9. Gerard H. Clarfield, *Timothy Pickering and the American Republic* (Pittsburgh, 1980), 163–269; Herbert S. Parmet and Marie B. Hecht, *Aaron Burr: Portrait of an Ambitious Man* (New York, 1967), esp. 285, 230–31.

10. John F. Kennedy, *Profiles in Courage*, (New York, 1956), 31–51; David Burner and Thomas R. West, *The Torch Is Passed: The Kennedy Brothers and American Liberalism* (New York, 1984), 58.

11. Ammon, *Monroe*, 273, 280, 337, 352–57; Ernst, *King*, 347–52.

12. Ammon, *Monroe*, 185–89, 522–23. Styron, *Last of the Cocked Hats*, 222–23, presents an old-fashioned view more sympathetic to Monroe than to the "Negroes."

13. Styron, *Last of the Cocked Hats*, 359–62; Ammon, *Monroe*, 454–56; Ernst, *King*, 369–75; Merrill D. Peterson, *Thomas Jefferson and the New Nation* (New York, 1970), 996.

14. C.F. Adams, ed., *Memoirs of John Quincy Adams, Comprising Portions of His Diary from 1795 to 1848*, 12 vols. (Philadelphia, 1874–77), 6:367; Ammon, *Monroe*, 472; James S. Young, *The Washington Community, 1800–1828* (New York, 1966), 235–36; Ralph Ketcham, *Presidents above Party: The First American Presidency, 1789–1829* (Chapel Hill, NC, 1984), 126; Richard Hofstadter, *The Idea of a Party System: The Rise of Legitimate Opposition in the United States, 1780–1840* (Berkeley, CA, 1969), 199; George Dangerfield, *The Era of Good Feelings* (New York, 1952).

15. Styron, *Last of the Cocked Hats;* Ernst, *King*, 407, 389, 393.

16. Ernst, *King*, 372; E.H. Brush, *Rufus King and His Times* (New York, 1926), 105.

Chapter 2. "Samson and the Temple of Slavery":
Thomas Hart Benton vs. John C. Calhoun (1820–1850)

1. Theodore Roosevelt, *Thomas H. Benton* (Boston, 1899; 1st ed., 1886), 301; William N. Chambers, *Old Bullion Benton: Senator from the New West* (Boston, 1956), 405.

2. Edward Pessen, *Jacksonian America: Society, Personality, and Politics* (Homewood, IL, 1969), 182–87; Charles M. Wiltse, *John C. Calhoun,* vol. 1, *Nationalist, 1782–1828* (Indianapolis, 1944), 221; John Niven, *John C. Calhoun and the Price of Union: A Biography* (Baton Rouge, 1988), 96–97; "Mark Twain" (Samuel L. Clemens), *The Adventures of Tom Sawyer,* chapter 22, in *Mississippi Writings* (New York, Library of America, 1982), 140.

3. Chambers, *Old Bullion,* 40, 17, 51.

4. Merrill D. Peterson, *The Great Triumvirate: Webster, Clay, and Calhoun* (New York, 1987), 23. Also see Margaret L. Coit, *John C. Calhoun: American Portrait* (Boston, 1950); Richard Hofstadter, "John C. Calhoun: The Marx of the Master Class," in Richard Hofstadter, *The American Political Tradition and the Men Who Made It* (New York, 1948), 68–92; Richard Current, "John C. Calhoun, Philosopher of Reaction," *Antioch Review* (summer 1943): 223–34.

5. Peterson, *Triumvirate,* 18, 95.

6. Chambers, *Old Bullion,* 112–14, 129, 304. Elbert B. Smith, *Magnificent Missourian: The Life of Thomas Hart Benton* (Philadelphia, 1958), 139. See M.W.M. Hargreaves, *The Presidency of John Quincy Adams* (Lawrence, KS, 1985).

7. Glyndon G. Van Deusen, *The Life of Henry Clay* (Boston, 1937), 219.

8. Benton, quoted in Chambers, *Old Bullion,* 162; Robert V. Remini, *The Life of Andrew Jackson* (New York, 1988).

9. John C. Fitzpatrick, ed., *The Autobiography of Martin Van Buren* (1920; reprint New York, 1969) 415; also Robert V. Remini, *Martin Van Buren and the Making of the Democratic Party* (New York, 1959).

10. Chambers, *Old Bullion,* 172, 184–85.

11. Smith, *Magnificent Missourian,* 164.

12. Ibid., 165; Chambers, *Old Bullion,* 156.

13. Major L. Wilson, *The Presidency of Martin Van Buren* (Lawrence, KS, 1984); Remini, *Van Buren and Democratic Party.*

14. Peterson, *Triumvirate,* 344–45; Charles M. Wiltse, *John C. Calhoun,* vol. 2, *Nullifier, 1829–1839* (Indianapolis, 1949) and vol. 3, *Sectionalist, 1840–1850* (Indianapolis, 1951); Norma L. Peterson, *The Presidencies of William Henry Harrison and John Tyler* (Lawrence, KS, 1989).

15. Peterson, *Triumvirate,* 347.

16. Smith, *Magnificent Missourian,* 199; Peterson, *Presidencies of Harrison and Tyler,* 230.

17. Wiltse, *Calhoun,* vol. 3, *Sectionalist,* 199–220; Smith, *Magnificent Missourian,* 211.

18. Smith, *Magnificent Missourian,* 214–15; Ernest M. Lander Jr., *Reluctant Imperialists: Calhoun, the South Carolinians, and the Mexican War* (Baton Rouge, 1980), 8, 10, 63, 71–72, 78.

19. Chambers, *Old Bullion,* 326.

20. Ferol Egan, *Frémont: Explorer for a Restless Nation* (New York, 1977), 46–48; Allan Nevins, *Frémont: Pathmarker of the West,* 2 vols. (New York, 1961).

21. Peterson, *Triumvirate,* 426–27; Chambers, *Old Bullion,* 314; Smith, *Magnificent Missourian,* 221; Thomas H. Benton, *Thirty Years' View,* 2 vols. (New York, 1856), 2:698–700.

22. Smith, *Magnificent Missourian,* 235–36; Wiltse, *Calhoun,* vol. 3, *Sectionalist*; Benton, *Thirty Years' View.*

23. Smith, *Magnificent Missourian,* 247–74; Peterson, *Triumvirate;* Chambers, *Old Bullion.* For Calhoun's virulent immortality, see Richard N. Current, *John C. Calhoun* (New York, 1963), esp. 150. Largely supporting my view of Benton is William W. Freehling, *The Road to Disunion,* vol. 1, *Secessionists at Bay, 1776–1854* (New York, 1990), 446–47, 541–44, 548. I agree with Freehling that Benton was in no way an

abolitionist but totally concerned with the preservation of the Union. But Benton was not "sphinx"-like by 1850, as the above speech on slavery as an "evil" reveals. While Benton concentrated on preventing the extension of slavery, he was abandoned by the Democratic Party in the 1850s. Benton's moral dilemma was that slavery was "incurable" without the dissolution of the Union. He tried to prevent its spread but was trapped like the nation in a moral contradiction. One can only speculate about the effect of the Democratic Party's adopting Benton's position instead of Douglas's. Would the Civil War have come sooner?

24. Smith, *Magnificent Missourian,* 279–80, 298.

25. Ibid., 319; Chambers, *Old Bullion.*

26. Coit, *Calhoun,* 459; Remini, *Life of Jackson,* 231; Roosevelt, *Benton,* 301.

Chapter 3. Lincoln's Prime Minister: William Pitt Fessenden vs. Charles Sumner (1850–1865)

1. J.S. Pike, *First Blows of the Civil War* (New York, 1879), 219. Though buried in the family plot of his father, Samuel, according to cemetery records, Pitt Fessenden and his wife and children have no grave markers and go unmentioned on the family monument, perhaps because of Pitt's illegitimacy or notoriety (personal observation).

2. Charles A. Jellison, *Fessenden of Maine* (Syracuse, NY, 1962), 76–78. Adequate until 1865, but unsympathetic, Jellison's *Fessenden* is inaccurate and unbalanced on the senator and Reconstruction, 1865 to 1868. For example, Jellison misinterprets Fessenden's draft of the Fourteenth Amendment. Most of Jellison's research and writing was done during the 1950s, before the revolution in studies of the Reconstruction during the past three decades. See Charles A. Jellison Jr., "William Pitt Fessenden, Statesman of the Middle Ground" (Ph.D. diss., University of Virginia, 1956). The concept of the "middle ground" distorts Fessenden's philosophy. In fairness to Jellison, it should be noted that a biographer of Fessenden faces a complex task more challenging than that of a Lincoln or Sumner biographer. Carl Sandburg's *Abraham Lincoln* 6 vols. (New York, 1950), presents a limited but very sympathetic portrait of Fessenden, who has been unlucky with biographers. See chapter 4, note 42, in this volume for an extended historiographical discussion of Fessenden.

3. William Pitt Fessenden (WPF) to "Father," October 30, 1827, Fessenden Family Collection, Bowdoin College; Jellison, *Fessenden,* 7.

4. David H. Donald, *Charles Sumner and the Coming of the Civil War* (New York, 1960), 1:7. I have generally accepted Professor Donald's interpretation of Sumner's motives.

5. Jellison, *Fessenden,* 5–15; WPF, quoted in Francis Fessenden, *Life and Public Services of William Pitt Fessenden,* 2 vols. (Boston, 1907), 1:12, 294.

6. Sandburg, *Lincoln,* 5:119–21.

7. WPF to Father, May 9, 1858, Bowdoin; Jellison, *Fessenden,* 112–13, 92–93; Fessenden, *Fessenden,* 1:88; Horace White, *The Life of Lyman Trumbull* (Boston, 1913), 83.

8. Fessenden, *Fessenden,* 1:96, 112–13; WPF to William, February 17, 1861, Bowdoin; R.W. Johannsen, *Stephen A. Douglas* (New York, 1973), 850.

9. Jellison, *Fessenden,* 129–32; Sandburg, *Lincoln,* 3:313–14.

10. Jellison, *Fessenden,* 133–39; Pamela Herr, *Jessie Benton Frémont: A Biography* (New York, 1987), 338–39; Ferol Egan, *Frémont: Explorer for a Restless Nation* (New York, 1977), 515–16.

11. Jellison, *Fessenden,* 141; George Julian, *Political Recollections, 1840 to 1872* (1st ed., Chicago, 1884; Miami, 1969), 212–13.

12. Jellison, *Fessenden,* 146–49.

13. WPF to James W. Grimes, September 25, 1862, Bowdoin.

14. *Diary of Orville Hickman Browning,* ed. James G. Randall, 2 vols. (Springfield, IL, 1925), 587–88.

15. Fessenden, *Fessenden,* 1:240–42.

16. Ibid., 242–44.

17. Sandburg, *Lincoln,* 3:650.

18. WPF to Elizabeth C. Warriner, January 10, 1863, Bowdoin.

19. *Congressional Globe,* January 26, 1863, vol. 31, part 1 (37th Cong., 3d sess.) 505–7; David A. Nichols, *Lincoln and the Indians: Civil War Policy and Politics* (Columbia, MO, 1978), 190. See David H. Donald, *Lincoln* (New York, 1995), 392–95. Just two months after the preliminary Emancipation Proclamation, Lincoln personally selected 38 Sioux men to be hanged from an original list of 303 after the Sioux rising in Minnesota.

20. Jellison, *Fessenden,* 170.

21. Joseph T. Glatthaar, *Forged in Battle: The Civil War Alliance of Black Soldiers and White Officers* (New York, 1990), 36; Fessenden, *Fessenden,* 1:256.

22. James M. McPherson, *The Struggle for Equality: Abolitionists and the Negro in the Civil War and Reconstruction* (Princeton, NJ, 1964), 216–17, states flatly that Fessenden "was a leading opponent of retroactive equal pay" because it would cost an extra $1.5 million; but see Fessenden's remarks to Sumner in debate February 29, 1864, *Congressional Globe,* vol. 35, part 2 (38th Cong., 1st Sess.) 868–73; also see March 3, 1865, *Congressional Globe,* vol. 35, part 2, (38th Cong., 2nd sess.) 1378.

23. *Congressional Globe,* March 28, 1867, vol. 38, (40th Cong., 1st sess.), 413. David Montgomery, *Beyond Equality: Labor and the Radical Republicans, 1862–1872* (New York, 1967), 241, 62, calls Fessenden the "most consistent and capable leader" of Senate conservatives because of his general opposition to trade unions and the federal eight-hour day. In focusing on labor issues, Montgomery misinterprets evidence of Fessenden's "radicalism" on racial and other political questions. Also see chapter 4, note 42, in this volume.

24. Fessenden, *Fessenden,* 1:276–77, 291–94. See Lew Wallace to Zach Chandler, June 30, 1868, Zach Chandler Papers, reel 2, Library of Congress. General Wallace, future territorial governor of New Mexico and author of *Ben Hur,* wrote to Chandler about being "deeply interested in a railroad project now pending in the form of a bill in the Senate. . . . If completed, it lays Mexico at our feet." See references to Chandler in chapters 4, 5, and 8 in this volume.

25. Jellison, *Fessenden,* 169.

26. William Salter, *William Pitt Fessenden* (Burlington, IA, 1908; reprinted from the *Annals of Iowa* [April 1908]), 10.

27. Lincoln to John Hay, July 1, 1864, in *Lincoln and the Civil War in the Diaries and Letters of John Hay,* ed. Tyler Dennett (New York, 1939), 202.

28. D.B. Cole and J.J. McDonough, eds., *Benjamin Brown French: Witness to the Young Republic, A Yankee's Journal, 1828–1870* (Hanover, NH, 1989), 452.

29. Jellison, *Fessenden,* 186–89.

30. *New York Tribune,* March 4, 1865 (editorial clipping, Fessenden Papers, Library of Congress); Robert P. Sharkey, *Money, Class, and Party: An Economic Study of the Civil War and Reconstruction* (Baltimore, 1959), 57. Robert Cook, " 'The Grave of All My Comforts': William Pitt Fessenden as Secretary of the Treasury, 1864–65," *Civil War History,* (41 no. 3, September 1995). 208–26. Cook, 219 n, states that Fessenden's "vanity" was "well known," based on Jellison's unsympathetic biography—a commonly held view among today's Civil War specialists. Even Lincoln's great champion Carl

Sandburg acknowledged Fessenden's "rare sense of justice." Vanity for some can be integrity for others.

31. Jellison, *Fessenden,* 193. Browning, *Diary,* 1:186–87.

32. WPF to Israel Washburn, December 29, 1864, Fessenden Papers, reel 3, vol. 5, Library of Congress.

33. Sandburg, *Lincoln,* 6:339.

Chapter 4. "Worthy of Plutarch": Fessenden vs. Sumner (1865–1870)

1. Allan Nevins, *Hamilton Fish,* 2 vols., rev. ed. (New York, 1957), 1:44; Allan Bogue, *The Earnest Men, Republicans of the Civil War Senate* (Ithaca, NY, 1981), 81–82, recognizes Fessenden's leadership but does not place in perspective his perhaps justified "ill-tempered outbursts" and "dislike of Sumner."

2. Charles A. Jellison, *Fessenden of Maine* (Syracuse, NY, 1962), 94.

3. Julian, quoted in David Donald, *Charles Sumner and the Rights of Man,* hereafter, *Sumner,* (New York, 1970), 2:250; L.E. Richards and M.H. Elliott, *Julia Ward Howe,* 1818–1910, 2 vols. (Boston 1916), 1:205.

4. Donald, *Sumner,* 2:251.

5. Ibid., 2:144–45.

6. Adam Gurowski, *Diary, 1863–5,* 219–20, quoted in Donald, *Sumner,* 145; Eric McKitrick, *Andrew Johnson and Reconstruction* (Chicago, 1960), 226–27.

7. Donald, *Sumner,* 1:129. See also Harvard alumni records. Don E. Fehrenbacher, "The Making of a Myth: Lincoln and the Vice Presidential Nomination in 1864," *Civil War History* 41, no. 4 (December 1995): 273–90, discusses the fluid situation but downplays Sumner's role and refers to Donald's account.

8. Fawn Brodie, *Thaddeus Stevens* (New York, 1959), 197; Shelby M. Cullom, *Fifty Years of Public Service* (Chicago, 1911), 152.

9. Sandburg, *Abraham Lincoln,* 6 vols. (New York, 1950), 6:79, 118–19.

10. Donald, *Sumner,* 2:244–45; Francis Fessenden, *Life and Public Services of William Pitt Fessenden,* 2 vols. (Boston, 1907), 2:25.

11. Donald, *Sumner,* 2:252, 248.

12. Phillips to Stevens, April 30, 1866, in Eric Foner, *Reconstruction: America's Unfinished Revolution, 1863–1877* (New York, 1988), 255; Anthony to Sumner, n.d. (appendix to "Equal Rights of All") in *Works of Sumner,* 15 vols. (Boston, 1870–1883), 10:266; Stanton to Phillips, December 26, 1865, in *Elizabeth Cady Stanton: As Revealed in Her Letters[,] Diary[,] and Reminiscences,* ed. Theodore Stanton and Harriot Stanton Blatch, 2 vols. 1st ed., 1922; New York, 1969), 2:109–11.

13. Sumner to Horatio Woodman, March 18, 1866, in Donald, *Sumner,* 2:247; B.B. Kendrick, *The Journal of the Joint Committee of Fifteen on Reconstruction* (New York, 1914), 49–53; Fessenden, *Fessenden,* 2:315.

14. *Congressional Globe,* vol. 36, part 1, February 5, 6, 7, 21, 1866, (39th Cong., 1st sess.) 673–74, 704–5, 951; part 2, March 9, 1866, 1278–79.

15. *Congressional Globe,* March 9, 1866, 1278–79; Fessenden, *Fessenden,* 2:59; Donald, *Sumner,* 2:251; William Pitt Fessenden to Elizabeth C. Warriner (ECW), February 25, 1866, Fessenden Family Collection, Bowdoin College; Seward comments quoted in Glyndon G. Van Deusen, *William Henry Seward* (New York, 1967), 428–29.

16. WPF to William Fessenden, March 31, 1866, Bowdoin.

17. WPF to William, April 21, 1866, Bowdoin.

18. McKitrick, *Johnson and Reconstruction,* 322, 89–90.

19. Ibid., 314.

20. Donald, *Sumner,* 2:263.

21. Fessenden, *Fessenden,* 2:81–82.

22. Andrew Johnson to A.J. Herron, July 30, 1866, quoted in McKitrick, *Johnson and Reconstruction,* 425; also, 426.

23. David H. Donald, *The Politics of Reconstruction, 1863–1867* (Baton Rouge, 1965), 53; Hans L. Trefousse, *Impeachment of a President: Andrew Johnson, the Blacks, and Reconstruction* (Knoxville, TN, 1975), 61–62; *Congressional Globe,* February 19, 1867, vol. 37, part 3 (39th Cong., 2d sess.), 1559; also February 15, 1867, 1384. Also see note 42 below.

24. Donald, *Sumner,* 2:319–20.

25. Jellison, *Fessenden,* 224, 222–23.

26. Quotes from Fessenden, *Fessenden,* 2:306–7. See Foner, *Reconstruction,* 241–42. Pitt Fessenden's views bear a remarkable similarity to those of the highly respected ex-governor of Massachusetts, John A. Andrew, who also believed that the "natural leaders" of the white South should be encouraged to grant African American suffrage voluntarily rather than have the North force it upon them.

27. "The Equal Rights of All," *Congressional Globe,* February 6, 1866, vol. 36, part 1 (39th Cong., 1st sess.), 685; Milton Viorst, *Fall from Grace: The Republican Party and the Puritan Ethic* (New York, 1968), 53.

28. Fessenden, *Fessenden,* 2:184–85.

29. "Opinion of Hon. William P. Fessenden," *Trial of Andrew Johnson, Congressional Globe,* vol. 39, supple., 452–57.

30. Donald, *Sumner,* 2:334; *Springfield Republican,* July 9, 1867, quoted in Donald, *Sumner,* 2:300; Sumner to Duchess of Argyll, June 30, 1868, quoted in Donald, *Sumner,* 2:336.

31. "Opinion of Hon. Charles Sumner," *Trial of Johnson,* 463–74; "Very Like Robespierre," Donald, *Sumner,* 2:218–67.

32. Michael Les Benedict, *The Impeachment and Trial of Andrew Johnson* (New York, 1973), 99; Fessenden, *Fessenden,* 2:149–50; Benjamin P. Thomas and Harold M. Hyman, *Stanton: The Life and Times of Lincoln's Secretary of War* (New York, 1962; Westport, CT, 1980), 565, 567, 614; Justin Morrill to WPF, May 10, 1868, letter quoted and described as "pathetic" in William B. Parker, *The Life and Public Services of Justin Smith Morrill* (Boston, 1924), 210–1.

33. Fessenden, *Fessenden,* 2:241–73.

34. Edmund Ross, *History of the Impeachment of Andrew Johnson, President of the United States* (1st ed., Santa Fe, 1896; New York, 1965), 137.

35. Fessenden, *Fessenden,* 2:219; Gene Smith, *High Crimes and Misdemeanors: The Impeachment and Trial of Andrew Johnson* (New York, 1977), 293–94; WPF to ECW, May 10, 1868, Bowdoin; Trefousse, *Impeachment,* 62–63.

36. William Salter, *William Pitt Fessenden,* (Burlington, IA, 1908; reprinted from the *Annals of Iowa* [April 1908]), 19; *Congressional Globe,* vol. 39, part 4, June 23, 1868 (40th Cong., 2d sess.) 3389–94; June 24, 1868, 3429.

37. Donald, *Sumner,* 2:345.

38. Fessenden, *Fessenden,* 2:347–49.

39. Donald, *Sumner,* 2:6.

40. *Autobiography of Andrew Dickson White,* 2 vols. (New York, 1905), 2:147; Fessenden, *Fessenden,* 2:300.

41. J.S. Morrill to Francis Fessenden, October 20, 1893, Bowdoin.

42. Eric Foner, *Reconstruction,* 308–9; also *Politics and Ideology in the Age of the Civil War* (New York, 1980), 142. Foner bases his categories of "moderate," "conserva-

tive," and "radical" on the quantitative study of Michael Les Benedict, *A Compromise of Principle: Congressional Republicans and Reconstruction, 1863–1869* (New York, 1974), 28, 153, 254, who labels Fessenden a "Consistent Conservative." In searching for evidence supporting the possibility of a workers' republic under "President" Ben Wade, endorsed by Karl Marx, Foner takes out of context Fessenden's cross-examination of Sumner on his proposal to give African Americans "a piece of land . . . where they are residing" from the confiscated land of pardoned Confederate whites. (See *Congressional Globe*, March 11, 1867, vol. 38 [40th Cong., 1st sess., 50–51.]) On this question, Fessenden was primarily concerned with Sumner's delaying the enactment of the right to vote, as the Massachusetts senator had delayed the Fourteenth Amendment for about four months to enhance his "radical" reputation back home.

Foner also (*Reconstruction*, 336) portrays four of the six who voted with Fessenden against impeachment as being disillusioned with Reconstruction and therefore joining the Liberal Republicans in 1872 against Grant. But so did Sumner! And one of the "Fessenden seven" was Lyman Trumbull, author of the Civil Rights and Freedmen's Bureau Bills of 1866.

Foner follows the interpretation of Fessenden by McKitrick, *Johnson and Reconstruction*, 269–73. James M. McPherson, *The Struggle for Equality: Abolitionists and the Negro in the Civil War and Reconstruction* (Princeton, NJ, 1964) 216–17, uncritically accepts the Garrison–Phillips view of Fessenden. Bogue, *Earnest Men*, proves the limits of quantitative studies on such qualitative questions as "leadership." A highly sophisticated, almost poetic, quantitative study is quite consistent with my interpretation of Fessenden and Sumner from 1864 to 1868 (i.e., the varieties and contrasting personal motivations of radical Republicans): see Dale Baum, *The Civil War Party System: The Case of Massachusetts, 1848–1876* (Chapel Hill, 1984). But William E. Gienapp, *The Origins of the Republican Party 1852–1856* (New York, 1987), 138 n, 220 n, 420 n, strongly criticizes Baum's view of the Know-Nothings as "an unimportant part of the Republican coalition in Massachusetts" during the mid-1850s. Though not focusing on Fessenden, Gienapp (129, 191) calls him "a moderate antislavery and temperance Whig" in 1854 and labels him a "Conservative."

David Montgomery, *Beyond Equality: Labor and the Radical Republicans, 1862–1872* (New York, 1967), 62, 352, equates Fessenden's views with Seward's and even goes so far as to state that "Senate Conservatives, led by William P. Fessenden, had fought to delete Negro suffrage from the Reconstruction Act of March 1867." Fessenden, of course, wanted a constitutional amendment. Montgomery relies on Jellison, *Fessenden*, 216, which describes Fessenden as "still shying away from unqualified Negro suffrage" and misconstrues his clear position as early as January 1866. Albert Castel, *The Presidency of Andrew Johnson* (Lawrence, KS, 1979), 254, is wide of the mark in claiming Jellison's *Fessenden* has "provided all that most people will want to know" about Fessenden. My interpretation of Fessenden's draft of the Fourteenth Amendment is supported by Mark M. Krug, *Lyman Trumbull: Conservative Radical* (New York, 1965), 235.

Sandburg's *Lincoln* does limited justice to Fessenden without covering his "Johnson" years. J.F. Rhodes's condescendingly racist *History of the United States from the Compromise of 1850* (1st ed., 1906; Port Washington, NY, 1967), 6:404, calls Fessenden "a model senator" and one of that chamber's "mightiest Conservatives." W.E.B. Du Bois, *Black Reconstruction in America* (New York, 1975), 286, would naturally call Fessenden (with a posthumous friend like Rhodes) "a Conservative . . . who wished to stand by President Johnson, and was strongly, and sometimes even bitterly, opposed to the radicalism of Sumner." Du Bois's research in primary sources was very limited.

Clearly, more detailed, nonideological research is needed on the Reconstruction in order to, in the words of Professor Donald, *Politics of Reconstruction,* 82, "take into account both the mixed motives of individuals and the mixed moral consequence of their actions."

See Parker, *Morrill,* 216.

43. *Congressional Globe,* December 14, 1869, vol. 42, part 1 (41st Cong., 2nd sess.), 113; Horace White, *The Life of Lyman Trumbull* (Boston, 1913), 324.

44. *Congressional Globe,* April 12, 1866, vol. 36, part 2 (39th Cong., 1st sess.), 1909–10.

Chapter 5. "Try Justice":
George Frisbie Hoar vs. John Sherman (1870–1900)

1. *New York Times,* October 23, 1900, p. 5 (obituary clipping, John Sherman manuscripts, Library of Congress); G.F. Hoar, *Autobiography of Seventy Years,* 2 vols. (New York, 1903), 2:19–20; Robert L. Beisner, *Twelve against Empire: The Anti-Imperialists, 1898–1900* (New York, 1968), 199.

2. Hoar, *Autobiography,* 1:196.

3. John Sherman to W.T. Sherman, April 12, 1861, in *The Sherman Letters: Correspondence between General and Senator Sherman from 1837 to 1891,* ed. R.S. Thorndike (New York, 1894), 110–11; J.P. Nichols, "John Sherman: A Study in Inflation," *Mississippi Valley Historical Review* 21 (September 1934): 183–84.

4. Richard E. Welch Jr., *George Frisbie Hoar and the Half-Breed Republicans* (Cambridge, MA, 1971), 193, 316–17, 325–26; Hoar, *Autobiography,* 1:8–9; Roger S. Boardman, *Roger Sherman: Signer and Statesman* (Philadelphia, 1938), 2, 332–33.

5. Theodore E. Burton, *John Sherman* (Boston, 1906), 18–19; Beisner, *Twelve,* 142; A.D. White, *Autobiography of Andrew Dixon White,* 2 vols. (New York, 1905), 1:218.

6. Welch, *Hoar,* 25.

7. C. Vann Woodward, *Reunion and Reaction: The Compromise of 1877 and the End of Reconstruction* (New York, 1956), 228–29.

8. See Harry Barnard, *Rutherford B. Hayes and His America* (Indianapolis, 1954); and H.J. Eckenrode, *Rutherford B. Hayes: Statesman of Reunion,* reprint (Port Washington, NY, 1963).

9. James M. McPherson, *Struggle for Equality: Abolitionists and the Negro in the Civil War and Reconstruction* (Princeton, NJ, 1964), 430–31.

10. *Congressional Record,* April 9, 1880, vol. 10, part 3, 2248–49. For the alleged mutilation of black cadet Johnson Chesnut Whittaker of South Carolina, and the court of inquiry's investigation pointing to his self-mutilation and concoction of the incident, see Thomas J. Fleming, *West Point: The Men and Times of the United States Military Academy* (New York, 1969), 226–31, and Stephen E. Ambrose, *Duty, Honor, Country: A History of West Point* (Baltimore, 1966), 234–35.

11. Ari Hoogenboom, *The Presidency of Rutherford B. Hayes* (Lawrence, KS, 1988), 139, 115.

12. John Sherman, *John Sherman's Recollections of Forty Years in the House, Senate, and Cabinet: An Autobiography,* 2 vols. (Chicago, 1895), 480, 484, 400–406, 823, 827; *Cleveland Leader,* December 21, 1882, in Constance M. Green, *Washington,* vol. 2, *Capital City, 1879–1950* (Princeton, NJ, 1963), 17.

13. Sherman, *Autobiography,* 774; Welch, *Hoar,* 97. Gaius Suetonius Tranquillus, *The Twelve Caesars,* trans. Robert Graves (Middlesex, U.K., 1985), 181: the Emperor Caligula threatened to appoint his horse Incitatus consul and senator for life.

14. Contemporary quotes from Beisner, *Twelve,* 141; Welch, *Hoar,* 100.

15. G.F. Hoar, "Woman's Right and the Public Welfare," before a Joint Special Committee of the Massachusetts legislature, April 14, 1869 (Boston, 1869), 4; see also Hoar, "Woman Suffrage Essential to the True Republic," An Address Delivered by the Honorable G.F. Hoar at the Annual Meeting of the New England Woman Suffrage Association, May 27, 1873 (Boston, 1873), Hoar Papers, Massachusetts Historical Society; Welch, *Hoar,* 29–30; Hoar, *Autobiography,* 2:125.

16. Richard E. Welch, Jr. *The Presidencies of Grover Cleveland* (Lawrence, KS, 1988), 54–56; H. Wayne Morgan, *From Hayes to McKinley: National Party Politics, 1877–1896* (Syracuse, NY, 1969), 339.

17. William C. Widenor, *Henry Cabot Lodge and the Search for an American Foreign Policy* (Berkeley, CA, 1980), 78.

18. Morgan, *Hayes to McKinley,* 341; G.F. Hoar, "United States Elections," a speech delivered to the Senate, December 29 and 30, 1890 (Washington, DC, 1891), 45.

19. Morgan, *Hayes to McKinley,* 342; Green, *Capital City;* Welch, *Hoar,* 161.

20. H.S. Merrill and M.G. Merrill, *The Republican Command, 1897–1913* (Lexington, MA, 1971), 17–19; Robert C. Byrd, *The Senate, 1789–1989,* 2 vols. (Washington, DC, 1988; vol. 1 ed. Mary Sharon Bell; vol. 2 ed. Wendy Wolff), 1:373; N.W. Stephenson, *Nelson W. Aldrich: A Leader in American Politics* (New York, 1930); Nelson W. Aldrich Jr., *Old Money: The Mythology of America's Upper Class* (New York, 1988), 19, 24.

21. T.M. Cooley to Hoar, January 12, 1889, Hoar Papers; Welch, *Hoar,* 163.

22. Wharton Barker to Hoar, May 28, 1891, Hoar Papers; Welch, *Hoar,* 168.

23. Welch, *Hoar,* 171.

24. Welch, *Hoar,* 183–87, 191, 197.

25. Beisner, Twelve, 148.

26. Welch, *Hoar,* 209.

27. Beisner, *Twelve,* 149.

28. Welch, *Hoar,* 212 and 212 n.

29. *Salt Lake City Tribune,* n.d., Scrapbook 613 (1897–1898), John Sherman Papers, Library of Congress.

30. Beisner, *Twelve,* 198–202; *Sherman's Recollections.*

31. Letter of Adams, quoted in Beisner, *Twelve,* 158.

32. John Braeman, *Albert J. Beveridge: American Nationalist* (Chicago, 1971), 22–23.

33. Braeman, *Beveridge,* 44–45.

34. Quoted in Welch, *Hoar,* 260; and Braeman, *Beveridge,* 46. William James to Hoar, May 11, 1900, Hoar Papers; Welch, *Hoar,* 267 n. 28.

35. Welch, *Hoar,* 299.

36. G.F. Hoar, "Popular Discontent with Representative Government," *Annual Report of the American Historical Association For The Year 1895* (Washington, DC, 1896), 21–43.

37. Welch, *Hoar,* 209; Beisner, *Twelve,* 158; Hoar, *Autobiography,* 1:259.

Chapter 6. The "Lamp of Experience" and "Bungalow Minds": Henry Cabot Lodge vs. Thomas J. Walsh (1900–1920)

1. Josephine O'Keane, *Thomas J. Walsh: A Senator from Montana* (Francestown, NH, 1955), 5–11; Tom to Ellen, July 7, 1889, in J.L. Bates, ed., *Tom Walsh in Dakota Territory: Personal Correspondence of Senator Thomas J. Walsh and Elinor C. McClements* (Urbana, IL, 1966), 242–43; John A. Garraty, *Henry Cabot Lodge: A*

Biography (New York, 1953), 9, 15; Lodge to Bancroft, May 28, 1878, quoted in Garraty, *Lodge,* 59; Van Wyck Brooks, *New England: Indian Summer, 1865–1915* (New York, 1940).

2. Lodge, *Studies in History* (Boston, 1884), 217–18, William C. Widenor, *Lodge,* 25.

3. Garraty, *Lodge,* 94; *Congressional Record,* vol. 22, part 2 (51st Cong., 2d sess.), 1211–13, 1265–67.

4. Thomas A. Bailey, *Woodrow Wilson and the Lost Peace* (Chicago, 1963), 99.

5. O'Keane, *Walsh,* 14–15.

6. Ibid., 16.

7. B.K. Wheeler with P.F. Healy, *Yankee from the West* (New York, 1962), 86–87; O'Keane, *Walsh,* 37.

8. O'Keane, *Walsh,* 39.

9. Thomas F. Gossett, *Race: The History of an Idea in America* (New York, 1965), 238, 268–69, 278–79.

10. F.P. Dunne, *Mr. Dooley Says* (New York, 1910), quoted in Garraty, *Lodge,* 268.

11. Garraty, *Lodge,* 288–90.

12. See Gabriel Kolko, *The Triumph of Conservatism: A Reinterpretation of American History, 1900–1916* (New York, 1963).

13. O'Keane, *Walsh,* 59–60.

14. Arnon Gutfeld, *Montana's Agony: Years of War and Hysteria, 1917–1921* (Gainesville, FL, 1987); D.M. Emmons, *The Butte Irish* (Urbana, IL, 1989), 378; Wheeler with Healy, *Yankee,* 137–41.

15. *Congressional Record,* April 4 to 8, 1918, vol. 56, part 5 (65th Cong., 2d sess.), 4560–785.

16. Wheeler with Healy, *Yankee,* 163.

17. O'Keane, *Walsh,* 78–79; J.L. Bates, "Senator Walsh of Montana: A Liberal under Pressure" (Ph.D. diss., University of North Carolina, 1952), 190–214; Stanley Coben, *A. Mitchell Palmer: Politician* (New York, 1963), 226–67, 208–9; *Congressional Record,* vol. 60, part 1 (66th Cong., 3d sess.), 149–50.

18. Thomas A. Bailey, *Woodrow Wilson and the Great Betrayal* (Chicago, 1963), 54; Bates, ed., *Walsh in Dakota Territory,* xiv: Senator Henry F. Ashurst of Arizona called Walsh the "soundest" of all the senators on constitutional law.

19. Garraty, *Lodge,* 191–92, 271–72, 319; Bailey, *Wilson and Lost Peace,* 92–93.

20. Bailey, *Betrayal,* 52; Woodrow Wilson, *Congressional Government,* 15th ed. (Boston, 1901), xi–xii; Robert C. Byrd, *The Senate, 1789–1989,* 2 vols. (Washington, DC, 1988; vol. 1 ed. Mary Sharon Bell; vol. 2 ed. Wendy Wolff), 1:420.

21. Byrd, *Senate,* 422–24; Widenor, *Lodge,* 315.

22. Bailey, *Great Betrayal,* 14–15.

23. Byrd, *Senate,* 426.

24. Bailey, *Great Betrayal,* 182–83.

25. Ibid., 229–32.

26. Walsh to Reinhardt Rahr, February 26, 1920, Walsh Papers, Library of Congress; Bates, "Walsh," 155 n; Bailey, *Great Betrayal,* 229–32; *Congressional Record,* March 19, 1920, vol. 59, part 5 (66th Cong., 2d sess.), 4581–85. See H. Trevor Colbourn, *The Lamp of Experience: Whig History and the Intellectual Origins of the American Revolution* (Chapel Hill, NC, 1965), xi: Patrick Henry remarked in 1775, "I have but one lamp by which my feet are guided, and that is the lamp of experience. I know of no way of judging the future but by the past."

27. Bailey, *Great Betrayal,* 267; Henry F. Pringle, *The Life and Times of William Howard Taft: A Biography,* 2 vols. (Hamden, CT, 1964), 2: 949.

28. Bailey, *Great Betrayal,* 300.

29. Karl Schriftgiesser, *The Gentleman from Massachusetts: Henry Cabot Lodge* (Boston, 1944), 355; Garraty, *Lodge,* 394; O'Keane, *Walsh,* 97.

30. O'Keane, *Walsh,* 105; Philip C. Jessup, *Elihu Root,* 2 vols. (New York, 1938), 2:412–14.

31. Garraty, *Lodge,* 397, 416; LeRoy Ashby, *The Spearless Leader: Senator Borah and the Progressive Movement in the 1920's* (Urbana, IL, 1972), 248–49.

32. Lodge to Sturgis Bigelow, February 5, 1924, Lodge Papers, quoted in Garraty, *Lodge,* 424.

33. "A Washington Correspondent," "The Progressives of the Senate," *American Mercury* 16 (April 1929), 385–93, in Richard Hofstadter, *Age of Reform* (New York, 1961), 283 n.

34. Burl Noggle, *Teapot Dome: Oil and Politics in the 1920's* (Baton Rouge, 1962), 71–72; Hasia Diner, "Teapot Dome, 1924," in *Congress Investigates: A Documentary, 1792–1974,* ed. A.M. Schlesinger and Roger Bruns, 5 vols. (New York, 1975), 2385–89; Byrd, *Senate,* 1:437–38; O'Keane, *Walsh,* 129–32.

35. J.L. Bates, *The Origins of Teapot Dome* (Urbana, IL, 1963), 209.

36. David Burner, *The Politics of Provincialism: The Democratic Party in Transition, 1918–1932* (New York, 1975), 109–10.

37. Burner, *Provincialism,* 115–27; Noggle, *Teapot Dome,* 163; *Proceedings of the [Democratic] Convention, 1924* (transcript), 972–1038; Supplement to *Political Science Quarterly* 15 (1925): 38.

38. David P. Thelen, *Robert M. La Follette and the Insurgent Spirit* (Boston, 1976), 176–84.

39. Richard Lowitt, *George W. Norris: The Persistence of a Progressive, 1913–1933* (Urbana, IL, 1971), 384–85.

40. James Cannon Jr., *Bishop Cannon's Own Story,* ed. Richard L. Watson Jr. (Durham, NC, 1955), 391–96.

41. Noggle, *Teapot Dome,* 203.

42. Roosevelt, quoted in O'Keane, *Walsh,* 275.

43. *Christian Century,* March 15, 1933, editorial clipping, Walsh Papers, Library of Congress.

44. Mencken, quoted in Schriftgiesser, *Lodge,* 355; T.R. Marshall, *Recollections of Thomas R. Marshall: A Hoosier Salad* (Indianapolis, 1925), 315.

45. *Nation,* March 14, 1925, editorial clipping, Walsh Papers, Library of Congress.

Chapter 7. "Senator-at-Large of the Whole American People": William E. Borah vs. George W. Norris (1920–1940)

1. Richard Lowitt, *George W. Norris: The Making of a Progressive, 1861–1912* (Syracuse, NY, 1963), 1–10, 63, 82–83; John M. Cooper, "William E. Borah, Political Thespian," *Pacific Northwest Quarterly* (October 1965), 145–58; Norman L. Zucker, *George W. Norris* (Urbana, IL, 1966), 24–25; George W. Norris, *Fighting Liberal: The Autobiography of George W. Norris* (New York, 1945), 19; William E. Leuchtenburg, "William Edgar Borah," *Dictionary of American Biography,* Supple. 3:49–53; Carol Felsenthal, "A Love Affair with Borah," in Carol Felsenthal, *Alice Roosevelt Longworth* (New York, 1988), 135–62.

2. Cooper, "Borah," 147; Zucker, *Norris*; Marian C. McKenna, *Borah* (Ann Arbor, MI, 1961), 107, 110, 1–47.

3. *Congressional Record,* December 12, 1913, McKenna, *Borah,* 132; also, 48–63.

4. *Congressional Record,* June 26–29 and October 2, 1914; McKenna, *Borah,* 132–

33; Richard Lowitt, *Norris: The Persistence of a Progressive, 1913–1933* (Urbana, IL, 1971), 197.

5. Lowitt, *Norris, 1913–1933,* 63–65.

6. Ibid., 70–73.

7. McKenna, *Borah,* 142–45.

8. Lowitt, *Norris, 1913–1933,* 90.

9. David P. Thelen, *Robert M. La Follette and the Insurgent Spirit* (Boston, 1976), 140–48.

10. Lowitt, *Norris, 1913–1933,* 122–23.

11. Robert J. Maddox, *William E. Borah and American Foreign Policy* (Baton Rouge, 1969), 42–44.

12. Lowitt, *Norris, 1913–1933,* 113, 122–23.

13. Thomas A. Bailey, *Woodrow Wilson and the Great Betrayal* (Chicago, 1963), 230–31.

14. "Newberry Election Case," extracts from 67th Cong., 1st and 2d Sess., January 10 and 11, 1922, 1183, 1239, Walsh Papers, box 423, Library of Congress.

15. LeRoy Ashby, *The Spearless Leader: Senator Borah and the Progressive Movement in the 1920's* (Urbana, IL, 1972); William A. White, *A Puritan in Babylon: The Story of Calvin Coolidge* (New York, 1938), 301; McKenna, *Borah,* 211; Donald A. Ritchie, *Press Gallery: Congress and the Washington Correspondents* (Cambridge, MA, 1991), 208.

16. McKenna, *Borah,* 251.

17. Arthur M. Schlesinger Jr., *The Imperial Presidency* (Boston, 1989), 94–95.

18. McKenna, *Borah,* 239, 244–49, 347, 237.

19. Lowitt, *Norris, 1913–1933,* 557.

20. *Congressional Record,* February 22 and 23, 1933, vol. 76, part 5 (72d Cong., 2d sess.), 4769–80.

21. Lowitt, *Norris, 1913–1933,* 330–47, 463.

22. Ibid., 466; Richard Lowitt, *George W. Norris: The Triumph of a Progressive, 1933–1944* (Urbana, IL, 1978), 25, 167; Leuchtenburg, "Borah," Supple. 3:49–53.

23. Lowitt, *Norris, 1933–1944.*

24. McKenna, *Borah,* 308–14.

25. Lowitt, *Norris, 1933–1944,* 178–91.

26. Arthur M. Schlesinger Jr., *The Age of Roosevelt,* vol. 3, *The Politics of Upheaval* (Cambridge, MA, 1960), 437–38.

27. McKenna, *Borah,* 31–32; Joseph P. Lash, *Eleanor and Franklin* (New York, 1971), 522.

28. The ratification in 1920 of the Nineteenth Amendment, providing for woman suffrage, did not significantly change the male-dominated Congress. In 1932, Hattie W. Caraway, who had been appointed to succeed her husband, Thaddeus, upon his death in 1931, became the first woman elected to a full six-year term in the Senate. Her campaign in Arkansas was greatly assisted by Huey Long, running for the Senate in Louisiana, who spread his "Share the Wealth" campaign to his neighboring state. She was elected to two six-year terms and then defeated by J. William Fulbright in 1944. "Silent Hattie" was hardly an inspiration to women, as she recorded in her journal when asked to "eulogize" the suffragette Susan B. Anthony, "nix on that." See Diane D. Kincaid, ed., *Silent Hattie Speaks: The Personal Journal of Senator Hattie Caraway* (Westport, CT, 1979), 76.

29. McKenna, *Borah,* 325, 137, 277, 283.

30. Norris, *Fighting Liberal,* 358: Norris considered the anti-poll-tax bill constitutional but not the antilynching bill. White to Norris, February 24, 1938, R.F. Wagner

Papers, quoted in J. Joseph Huthmacher, *Senator Robert F. Wagner and the Rise of Urban Liberalism* (New York, 1968), 242; White to Norris, March 4, 1940, Norris Papers, box 147, Library of Congress.

31. Lowitt, *Norris, 1913–1933*, 387–89, 452.

32. Mary Borah, *Elephants and Donkeys: The Memoirs of Mary Borah as Told to Mary Louise Perrine* (Moscow, ID, 1976), 138; McKenna, *Borah*, 349–68.

33. Lowitt, *Norris, 1913–1933*, 251–53.

34. McKenna, *Borah*, 354–61.

35. Ibid., 365; Maddox, *Borah and Foreign Policy*, 242.

36. Ashby, *Spearless Leader*, 16.

37. Lowitt, *Norris, 1933–1944*, 259–60.

38. Ibid. 294–97, 293; "Report of the Special Committee on the Senate Reception Room," appendix C (85th Cong., 1st sess.), 1, insert; Stephen E. Ambrose, *Nixon*, vol. 2, *The Triumph of a Politician, 1969–1972* (New York, 1989), 330.

39. Lowitt, *Norris, 1933–1944*, 435–39.

40. Ashby, *Spearless Leader*, 15; Zucker, *Norris*, 29.

Part IV Introduction.
The Imperial Presidency and the Supine Senate (1940–1990)

1. Arthur M. Schlesinger Jr., *The Imperial Presidency* (Boston, 1989), 421.

2. Constance M. Green, *Washington*, vol. 2, *Capital City, 1879–1950* (Princeton, NJ, 1963), 466–87, esp. 469.

3. Christopher Lasch, *The Culture of Narcissism: American Life in an Age of Diminishing Expectations* (New York, 1979); Ralph Ketcham, *Presidents above Party: The First American Presidency, 1789–1829* (Chapel Hill, NC, 1984), 175; W.E.H. Lecky, *Democracy and Liberty*, 2 vols. (New York, 1896), 1:397. For the role of the media in the 1988 presidential campaign, see Peter Goldman and Tom Mathews, *The Quest for the Presidency 1988* (New York, 1989).

Chapter 8. Shaping Pax Americana:
Robert A. Taft vs. Arthur H. Vandenberg (1940–1950)

1. D.R. Kepley, *The Collapse of the Middle Way: Senate Republicans and the Bipartisan Foreign Policy, 1948–1952* (Westport, CT, 1988), 124–25.

2. James T. Patterson, *Mr. Republican: A Biography of Robert A. Taft* (Boston, 1972), 285–86; Richard M. Freeland, *The Truman Doctrine and the Origins of McCarthyism* (New York, 1972).

3. C. David Tompkins, *Senator Arthur H. Vandenberg: The Evolution of a Modern Republican, 1884–1945* (Lansing, MI, 1970), 34; Alvin M. Josephy Jr., *On the Hill: A History of the American Congress* (New York, 1980), 333, 352.

4. Wayne S. Cole, *Roosevelt and the Isolationists* (Lincoln, NE, 1983), 350–51, 518–19; Tompkins, *Vandenberg*, 34–35; Patterson, *Taft*, 44–46, 60–65, 74–78, 90–105, 160–79; George H. Mayer, *The Republican Party, 1854–1966* (New York, 1967).

5. Arthur H. Vandenberg Jr., ed., *The Private Papers of Senator Vandenberg* (Boston, 1952), 130–39; Wayne S. Cole, *Senator Gerald P. Nye and American Foreign Relations* (Minneapolis, 1962), 191–98, 211–16.

6. Vandenberg, ed., *Vandenberg*, 129–30.

7. Ibid., 132–39; Gabriel Kolko, *The Politics of War: The World and United States Foreign Policy, 1943–1945* (New York, 1968), 109, 164.

8. Vandenberg, ed., *Vandenberg,* 146–51.

9. Robert L. Messer, *The End of an Alliance: James F. Byrnes, Roosevelt, Truman, and the Origins of the Cold War* (Chapel Hill, NC, 1982), 137–216.

10. Vandenberg, ed., *Vandenberg,* 305–10, 93; Clark Clifford with Richard Holbrooke, *Counsel to the President* (New York, 1991), 83; Randall B. Woods, *Fulbright: A Biography* (New York, 1995), 102–4, 122–26, 142, 245, 585.

11. Booth Mooney, *The Politicians: 1945–1960* (Philadelphia, 1970), 41–59.

12. Joseph M. Jones, *The Fifteen Weeks: February 21–June 5, 1947* (New York, 1955), 121–25; Stephen E. Ambrose, *Rise to Globalism: American Foreign Policy since 1938,* 3d ed. (New York, 1983), 132, 131, 129–34; Vandenberg, ed., *Vandenberg,* 341–42. David McCullough, *Truman* (New York, 1992); Alonzo M. Hamby, *Man of the People: A Life of Harry S. Truman* (New York, 1995).

13. Patterson, *Taft,* 370–71.

14. Jones, *Fifteen Weeks,* 31–36; Ambrose, *Globalism,* 138–39; Walter LaFeber, *America, Russia, and the Cold War, 1945–1984* (New York, 1985).

15. Patterson, *Taft,* 381–87; Robert Griffith, *The Politics of Fear: Joseph R. McCarthy and the Senate,* 2d ed. (Amherst, MA, 1987), xiii.

16. Vandenberg, ed., *Vandenberg,* 384–86; Patterson, *Taft,* 392.

17. Ambrose, *Globalism,* 142–43; Vandenberg, ed., *Vandenberg,* 406–8.

18. David Calleo, *The Atlantic Fantasy: The U.S., N.A.T.O. and Europe* (Baltimore, 1970), 151 n; Stephen E. Ambrose, *Eisenhower,* vol. 1, *Soldier, General of the Army, President-Elect, 1890–1952* (New York, 1983).

19. Dean Acheson, *Present at the Creation: My Years in the State Department* (New York, 1969), 71–72; *Executive Sessions of the Senate Foreign Relations Committee,* Historical Series, vol. 2, 81st Cong., 1st and 2d sess., 1949–1950 (Washington, DC, 1976), 3, 15.

20. Vandenberg, ed., *Vandenberg,* 479–80, 498, 515; Patterson, *Taft,* 435–39.

21. Vandenberg, ed., *Vandenberg,* 515–16; Eric Goldman, *The Crucial Decade— And After: America, 1945–1960* (1st ed., 1960; New York, 1966), 113; Thomas C. Reeves, *The Life and Times of Joe McCarthy* (New York, 1982), 212–15; *Congressional Record,* January 25, 1949, vol. 95 (81st Cong., 1st sess.), 532–33.

22. Reeves, *McCarthy,* 221–23; Griffith, *Politics of Fear,* 48–49.

23. Vandenberg, ed., *Vandenberg,* 499; Patterson, *Taft,* 341, 448, 328–31; Ambrose, *Globalism,* 157; Robert Griffith, "Dwight D. Eisenhower and the Corporate Commonwealth," *American Historical Review* 87, no. 1 (February, 1982): 87–122.

24. *Congressional Record,* January 5, 1951, quoted in Arthur M. Schlesinger Jr., *The Imperial Presidency,* 2d ed. (Boston, 1989), 354.

Chapter 9. The "Politics of Joy" and "Uncle Strom's Cabin": Hubert H. Humphrey vs. Strom Thurmond (1950–1990)

1. Carl Solberg, *Hubert Humphrey: A Biography* (New York, 1984), 17–18; Alberta Lachicotte, *Rebel Senator: Strom Thurmond of South Carolina* (New York, 1967), 40–44; Donald R. McCoy, *The Presidency of Harry S. Truman* (Lawrence, KS, 1984), 154–58; Richard Hofstadter, "From Calhoun to the Dixiecrats," *Social Research* 16 (June 1949), 136–50. Nadine Cohodas's *Strom Thurmond and the Politics of Southern Change* (New York, 1993) is a hagiography, fairly good on racial matters but ignoring many of the issues raised in this chapter.

2. Solberg, *Humphrey,* 1–130: quotes, 89, 116.

3. *Time,* January 17, 1949, quoted in Solberg, *Humphrey,* 133; also, Humphrey quoted in Solberg, *Humphrey,* 157–59, 468. See also Robert A. Caro, *The Years of Lyndon Johnson,* vol. 1, *The Path to Power* (New York, 1982); vol. 2, *Means of Ascent* (New York, 1990).

4. *Life,* quoted in Lachicotte, *Thurmond,* 26.

5. Garry Wills, *Nixon Agonistes: The Crisis of the Self-Made Man* (Boston, 1970), 271. See also Jill Abramson, "Strom Thurmond Springs Eternal in the U.S. Senate," *Wall Street Journal,* October 18, 1990, 1, A6; press release, *New York Times,* March 29, 1991, B4. The divorce has been finalized, and Senator Thurmond is running for reelection in 1996. See Kevin Sack, "The Age Issue Dogs Senator Thurmond, 93," *New York Times,* June 11, 1996, A1, B8.

6. Lachicotte, *Thurmond,* 77–104.

7. Ibid., 105–39; David J. Garrow, *Bearing the Cross: Martin Luther King, Jr.* (New York, 1986; paperback ed., 1988), 11–74; Robert Dallek, *Lone Star Rising: Lyndon Johnson and His Times, 1908–1960* (New York, 1991), 517–28.

8. Solberg, *Humphrey,* 216–17, 462–63.

9. Ibid., 170–71, 178–80; Garrow, *Bearing the Cross,* 98, 139, 173, 411; Taylor Branch, *Parting the Waters: America in the King Years, 1954–63* (New York, 1988), 220–22.

10. Solberg, *Humphrey,* 174–77; Theodore C. Sorensen, *Kennedy* (New York, 1965), 91–92.

11. Solberg, *Humphrey,* 199–213; Thomas C. Reeves, *A Question of Character: A Life of John F. Kennedy* (New York, 1991), 161–67.

12. Oscar Wilde, *Lady Windemere's Fan* (1892), act III; Doris Kearns, *Lyndon Johnson and the American Dream* (New York, 1976), 202; David Halberstam, *The Best and the Brightest* (1st ed., 1972; paperback ed., New York, 1983), 647; Solberg, *Humphrey,* 270–84.

13. Allen J. Matusow, *The Unraveling of America: A History of Liberalism in the 1960's* (New York, 1984), 156–57; Solberg, *Humphrey,* 287–90.

14. Solberg, *Humphrey,* 332–33, 339.

15. Statistics from Matusow, *Unraveling,* 409–10.

16. Lachicotte, *Thurmond,* 162, 175, 236.

17. Strom Thurmond, *The Faith We Have Not Kept* (San Diego, 1968), 15–16; Lewis Chester, Godfrey Hodgson, and Bruce Page, *An American Melodrama: The Presidential Campaign of 1968* (New York, 1969), 479. With a special sense of irony, if not hypocrisy, see Marilyn W. Thompson, "Thurmond and the Girl from Edgefield," *Washington Post,* August 4, 1992, E1–E2, which claims Thurmond has an illegitimate African American daughter, now seventy years old, named Essie Mae Washington. Both Thurmond and Ms. Washington have denied the reports.

18. *Congressional Record,* August 13, 1963, vol. 109 (88th Cong., 1st sess.), 14836–44, 13968–75, 14454–63; Branch, *Parting the Waters,* 861–62.

19. Lachicotte, *Thurmond,* 237–39.

20. I.F. Stone, *Polemics and Prophecies: 1967–1970* (New York, 1970), 461; Kevin P. Phillips, *The Emerging Republican Majority* (New Rochelle, NY, 1969), 462–63; Wills, *Nixon Agonistes,* 272.

21. Solberg, *Humphrey,* 456, 407; also based on personal recollections of this author. For Humphrey's comparison of the roles Thurmond played in 1948 and 1968, see Albert Eisele, *Almost to the Presidency: A Biography of Two American Politicians* (Blue Earth, MN, 1972), 375.

22. Ronnie Dugger, *On Reagan: The Man and His Presidency* (New York, 1983), 178, 212–13; Gwen Ifill, "Senate Defeats Measure Backing Searches without Warrants," *New York Times,* June 26, 1991, A19.

23. Bob Schieffer and Gary Paul Gates, *The Acting President* (New York, 1989), 182; Peter Goldman and Tom Mathews, *Quest for the Presidency 1988* (New York, 1989), 278–84. See also Bruce J. Schulman, *From Cotton Belt to Sun Belt: Federal Policy, Economic Development, and the Transformation of the South, 1938–1980* (New York, 1991), esp. 135–73: "Missiles and Magnolias."

24. Garry Wills, *Lead Time: A Journalist's Education* (New York, 1983), 121; Edward M. Kennedy, "The Return of Public Service," address to the National Press Club, May 2, 1990, 2.

25. Gaius Suetonius Tranquillus, *The Twelve Caesars,* trans. Robert Graves (Middlesex, U.K., 1985), 127.

Epilogue. Virtue Misapplied:
Modern Heroes in an Age of Hubris

1. Robert Griffith, *The Politics of Fear,* 103–4; Robert C. Byrd, *The Senate, 1789–1989,* 2 vols. (Washington, DC, 1988; vol. 1 ed. Mary Sharon Bell; vol. 2 ed. Wendy Wolff), 1:571; John F. Kennedy, *Profiles in Courage* (New York, 1956), 237; Margaret Chase Smith, *Declaration of Conscience,* ed. William C. Lewis Jr. (Garden City, NY, 1972), 430–41.

2. Herbert S. Parmet, *Jack: The Struggles of John F. Kennedy* (New York, 1980), 395–98, 312–33; Richard J. Whalen, *The Founding Father: The Story of Joseph P. Kennedy* (New York, 1966), 430–31; David Burner and Thomas R. West, *The Torch Is Passed: The Kennedy Brothers and American Liberalism* (New York, 1984), 56–60. See Thomas C. Reeves, *A Question of Character: A Life of John F. Kennedy* (New York, 1991): my own research and writing were completed before reading this book, though we used virtually the same sources.

3. Byrd, *Senate,* 1:638–40.

4. David Halberstam, *The Best and the Brightest* (New York, 1972), 503; Doris Kearns, *Lyndon Johnson and the American Dream* (New York, 1976), 110, 152, 198; Lee Wilkins, *Wayne Morse: A Bio-Bibliography* (Westport, CT, 1985), 3–54; A. Robert Smith, *The Tiger in the Senate: The Biography of Wayne Morse* (New York, 1962); Ernest Gruening, *Many Battles: The Autobiography of Ernest Gruening* (New York, 1973), 28–29, 156–57, 280, 510–11.

5. Byrd, *Senate,* 1:621; Halberstam, *Best and Brightest,* 509; Gruening, *Autobiography,* 473.

6. Tristram Coffin, *Senator Fulbright: Portrait of a Public Philosopher* (New York, 1966), 13, 19; J. William Fulbright, *The Arrogance of Power* (New York, 1966), 3–22; Halberstam, *Best and Brightest,* 504–11; Randall B. Woods, *Fulbright: A Biography* (New York, 1955).

7. Byrd, *Senate,* 1:673–79, 690–93; Bobby Baker, *Wheeling and Dealing: Confessions of a Capitol Hill Operator* (New York, 1978), 87, 140, quoted in Byrd, *Senate,* 1:678–79; Halberstam, *Best and Brightest,* 256–57, 729; Lyndon B. Johnson, "Peace without Conquest," address at Johns Hopkins University, April 7, 1965, in *Public Papers of the Presidents of the United States* (Washington, DC, 1966), no. 172.

8. Lewis Chester, Godfrey Hodgson, and Bruce Page, *An American Melodrama: The Presidential Campaign of 1968* (New York, 1969), 79, 125–26; Garry Wills, *The Kennedy Imprisonment: A Meditation on Power* (New York, 1983), 105.

9. Jack Newfield, *Robert Kennedy: A Memoir* (New York, 1969), 58; Eugene McCarthy, *Up 'Til Now: A Memoir* (New York, 1987), 193; Peter Collier and David Horowitz, *The Kennedys: An American Drama* (New York, 1984), 343–44; Eugene McCarthy, *The Year of the People* (Garden City, NY, 1969).

10. Chester, Hodgson, and Page, *American Melodrama*, 71.

11. Milton Viorst, *Hustlers and Heroes: An American Political Panorama* (New York, 1971), 233; Wills, *Kennedy Imprisonment*, 102; Albert Eisele, *Almost to the Presidency* 299–321; personal recollections.

12. Newfield, *Robert Kennedy*, 304; Jeanne Shaheen, quoted, in Susan B. Casey, *Hart and Soul: Gary Hart's New Hampshire Odyssey ... and Beyond* (Concord, NH, 1986), 306.

13. Edgar Berman, *Hubert: The Triumph and Tragedy of the Humphrey I Knew* (New York, 1979), 171, 246–47; McCarthy, *Up 'Til Now*.

14. Paul R. Clancy, *Just a Country Lawyer: A Biography of Senator Sam Ervin* (Bloomington, IN, 1974), 18.

15. Clancy, *Ervin*, 178, 181–82.

16. For an evaluation of Ervin on Vietnam, see Dick Dabney, *A Good Man: The Life of Sam J. Ervin* (Boston, 1976), 288; Clancy, *Ervin* 240–42, 205, 194.

17. Sam J. Ervin, Jr., *The Whole Truth: The Watergate Conspiracy* (New York, 1980); Clancy, *Ervin*, 273–74, 280–82.

18. Jeffrey C. Goldfarb, *The Cynical Society: The Culture of Politics and the Politics of Culture in American Life* (Chicago, 1991), esp. 131, 142, 152; Alexis de Tocqueville, *Democracy in America*, 2 vols. in 1, ed. J.P. Mayer, trans. George Lawrence (Garden City, NY, 1969), 694.

Afterword

1. Andrew D. White, "On Studies in General History and the History of Civilization," *Papers of the A.H.A.* 1, no. 2 (New York, 1885): 70, 72.

2. Christopher Lasch, *The Culture of Narcissism: American Life in an Age of Diminishing Expectations* (New York, 1979), 19, 24–25, quotes David Donald on the irrelevance of history, *New York Times*, September 8, 1977; David H. Donald, *Lincoln* (New York, 1995), 9, highlights this remark of Lincoln's on the frontispiece to his biography; David H. Donald, *The Politics of Reconstruction, 1863–1867* (Baton Rouge, 1965), xii; G.M. Trevelyan, quoted in Joseph M. Hernon Jr., "The Last Whig Historian and Consensus History: George Macaulay Trevelyan, 1876–1962," *American Historical Review* 81 (1976): 72.

3. Draft of speech, Walsh Papers, box 421, Library of Congress; William Pitt Fessenden to his son William, January 22, 1859, Fessenden Family Collection, Bowdoin College. The senator had four sons and a daughter, Mary, who had died of scarlet fever.

Index

Born in Washington, DC, Joseph Martin Hernon is the author of three books, more than twenty articles, and dozens of poems. He taught at the university level for thirty-two years and is currently Professor of History Emeritus from the University of Massachusetts, Amherst. With a Ph.D. from Trinity College, Dublin University, he was also elected Fellow of the Royal Historical Society and selected Theodore Sorensen Fellow of the John F. Kennedy Library Foundation for 1991–1992.

As a student, Mr. Hernon worked in the U.S. Senate, the House of Representatives, the Library of Congress, and the Democratic National Committee. He led one of the earliest demonstrations in the North to support Dr. Martin Luther King and the student sit-ins, in front of the White House on March 23, 1960. Elected a member of the first national Executive Committee of the College Young Democrats, he served as a delegate to the North Atlantic Treaty Organization (NATO) Conference of Young Political Leaders in May 1960. And in May 1970, he formed the National Movement to Impeach Nixon and Agnew in response to the invasion of Cambodia. He has pursued an independent voting pattern during the past twenty years: Ford (1976), Anderson (1980), Mondale (1984), Bush (1988), Clinton (1992).